OPEN FIRE

To Ed—
I hope you enjoy this little piece
of Utah History. Never be afraid
to raise a Righteous Ruckus!

OPEN FIRE

J. GOLDEN KIMBALL

TAKES ON THE SOUTH

SCOTT M. HURST

BONNEVILLE BOOKS
AN IMPRINT OF CEDAR FORT, INC.
SPRINGVILLE, UTAH

ISBN 13: 978-1-59955-907-0

Published by Bonneville Books, an imprint of Cedar Fort, Inc.
2373 W. 700 S., Springville, UT, 84663
Distributed by Cedar Fort, Inc., www.cedarfort.com

LIBRARY OF CONGRESS CATALOGING-IN-PUBLICATION DATA

Hurst, Scott M., 1973- , author.
Open fire : J. Golden Kimball takes on the South / Scott M. Hurst.
pages cm.
Summary: Focuses on the early years of Kimball's life and his two missions to the Southern States.
ISBN 978-1-59955-907-0
1. Kimball, Jonathan Golden, 1853-1938. 2. Church of Jesus Christ of Latter-day Saints--Missions--Southern States. 3. Mormon Church--Missions--Southern States. 4. Mormon missionaries--Southern States. 5. Mormons--Biography. I. Title.

BX8695.K52H87 2012
289.3092--dc23
[B]

2012006302

Cover design by Brian Halley
Cover design © 2012 by Lyle Mortimer
Edited and typeset by Kelley Konzak

Printed in the United States of America

10 9 8 7 6 5 4 3 2 1

Printed on acid-free paper

Special thanks to James Kimball

For taking the time to answer a random letter from a complete stranger. I know you're on the other side raising a righteous ruckus with Uncle Golden and carrying on the good work of the Lord. God bless you, Jim. This one's for you.

PRAISE FOR *OPEN FIRE*

FOREWORD

We must never underestimate the influence we may have on those around us. For instance, one of my junior LDS missionary companions was an aspiring writer. He spoke of his dreams of writing as endlessly as he turned superbly unique phrases, and though at the time I simply marveled and enjoyed, the day came when I dared make my own literary attempts because of his courage and fierce determination.

While my efforts seemed to take wing, my companion's writing career was cut short by a long bout with cancer. Nevertheless, I have been fortunate to stay in intermittent contact with his wife and son, who is the author of this book. It comes as no surprise that Scott would also follow his father's dream, but tweak it to better fit his own unique perspective.

J. Golden Kimball was another who had a perspective all his own. Becoming one of the best-loved General Authorities in history wasn't his original plan, but he went on to touch countless lives and continues to do so nearly one hundred years after his passing. He taught us so many things, some on purpose and some quite unintentionally. He exemplified not getting hung up on our imperfections and especially not getting hung up on the imperfections of others. More than anything else, he taught us to trust in the Lord and believe that all things would work together for our good.

In *Open Fire*, Scott Hurst fulfills the promise of his father and more, bringing the story of J. Golden Kimball to life in a wonderful and entertaining way. This loving exploration—celebration, really—of the life of J. Golden Kimball is a must-read for anyone who is going to serve or has served a mission or even anyone who just knows a missionary. It is a story of faith and doubt, hope and redemption. It is a tale of love and loss, trial and tribulation, and ultimately conquering our own fears. In short, it is a story for all of us.

Blaine M. Yorgason
Author

AUTHOR'S NOTE

When you have to choose between the truth and the legend—print the legend.

—*John Ford*

If the history of the LDS Church were a quilt, then J. Golden Kimball would be one of the most colorful swatches to ever exist. Most every Mormon can tell you a J. Golden story or two. Called the swearing apostle (although he was never actually an apostle), he is the only General Authority of the Church known for cussing from the pulpit. He was a second-generation Mormon, born of pure pioneer stock in the Wild, Wild West. People often questioned his vocabulary, questioned his methods, and even questioned his manhood, but no one has ever questioned his loyalty to the Church.

There are many stories about Uncle Golden in circulation. Some are apocryphal, some are anecdotal, and some are common folklore that have become attributed to him over time. Most of what you'll find here is based on verifiable, true accounts; however, I have made no real effort to discriminate between fact and fiction. Events, places, and people have been condensed and shuffled in order to achieve better story flow. I hope I will be forgiven for these liberties.

I have made every attempt to hold true to the spirit of the

man, whom I honor greatly. Golden was much like the rest of us: rough around the edges, a human being of weaknesses and shortcomings. Nobody was ever more aware of their own imperfections than Golden, and he never pretended to be anything other than who he was. Perhaps this is why people related to him then and so many still do.

Golden was a man of great faith and was steadfast in his love for the gospel of Jesus Christ. He was the living embodiment of holding to the rod and enduring to the end. He persevered, even when he didn't want to. Perhaps, more than anything else, what made him great was his profound sense of compassion for his fellow men. Golden understood that no matter who we are, we all have challenges and difficulties in our lives. It is how we deal with them that determines the kind of person we are.

Golden used to joke that he was so thin he didn't cast a shadow. He was wrong. His shadow is immense. He has become more than just a man. J. Golden Kimball is the stuff of legend.

Like any great legend, Golden's story begins with four magical words . . .

CHAPTER 1

THE STUBBORN BULL

I can tell my whole life story in five minutes, if I leave out all the bad parts.

—*J. Golden Kimball*

Once upon a time, when the world wasn't quite so modern and the West wasn't quite yet won, there was a bull. It was springtime in the western plateaus of the Rockies. The warming sun and budding sagebrush had finally dug Old Man Winter out like a begrudging tick, and the bull was flush with the vigor of youth and feeling his oats.

The grass was high and green, just the kind a bull would favor, and he wandered where he liked, when he liked, grazing at his leisure. He was a handsome specimen of goodly size and proportion, powerfully built, with muscles that rippled like the waves of the Colorado and horns that ended in tips as keen as his newfound sense of independence. He had survived the bitter harshness of winter, a yearling in his prime. The world was his oyster (if bulls cared for that sort of thing), and he was just as free as a bird, with no one to tell him what to do or where to go, and he preferred things that way.

The morning had been spent sampling grass in the ditches and gullies of the lower foothills, and by midday his meandering found him loitering in a stretch of highland pasture. He had grazed his fill, and thinking of little more than a drink before lying down beneath a shady cedar tree for a nap, he sauntered over to a thin stream snaking its way through the meadow. His muzzle was inches from the water when the smell hit him.

Pungent, unnatural. It was the smell of fire. It was the smell of men.

Memory came like a lightning bolt scorching the earth where it strikes—memory of man's fire, of his iron burning red, the searing pain on his flank. Memory of fences and corrals. Confinement. No more open range. No grazing when and where he wanted.

Any thoughts of dozing were gone. Deep in his mind, a decision was being made, firm and irrevocable. There would be no going back, not this spring or any spring—not for this bull. He would keep his freedom, no matter the cost. Let them come with their horses and their lassoes. Let them come and see.

The smell had been faint. They had been a ways off yet, but come they did. Three of them, roughnecks down to the last man, as tough and wiry as the broncos they rode. They spotted him the instant they entered the field, where he stood waiting and ready. They were closing in now, reaching for their lassoes.

High above them, the sun carved its eternal march across the sky; it was high noon on the plateau. The bull set his horns square to the cowboys and charged.

Once upon a time, shortly after the bull's showdown in the foothills, there was a cowboy. His Stetson sat low and sharp on his brow, casting its shadow across his strong-set eyes, which squinted slightly in the harsh sun, peering out like a hawk. Two days of whiskers covered his cheeks like a fine pelt, adding to the masculine physique of his rugged features and chiseled jaw. Years of hard labor had sculpted his body like a richly tanned David even Michelangelo would envy. Sweat glistened on his bare chest where his shirt lay open, his supple leather vest lying across his broad shoulders, draping down to caress the six-shooter strapped to his waist. The very essence of the rugged West seemed to flow in his veins as if he were the living embodiment of all that was wild and untamed.

But this story isn't about that cowboy. It's about the tall, lanky fellow standing next to him. By all accounts, J. Golden Kimball wasn't the skinniest man to ever walk the face of the earth, but he sure gave that hombre a run for his money. He was so thin he could find shade in a fence post. His ten-gallon hat fit loosely around his head, its wide brim crossing him like a T. His gun belt seemed to defy gravity, refusing to fall despite the lack of bodily territory on which to find purchase. He hadn't shaved in several days either, as the scruffy patches of hair scattered about his face testified. His Adam's apple stuck out so far from his beanpole neck that his bandanna practically hung from it. And, as if all that weren't enough to go against the traditional cowboy grain, perched on the end of his long nose was a pair of round-lensed, wire-frame spectacles. Golden looked like a librarian stuffed into a scruffy cowboy outfit.

In Golden's defense, he did stand nearly a full head taller than anyone else around him. Where this sort of height might usually make a man seem bigger and more intimidating, in Golden's case it only added to his awkwardness, making him stick out like a sore thumb wherever he went. You could tell right away that the road Golden traveled wasn't only dusty, it was covered with a fair amount of cow manure as well.

Make no mistake, all appearances aside, Golden was a cowboy to the manner born, tough as a pine knot and dogged as they came, more than able to hold his own against any buckaroo that ever lived. It was for that reason he found himself among the handful of men chosen to go and fetch that Stubborn, Obstinate Bull.

Word was the critter had dragged poor Hanson clean off his horse by his own lasso, trampling him until the others could scare the bull off with shots from their pistols. Hanson had been hauled into camp on a makeshift stretcher, broken up mighty fierce. Golden didn't know the first thing about medicine, but the doc had looked awful grim as they carried the poor fellow into the ranch house.

Golden took a bite of his tobacco, tucking the wad firmly in his lip. He chawed the dark goo pensively while he waited for the other men to finish strapping their saddles on. His expression was severe, his eyes filled with concern. Anyone who knew the slightest thing about Golden knew he felt awful for poor Hanson. You see, Golden was the kind of man who felt others' pain deeper than his own. He didn't have the slightest notion of what he could do to help, but if there had been anything at all, you better believe he would have done it.

Golden stood by his brother Elias, who was four years junior. Neither as tall nor as thin as Golden, Elias was less of a spectacle but no less a cowboy. They both winced as another agonized groan drifted from the ranch house.

"Prize bull or not," Elias said, his voice grim, "if that critter tries anything like that again, I'll kill him, I swear to G—"

"What'd I say about taking the name of the Lord in vain?" Golden asked, chastising his brother. As if being scrawny as a toothpick wasn't enough, Golden's voice was high pitched and thin as his hair. It sounded pinched, as if his skinny neck were too narrow to let it all through.

"Sorry, Golden," Elias apologized.

"It's all right." Golden spat with the unconscious precision of long practice, the dry earth quickly absorbing the tobacco where it landed by his boots. Then he said what any self-respecting Mormon cowboy might have said. "Well, let's go get that damn bull."

That's right, despite his rootin', tootin', roughshod appearance, Jonathan Golden Kimball was a Mormon, born and bred from bona fide, dyed-in-the-wool Latter-day Saint stock. His father was no less than Heber C. Kimball, first counselor to the prophet Brigham Young himself. Ferociously loyal to the

Church, Heber was the living embodiment of a first-generation Mormon pioneer if ever there was one. With a grand total of forty-three wives, Heber had the distinction of being the most married polygamist (not that it was a contest or anything) and fathering sixty-five children. In addition to his copious contribution to propagating the species, the stout, barrel-chested man was also known for having the strength of a bear. Once, when his mule got stuck in a ditch, Heber reached in, grabbed hold of its harness, and pulled it out with one hand.

Golden received his rather unique name and his lean build from his mother's side of the family. Tall and stately, Christeen Golden Kimball was a right impressive woman by all accounts. A convert from Pennsylvania, she had married Heber in Nauvoo shortly before the exodus west. Officially counted as Heber's tenth wife, she was the only member of her family to join the Church. Converting to a strange religion and moving clear across the country to the undeveloped frontier takes more courage and faith than most of us can comprehend today. Like so many of her generation, she faced the challenge with bravery and conviction. Throughout his life, Golden always carried the deepest love and respect for his parents and the fearlessness of their sacrifice and dedication.

Christeen and Heber had four children together, though sadly the oldest passed away when she was only three. Golden was born in 1853, the second child and oldest boy. Elias was next and then their baby sister, Mary Margaret. Golden was a favored son of Heber's and one he marked as a boy of unusual promise.

This sort of distinction might usually mean that the boy was destined for greatness, and in many ways he was, but this time around, Heber's emphasis might have been more on the unusual part. That's not to say that Golden was weird, but he was definitely one of a kind, and his father knew it. Once, when pronouncing a blessing upon young Golden, Heber declared, "He shall have strong mental power and be stupid in his own way." Golden was indeed a boy of great potential, and time would come to show that he certainly had his own unique way of doing things.

The elegant Kimball Estate took up most of what the locals called Heber's Bench, the area now known as Capitol Hill. The great Salt Lake City, still in its humble beginning stages, was growing fast, and Golden was growing right along with it. It was a paradise for a whippersnapper like Golden. When he wasn't playing in the creek, conquering Ensign Peak, or sneaking fruit from the walled-in family gardens, he was being groomed under Heber's watchful care as his father's personal secretary. It was here that Golden learned bookkeeping and penmanship, but more than anything what he learned was a profound admiration for his father.

Tragedy came early to Golden's life when Heber passed away in June of 1868. His untimely death was the delayed result of a buggy accident a few days prior. Golden was only fifteen years old, and he took the loss hard. With Heber gone, the family fell on tough economic times. Christeen took up work sewing for a pittance in the ZCMI store, and when that wasn't enough, she took in boarders to help make ends meet.

To Golden it simply wasn't fair that his mother had to work so hard to be their sole support. She was a good woman and deserved better. He was bound and determined to fight the good fight. He knew his father would expect it, and Golden expected nothing less from himself. He was the oldest son; the obligation to provide for the struggling family fell to him now, and, by George, that's just what he was going to do.

In those days, following a profession of any kind was not urged upon young men or women, and his mother wanted him to continue with his schooling. Normally Golden wasn't the sort to disobey his mother, but he felt that his responsibility to his family outweighed his personal needs. Against Christeen's wishes, the gangly teenager gave up a scholarship to the University of Deseret and got a job driving a mule team. Mule skinning, as it was called, was no easy task, let alone for such a young man, but Golden was up to the challenge and proved to be one of the best around. A mule will work harder than any other creature alive if you can get it to work in the first place. Turns out that Golden had an affinity for the stubborn critters, and when it came to motivating them, he was a bit of a natural.

Golden started out hauling wood and ore for the railroads, a job that provided him with steady wages until the joining of the Union Pacific and Central Pacific railroads at Promontory Point in 1869. He had no way of knowing at the time that the very railroad he was helping to build would one day carry him to the hardest and most rewarding experience of his life.

Golden earned additional money by digging cellars for folks around town. It was hard, backbreaking labor, hardly work fit for a child. Golden's day often began at four in the morning and didn't end until the sun was tucked away behind the mountains again. Golden made sure the job was always done right and that his price was always reasonable, and he soon earned a reputation for his honesty, punctuality, and fairness. Unfortunately in the end, despite his and his mother's best efforts, it wasn't enough to stay afloat.

So, in 1875, Christeen and her children packed up their meager belongings and moved north to Rich County, an ironic name since they were anything but wealthy. They settled in Meadowville, a small lick of a town roughly four miles west of the southern tip of Bear Lake, near the Idaho border. Eleven of Heber's sons were already living in the area with their families, and it was from Isaac and Solomon Kimball that they bought a small parcel of property to homestead on.

The new family home wasn't much to brag about. Located among the dry grass and sagebrush, the austere log cabin measured only sixteen by twenty feet, not exactly luxury living for a family of four. A lean-to kitchen was later added, but other than that, the property was without amenities or improvements. It was here in the stark, northern Utah scrub that they commenced a fight for life, struggling daily to survive against poverty and the harshness of the high country climate. Golden would later recall

Meadowville as having nine months of winter and three months of late fall.

It was here in this unforgiving place that Golden began his illustrious career as a cowboy. He took a cotton to it, and it wasn't too long before he'd mastered all the great cowboy arts—roping and riding, wrangling, and most particularly, cussing. As good as he was at riding and roping, his skill with the stronger words of the English language was unparalleled and remains, as far as anyone knows, unmatched to this day. A few choice words from Golden and even the most stubborn of animals would hop to work.

For those of you who have never had the pleasure, let me tell you that ranching is a hard way to make a living, perhaps one of the hardest. There is always some job or another that needs doing, and you are constantly at the mercy of old Mother Nature. If a fence needed mending or an animal needed tending to, it had to be done whether morning, noon, or night, rain or shine, or— as often as not—snow. In Rich County, Mother Nature wasn't often very merciful at all. No, sir.

Golden didn't mind though. When something needed doing, he'd get it done. That's all there was to it. The constant work kept Golden busy and out of trouble. It also kept him out of regular activity in the Church. Now, to say that the gospel wasn't part of his life would be doing Golden a great injustice. He could never be accused of any gross misconduct or sin, but active involvement in the Church simply wasn't his way of life since his father passed on.

"Golden," said his mother one afternoon.

"Yes, Mother?" Golden knew the tone in his mother's voice. She had something on her mind. He set his well-used saddle on the fence where he'd been oiling it. He wiped his hands on his denim trousers as he crossed to her, his spurs chiming and his boots kicking up dust with each step.

Christeen Kimball sat on what passed for a porch in the small cabin. She was a dignified woman by any standard even though years of hardship had etched their mark into her face. This morning she had sent Mary Margaret on some errand or another, probably to fetch flour from Bishop Nebeker's, and only she and Golden were at home.

"Have you given any more thought about what we talked about?" she asked.

Golden knew she meant him going on a mission. It was one of those kinds of conversations, the ones you've had with your parents over and over again. Golden almost knew it by heart. Being raised Mormon, he wasn't particularly surprised that his mother would ask him. In fact it was a perfectly normal question, but confessedly, he wasn't big on the idea. Spending two or three years confined in a suit and tie simply didn't appeal much to him, not when he could be out on the range, free as a bird that flies in air, so to speak. No man's hand was stretched out to guide him in the footsteps of his father, or in anyone else's footsteps for that matter, and he preferred it that way. Besides, with the way life was turning out so far, it didn't appear that God had shown much interest in J. Golden Kimball, so J. Golden Kimball wasn't sure why he should show much interest in God.

Golden knew that his mother was only asking out of love and concern for his well-being. So he wasn't upset when she brought it up again, just simply resigned to it. Golden didn't think like a parent, but if he did, he would have known that Christeen wasn't only worried about him, she was worried about both her boys. She knew that whatever choice Golden made, Elias would follow his example, for better or for worse.

Golden carried a deep respect and affection for his parents, and he truly hated to disappoint his mother. So even though he hemmed and hawed plenty, when she rested her hand gently on his cheek and asked if he would at least ask President Taylor about serving, Golden nodded and obediently agreed to do so.

"I'll get around to it, first chance I get, Mother." He sincerely meant it. There was no way he would ever go back on a promise, especially one made to his mother. He really would go the first chance that came along, he just wasn't sure when that would be. With the roundup starting and all, it was a busy time on the ranch, a busy time indeed. In fact, with everything going on, it was busy enough to make even the most genuine of promises slip from a young man's mind.

Christeen watched her oldest son step from the porch and back to his ranch duties, her eyes bright with hope and expectation. Golden may not have thought like a parent, but Christeen certainly did. She knew her son; she knew the quality of his heart but also the stubbornness of his head. And so, watching him walk off toward his patiently waiting horse with his saddle in hand, she prayed for a miracle, one that would turn both of her sons' hearts to their father's. She prayed not only for a miracle, but also that her headstrong son would have the wisdom to recognize it as such when he saw it. If there is one thing that history has proven time and time again, it's to never underestimate the power of the faith of a good woman. Especially if that woman is your mother.

CHAPTER 2

IF COWS COULD FLY

Never kick a cow chip on a hot day.

—*Cowboy Proverb*

I don't care how many pails of milk I lose, as long as I don't lose the cow.

—*Unknown*

Despite the morning's events, the day was a beautiful one, just as perfect as spring can provide. The greens of the early growth were as vivid as the blue of the sky, and Golden was soaking in every bit of it. After a long winter, every day of the warm sun on his shoulders was a blessing. It was the sort of day when Golden couldn't think of anything he'd rather be doing than riding with his brother, who always made for good company.

"What a way to spend the Sabbath," Elias said. It sounded like he only half believed it.

Golden flashed Elias a wry grin. "Sure beats sitting in church."

Golden took another bite of his tobacco. The Word of Wisdom, a caution for members of the Church against the use of tobacco, coffee, and alcohol, existed in Golden's time but wasn't yet a hard, fast rule. That was a challenge for Golden that would come later on. For now, chewing was merely discouraged and was something that Golden, like many cowboys, took part in freely.

In the meantime, while Golden was making full use of his right to stuff noxious brown goop in his cheeks, the bull was making full use of its range and leading the cowboys in a chase out along the far edges of the ranch.

The foreman, John Stokes, spotted the critter first. It was moving along the invisible line across the upper bench where the sagebrush begins fighting the juniper trees. He whistled for everyone's attention, and the rest whistled in amazement.

"You sure that's a yearling?" Hans Sorenson was the newest cowboy on the ranch and hadn't seen the bull yet.

"Big feller, ain't he?" grinned Stokes and not without pride. That bull had won the blue ribbon at the county fair hands down, and it was upon its offspring that the ranch looked to make its keep this season. It was, quite literally, their cash cow.

The bull spotted the cowboys at the same time and began to move away from them, climbing ever higher along the ridgeline.

"I'd say it knows why we're here," Elias chipped in.

"He ain't gonna make this easy for us," agreed another cowboy.

Golden spit again, then raised his high voice. "That's a relief. For a minute there I thought this might get boring."

The group of cowboys began working their way up the hillside again, the horses' hooves sending loose rocks tumbling down the steep slope. They fell with a hollow skittering sound, reminding everyone how dangerous riding here could be. The small, wiry horses were mountain born and bred and moved cautiously but easily up the rocky terrain; the experienced cowboys were wise enough to trust them to their pace. They could rush the bull, possibly surround it or catch it up in the trees, but there was no sense in being hasty and ending the chase with a broken leg or worse. The cowboys held the upper hand; they'd worked this range for years and knew the lay of the land. The bull had pushed far beyond its familiar range, and slowly but surely the men were closing in.

"Bring him around boys. Drive him to the point." The foreman motioned with his arm, and the cowboys spread out toward the right to steer the bull to the left. They were against the edge of the property line and hoped to trap it up against the fence.

Man and animal were less than a hundred feet apart when the bull kicked up its heels and started running three ways from Sunday. The chase was on.

"Let's go, girl." Golden slapped his horse's shoulders lightly with the long end of the reins, and the cayuse took off like a brush fire. With a whoop, the other cowboys spurred their horses to a gallop. Golden could feel the wind against his face, the rhythm of his horse beneath him. This is what he lived for. The bull was bigger than any of them, but when it came to running on the rocky ground, the lighter broncos held the advantage. They covered ground quickly, closing the gap.

Elias's horse had always been one of the swiftest on the ranch. He passed the head of the charge easily and was the first to close in on the flank of the bull by several lengths. He raised his lariat high in the air and was poised to throw when the bull darted like a rattler, cutting him off violently. Elias lurched from his saddle, clinging on for dear life as his mount rose on its forelegs, skidding to a halt. The horn of that bull was so close to the horse's belly it must have shaved several hairs loose. By the time Elias made a hurried recovery, the bull was beyond them and storming toward the crest of a nearby plateau.

Normally a missed throw would end with a lot of jokes and genial ribbing regarding Elias's cowboy skills and manhood, but not today. The mood simply wasn't there. Golden saw what had happened as clear as day, and he knew the others had as well—that bull had been waiting, drawing the cowboys in close on purpose. It had intentionally tried to gore Elias's horse. Only by the swiftness of its reflexes had Elias's mount saved itself and its rider. The horses knew this too, in the instinctive way that animals do.

They grew jumpy and skittish, forcing the cowboys to struggle to keep them under reign. This bull was out for blood. Prized animal or not, it looked like they'd gotten a bum steer.

Ahead of them, the bull bolted up the hillside. In its rush, there was one minor detail it failed to notice about its escape route—it was a dead end. Sheer granite cliffs dropped hundreds of feet to the valley floor on every side except one, and that way was blocked by a scraggly band of cowboys. The bull whirled around, but it was too late. It was cornered, and it knew it. It eyed the approaching cowboys, warily pawing at the rocky earth with its great hooves, hot breath flaring its nostrils.

"We've got him, boys. Careful now."

They fanned out, forming a line; Golden rode near the middle, next to Elias. The scent of dust and trampled sage drifted through his nostrils, and the reins felt tense in his hand. He knew there wasn't a creature alive that wouldn't fight like the devil himself when its back was against the wall. They had the beast trapped, and it would be more dangerous than ever. Sure, they had pistols, but they were only loaded with snake shot, powerful enough to kill a rattler but hardly enough to do more than tick the bull off even worse. The sound of the guns might have scared the animal off once before, but who knew if it would again. Shooting it wasn't an option.

The bull realized what was going on, and he didn't like it one bit. Even if he got out of this one, these men would keep coming, with their horses and their ropes and sticks of thunder. Eventually his precious freedom would be lost. Still, he had a choice. He could let the men take him or . . .

He got mad. I'm talking blood-boiling mad. So gall-durned mad that he began to see red, which is no small trick for a critter that has been proven by scientific method to see only black and white. And in his haze of red, the only thing he could see was Golden perched in his saddle like a lightning rod.

Froths of sweat lined the bull's sides like foam on a stormy sea. It snorted, sending a spray of spit and snot into the air. The horses fidgeted beneath their riders.

"Easy, girl." Golden patted his horse on the neck. The way the bull was winding up meant this was it. All or nothing. Golden picked up his lariat and began twirling it in wide, looping circles. The others followed suit, edging slowly closer to the bull. The cowboys' lariats floated above their heads like oversized halos.

The first rule of bulldogging is "keep your eye on the bull." Golden leaned over a bit, never taking his eyes off the critter, and said, "Stick with me, Elias." Even in times of danger, Golden was more concerned for his brother than for himself.

As if by some silent cue from the gods, the bull bellowed and charged. The men held their line as the bull freight-trained closer, massive hooves punishing the earth, kicking up clouds of soil and dust with each thunderous step. Its head was low, its deadly horns pointed like spears. It didn't take more than a hair's breadth for the cowboys to realize where it was going—it was heading straight for Golden!

If that bull was a ten on the stubborn meter, J. Golden Kimball was an eleven. There was no way he was going to back down—no, sir. He was made of truer grit than that. The challenge had been given, the ultimate game of chicken begun. Bull versus Golden. Sizing up the oncoming battering ram, Golden squared his jaw, letting forth as fierce a war whoop as his turkey neck would allow, and got set to throw.

Now, having true grit is a good thing. Sometimes it can be the greatest compliment you can give a man. But having true grit isn't always the same thing as being wise. In fact, the smartest thing Golden could have done was step aside and let that bull go through. A beast that size could take on horse and rider both and still have poundage to spare. Fortunately for the skinny cowboy, even though he refused to budge, his bronco had truer horse sense than its rider and decided it would be a good idea to get out of the way. And fast.

The bronco reared up in panic. Golden was concentrating so hard on the bull that the sudden motion caught him off guard. He had rarely been thrown from a horse, but like everything else he did, he didn't do it halfway. Choking on his war cry, he flew from the saddle, catching his foot in the stirrup and flipping hind end over head bone. If you've ever had your wind knocked loose, whirligigging into rocky ground while getting twisted up in your own lasso, you'd know just how painful kissing dirt can be. His vision blurred, and his head thrummed like a gong as he chewed gravel. He swore he could taste tinfoil. Even worse, he could feel the earth trembling beneath him. As painful as his landing was, it was guaranteed to pale in comparison to the damage about to be inflicted by the sixteen-hundred-pound avalanche of beef looming over him.

Golden's entire twenty-eight years of life flashed before his eyes like a bad cliché. All the things he wished he had done and all the things he wished he hadn't fired through his mind at lightning speed. Twenty-eight might seem like it's old to some, but those who have reached or surpassed that milestone know it comes and goes mighty fast and in truth isn't a very long time at all. Particularly when it's about to be cut eminently short by a towering ton of T-bone.

Was this the end of J. Golden Kimball? One glance at the number of pages left in this volume will tell you it most certainly was not. But it could have been. In all likelihood it should have been. That bull had him dead to rights, but then, right at the very last of seconds, the most peculiar thing happened.

Instead of giving Golden the business end of the hoof, that bull up and turned, just like that. Still barreling full speed, it ran to the edge of the plateau, leaping off the cliff in the greatest bovine swan dive the world has ever seen. The launch was immaculate; the arc as graceful and smooth as a crescent moon. Why, if you were a professional judge of diving, you would have given that bull a perfect ten and a standing ovation, you surely would have.

The bull could feel the rush of the air, the sky around him. It was exhilarating. He'd never been so liberated. He was as free as the birds that fly in the air, so to speak. But while there is such thing as a cowbird, it still doesn't make a cow a bird, and even the mightiest of creatures must bow down to gravity, especially ones weighing nearly a ton. The bull, being no exception to the rule, plummeted from sight below the rocky lip of the plateau, issuing a last defiant *moooooo* that echoed for miles.

Elias was off his horse lickety-split, sprinting over to where Golden lay on the ground, spluttering and hacking. He was covered head to heel in dirt and tangled up in his own lasso.

"Golden! Golden!"

Golden barked out a fit of coughing, expelling dirt and spit. His stomach churned as he sat up in a doozy of a daze, his head spinning with shock.

"Are you all right?" Elias asked in a panic.

Golden looked at his brother in a wide-eyed stupor. "I think I swallowed my tobacca."

Elias laughed with great relief. That was the Golden he knew and loved. "Let's get you untangled from that rope."

The other cowboys gathered around as Golden's wits returned. One hunted up his glasses and handed them back to him. Golden felt achy. Pinprick tingles raced up and down his body. He checked himself over. All his parts seemed to be intact, even if a bit more loose than before. He was tenderized in more than a few places, but he hadn't suffered anything he wouldn't recover from in a few days' time. Much to everyone's surprise, Golden's included, he was fine. Shaken and stirred, but fine.

The horses were collected. Jokes and genial ribbing were made about Golden's cowboy skills and manhood. Then with great caution, paying careful mind to their footing, the cowboys stepped to the cliff's edge, peering down to see what had become of their prize bull. Its dive might have been world class, but the plateau wasn't a swimming hole and sadly, that bull was no longer in any condition to accept any medal or trophy. In kinder terms you might say he'd gone to the great pasture in the sky. In simpler terms you'd say he was hamburger.

"Well, looks like we're gonna have to get ourselves a new bull.

Whatya think?" Usually Elias's knack for the obvious would have earned a laugh from his brother, but Golden kept staring down at the bull, remaining silent longer than was comfortable.

By all accounts there was no dadgum reason for him to be standing here instead of the bull. He should have been nothing more than mush stuck to the bottom of the critter's enormous hooves. Yet here he was, more or less fully intact. It was a miracle he was still alive. Simply a miracle. Somewhere in his slightly addled mind it occurred to Golden that if this wasn't proof of God showing at least a little interest in him, then he didn't know what was.

"Golden? You all right?"

When he finally looked up from the bull to his brother, Golden's high voice was as serious as a heart attack.

"Elias, that's the way it's going to end for me if I don't change my ways."

He had told his mother that he would talk to President Taylor whenever he next got to town. How long ago had that been now? Glancing down at the bull again, he decided he'd better quit beating the devil around the stump and make it a priority.

CHAPTER 3

CALLED TO SERVE

Life is either a daring adventure, or nothing.

—*Helen Keller*

And so Golden cleaned up his act. Mostly. "If I can quit swearing," he told one friend, "by hell, you can too!"

As promised, he put in for a mission call and waited. And waited. And waited. But to his surprise, the call never came. It didn't appear that God was in any hurry for Golden to serve any time soon. In the meantime, inspired by a lecture from Karl G. Maeser, Golden decided to attend the Brigham Young Academy in Provo and get himself an education. Ever loyal, Elias followed him there. Golden studied at the Academy for two years, where he received schooling in bookkeeping and commercial arithmetic.

And still he waited for his mission call, but it never came. After a while, Golden began to think that he had missed his window of opportunity. He was rounding thirty now. Perhaps the chance to serve really had passed him by. He guessed it was time to settle down and get married and start a family. That was one prospect that definitely perked his interest. With that thought in mind, Golden returned home to Bear Lake.

He hadn't been home long when ranch business brought him back to Salt Lake City. They were in need of a few new animals, and Golden had been sent to see what the stock house had to offer. The ride from Meadowville took three days on horseback, and Golden had arrived in town late at night. He rose early the next day and spent most of the morning negotiating on a draft horse and a pair of sows. He was just leaving the stock house when he ran into William C. Spence, who was serving as secretary to the First Presidency at the time. Brother Spence quickly informed Golden that President Taylor, the third prophet and current leader of the Church, was looking for him.

Golden was as unshaven as his patchy whiskers allowed him to be and was still dressed in the clothes he'd worn riding into town. He hadn't planned on doing anything formal, especially talking with the prophet, so he hadn't brought any clothes other than his work duds. His boots and spurs were covered in mud and manure, and his chaps were as stained and filthy as his shirt, which was dirty enough to make a hog wallow look clean. It's even been told that he was wearing his six shooters and a bowie knife. Yup, he was a real mess, and a frightful one at that. But the president wanted to see him, so despite the embarrassment at his own appearance, Golden climbed on his horse and rode over to the church offices.

In those days, Salt Lake City wasn't a thriving metropolis by any standard, but it was definitely outgrowing its frontier status. It didn't boast any skyscrapers like some of the cities back east, and the clamorous automobile had yet to be invented, so the hard-packed earthen roads were still traveled by horse and buggy. Most of the major roadways were already outlined, if not yet fully created, carefully following the grid system set forth by Brigham Young. The modern miracle of electric lights, the first in town, had been installed along Main Street, earning it the nickname "The Great White Way." The temple remained under construction, as it would for years to come, its steadily rising walls shrouded in scaffolding and workers. Behind it, Capitol Hill was bare but for a few homes, including many of Heber C. Kimball's households.

The rapid growth of the city never ceased to amaze Golden.

It was bigger every time he came. All about, there were houses or the beginnings of houses where once there had been nothing but untouched desert. Even the field where he and his brothers used to play stickball was now lined with Victorian-style houses. He had a strange feeling of nostalgia, but Golden supposed it was the price of progress.

The office of the president had been kept in the Beehive House ever since it had first been built. After the passing of Brigham Young, more and more of the house had been converted into offices to keep pace with the continuing growth of the Church. If the great granite temple was the heart of Mormondom, the Beehive House, with its columned porches and wrought iron lacing, was its brain.

Golden rode up and tied his horse to one of the hitches out front. It whinnied quietly, and he patted it gently on the neck. Golden had grown up on the hill above here. He remembered playing "kick the can" or "sheepy come home" with his siblings and other children in the neighborhood and swimming in City Mill Creek right behind it. It was as familiar to him as his nose was to his face, but never before had the house seemed so intimidating.

Men hurried in and out of the front door, all on some important errand or other. Much to Golden's consternation, every one of them was neatly groomed and in pressed suits and ties, none of which helped Golden feel less of a clodhopper. With Salt Lake being pretty much smack dab in the middle of the western frontier, folks didn't even bat an eye at the sight of a cowpoke or two running around. But the sight that met them this morning was something else entirely. Why, the average cowboy looked like he was dressed in a tuxedo compared to the ragged outfit Golden was wearing.

He wiped his boots on the porch mat the best he could, but it didn't make much difference. They were so dirty he supposed if he got all the soil off of them there wouldn't be anything left. He considered taking them off but knew his socks were no real improvement. So he wiped his feet again for good measure, then stepped inside.

The Beehive House, as its name implies, was a busy place, well maintained and clean. People bustled back and forth, hard at work. The skylight and large windows allowed plenty of light inside, giving the place a relaxed feel, like a cozy living room on the kind of day where there's nothing better to do than lie down on the sofa and take a nap. Sporting whitewashed walls and natural wooden panels, the home was elegant but not what you'd call excessive, luxurious but not highbrow. President Young had surely known how to keep a house. The cabin in Meadowville was a downright shanty by comparison. It wasn't even as nice as the Beehive House's woodshed, all of which made Golden feel even more out of place.

Golden decided that if he ever made it big time he would have a house like this, something his father would have liked. Maybe he'd even build it back on the hill north of the city, where the old homestead had been. That would be nice.

He wound his way to the president's office, leaving a trail of dirty footprints and shocked expressions behind him. The door was open a crack. Golden knocked lightly and peeked his head in. "Excuse me, President Taylor. I understand you wanted to see me."

At seventy-five, John Taylor's features were weathered with age, but his eyes were still as bright as the day he was born. Warm in spirit and manner, he had the most pleasant countenance that a fellow could ever ask for. With his hair white as bleached linen, he was the portrait of the kindest man in the whole world, even better than Santa Claus. Seeing Golden, a smile crossed his face, melting away years. He rose and moved slowly around the desk to greet the grubby and mighty self-conscious Golden.

"Brother Kimball, come in, come in."

"I apologize for my outfit," Golden said. "I was at the stock house pricing some beeves. Brother Spence grabbed me right off the street."

By this time Golden was embarrassed enough by his own appearance that he was sure his face must have been red as a tomato, if it was visible at all beneath the scruff and dirt. The prophet didn't seem to give it a second thought. There are some folks to whom a person's outward appearance means very little, especially when compared to the quality of his heart. John Taylor was such a man. He continued to smile utterly unfazed, genuinely pleased to see Golden.

"Please, don't mention it. I'm glad you're here." President Taylor said. It wasn't just lip service; he meant it. He reached up an aged hand and held Golden at arm's length, looking him over. His hand was shaky, but his grip was firm as a vice. The years had done very little to diminish his strength. "I don't think I've seen you since your father's funeral, may he rest in peace. My, you've certainly grown!"

He motioned to the chair by the desk, and Golden sat down.

"I understand you're working as a ranch hand now," President Taylor asked.

"Yessir."

"Good work, ranching. Honest work. Hard work." He emphasized "hard work," indicating it was a good thing. The prophet found his own chair again and sat down, the pleasant smile never leaving his face. "And how is your mother doing? She is such a wonderful soul." Many of the brethren knew Christeen from when she and the children had lived in town.

"She works very hard to take care of my brother and sister and me," Golden answered. "Too hard, I fear."

"Bless her heart. She's always been a good woman." President Taylor leaned forward, resting his arms on the edge of his desk. "Brother Kimball, I'm very pleased that you're here. I sent you a letter a while ago, yet I hadn't heard anything back. I was growing concerned."

"A letter?" Golden was perplexed. He didn't know anything about a letter. Mail of any sort was still enough of a rarity in Meadowville to be news. Even if Golden hadn't seen it, someone else surely would have mentioned it to him. "I never received any letter, sir."

The postal service at the time was leisurely to say the least, especially out in the boonies of Bear Lake. It was, for the most part, quite reliable, but it wasn't uncommon for a letter to take a good month or more to arrive. On rare occasions, letters were simply lost. Whatever its fate may have been, neither man was surprised or upset that Golden hadn't received any letter.

"Well, Brother Kimball, I have good news for you. You have been called to serve as a full-time missionary to the Southern States."

Golden's jaw dropped.

"A mission? Now? But President, I'm thirty. I was beginning to think about settling down. I've got a good horse and a girl in mind and everything!" he protested. It's not that he didn't want to go. Golden felt it was an honor to be called but wasn't sure if it was the right place for him anymore, especially at his age.

President Taylor nodded with a look of understanding. He rose again from his chair. "Would you take a walk with me?"

With the grand temple, which would pass it up as the crown jewel of the Church, still ten years from being finished, the Salt Lake Tabernacle stood as the central feature of Temple Square. Completed in 1867, the Tabernacle was less than twenty years old, still quite young in building years. Metal was in short supply at the time, and the building was constructed entirely out of timber, using wooden pegs and rawhide straps instead of nails, a right smart solution. The final building was one hundred fifty feet wide, two hundred fifty feet long and would seat over eight thousand people. Graceful in both design and construction, it was a true wonder in its time. Many years later, a young architect-type fellow by the name of Frank Lloyd Wright would dub the building as "one of the architectural masterpieces of the country and perhaps the world."

Golden and President Taylor entered at the eastern doors, the side closest to the Beehive House. Golden's lanky frame towered over the prophet's bent figure like a lamppost. The elderly man held Golden's arm for support as they walked down the long central aisle toward the main stand on the far side. Besides themselves, the building was empty, and the massive space dwarfed the two men.

The long benches and the columns supporting the balcony were made from white pine, though you'd never know it to look at them. Everything had been painstakingly painted by hand so that the benches resembled oak and the pillars looked like Tennessee marble. At the head of the room, the grand organ stood looking over everything. The lumber to craft it had been carted in from over three hundred miles away, and the original organ sported seven hundred pipes, all run by hand-pumped bellows. As impressive as all this was, it was still modest by comparison. There were much larger pipe organs in the world, and it was just an obscure instrument in the middle of nowhere. There was no way of knowing that one day it would have almost twelve thousand electrically powered pipes and become one of the largest and most famous organs in existence. Organs, just like the rest of us, don't have any real idea of what grand things might lay ahead of them in their future.

Golden had been here many times before, whenever the family would make the trek down for conference. The Tabernacle was always busy then, packed to bursting with Saints attending church meetings. Golden had never paid much attention to the interior work before. Now, with the main hall empty and quiet, he had a chance to really give it a gander for the first time. It surprised him that he'd never noticed how fine the craftsmanship was before.

"Magnificent, isn't it?" President Taylor broke the silence.

"I hardly feel worthy to step foot in it." It was the truth. This was where the Saints gathered to hear the prophet and the apostles distill the word of the Lord. Golden felt he hadn't always lived up to snuff, which, in his mind, made him the last person on earth who should be standing in here. But here he was, walking side by side with the living, breathing prophet of God.

President Taylor led him up the steps onto the stand, walking past the seats where the apostles sat every conference. Passing his own seat, he finally stopped at the elegantly carved podium and looked out over the room. From up here the space looked even bigger than it had from down below. Golden tried to imagine it filled to the brim with people and found the thought overwhelming.

"What's it like to stand here and preach to the Saints?" Golden asked.

"It's the most humbling thing in my entire life." President Taylor rested his hand on Golden's arm again. "Are you old enough to remember, I wonder, the time before this was built? Where we stand now on wooden floors there was once nothing but dirt and scrub brush."

Golden remembered, all right. He was eleven years old when the construction began. He still recalled his father meeting with Brigham Young, discussing plans for the building that would eventually cover the flat piece of desert that would become downtown Salt Lake City. The Tabernacle had taken the Saints a scant three years to complete, a real testament to their industriousness and hard work.

President Taylor continued, "Many faithful Saints have put long hours and much sacrifice into the building of this Tabernacle. Men such as your father. He was a great man. A great man."

Completed roughly a year before Golden's father passed away, the Tabernacle was the last thing Heber C. Kimball had been directly involved in before his death. Heber had put everything he had into the work until his dying day, into building not only the Tabernacle but also the kingdom of God. No doubt this was one of the reasons that Golden looked up to his father so much.

"Yes, sir," Golden agreed. His voice was quiet, his mind lost in reflection. "My only real hope is that I can live up to his name."

"Don't worry about his name. It will take care of itself. The important thing is that you live up to your own." President Taylor faced him directly now, looking at him with the same eyes that had born witness to the martyrdom of the prophet Joseph Smith. The kindness never left his eyes, but there was something else there, an almost palpable strength, well tempered by time and trial.

Golden was up a tree. He understood what President Taylor was saying, clear as day. And he knew that the prophet was right. To become anything in life he'd have to do more than just wish for it. He'd have to earn it for himself.

"When do I leave?" Golden asked, humbled.

"In one week."

CHAPTER 4

AWAY DOWN SOUTH IN DIXIE

I believe it to be the duty of everyone to unite in the restoration of the country and the reestablishment of peace and harmony.

—General Robert E. Lee

Next thing he knew, Golden found himself on Union Pacific #9, traveling from purple mountain majesties, across the fruited plains, through amber waves of grain, and headlong into the land of cotton. The steam engine chugged its rhythmic march across the endless miles of track created by the labor of the thousands of workers who literally pounded the steel trail into being.

The year was 1883, a busy year in the annals of history. A writer type going by the handle of Mark Twain was getting ready to introduce the world to Huckleberry Finn, and an odd contraption called the bustle was mode du jour for the lady folk, if you'll pardon my French. It was, as far as I know, the only time women have ever wanted something that made their hindquarters look bigger. The Civil War had been over for eighteen years, and even though the Emancipation Proclamation was written in the history books, it had yet to be fully etched into the hearts of the people. Jim Crow laws were in effect, and segregation, bitterness, and anger festered in the wounds left over from the war like gangrene. In the wake of the collapse of the Confederate way of life, poverty held sway in the South. Battle scars remained on both the land and the people; some were visible while others lay buried deep within. Divisions still ran strong along lines of race, politics, and especially religion. If anyone told you things were settling down in the South, they deserved to get their mouth washed out with soap. Things were settling down all right, like powder settling into a keg, waiting for a spark.

It was also a time when anti-Mormon sentiment was growing across the nation. Congress passed the Edmunds-Tucker Act without the approving signature of President Cleveland. It outlawed polygamy and threatened to disenfranchise the Church, which is a highfalutin way of saying nearly wrecking something. Mormons often made national news. The headlines were always lurid or fantastic, lambasting Mormons as wife stealers and harem-holding heretics.

In defense of the papers, they weren't picking exclusively on the Mormons (usually). They lambasted everything they didn't care for: carpetbaggers, Northerners, Catholics, whatever. But in a time and place when gossip and superstition were easier to print and more widely believed than truth or fact, taking potshots at the Mormons was easy.

As it happened, "Mo-muns" were gracing the headlines again on the day that Golden found himself rolling along into Tennessee. In typical fashion, it was something silly again—*Mormons Challenge Government!* or *Mormon Leaders Call for War!* or some such nonsense—but it was enough to raise a few eyebrows and garner some heated discussion on the train.

The passenger car was plenty crowded and not as pleasant smelling as a fellow might hope. It wasn't just the smoke and the steam from the engine. It wasn't even the cars filled with livestock; they were located downwind near the rear of the train. No, the odor was entirely due to the huddled mass of humanity crowded together in the passenger car like cattle in a chute. The South was nothing if not hot and muggy, and the high temperature crossed with the cramped quarters made for a sweaty ride indeed. Even with all the windows open, the car refused to breathe.

Golden was no desert rose himself, but he paled in comparison to the men sitting around him. The fellow next to him smelled identical to the contents of the metal flask he was waving around. The sharp scent was unfamiliar to Golden, but he knew it wasn't water. Several of the men were drunk as a skunk, and those that weren't were well on their way. The worst thing about drunk people, Golden realized, was the stench thick as soured milk.

This man, like many the missionaries had encountered in the Tennessee region, was coarse in manner and dress. It wasn't that he didn't shop from the Sears and Roebuck catalog; Golden couldn't have cared less about that. But the clothes he did have were filthy and unkempt. Heaven alone knew the last time they had been washed, or the man wearing them, for that matter.

Much to his own chagrin, it occurred to Golden that he must have looked similar to this fellow only a few weeks before as he walked to the Tabernacle with President Taylor, minus the drunkenness. He made a silent promise that he would never let himself become so poorly groomed ever again. Golden supposed that the man could have been clean this morning and was returning from a very, very dirty job. But the man's odor made him doubt it.

"Them Mo-muns is a blot on this nation, Ah tell you what." The flask-waving man spoke in a heavy Southern drawl, the clarity of his speech not helped at all by his drink. He made his pronouncement with the surety of the drunkard who knows his audience would agree, holding up his flask like a toast.

He was sloshed all right, and his companions were little better. "I think them Missurans had it right—they ought to be exterminated," one of them slurred. Whereas the first man might have been drunk, the second man erased all doubt. And the third? Well, he made the first two seem sober as judges by comparison.

"They think jusht cuz they live in the territoriesh they can git away with their shenanigansh," he slurred.

Golden was shocked that people had the brass to tongue-lash Mormons like that. He knew Mormons weren't much liked, but he had no idea things were so downright hostile. Everyone on the train seemed to agree with the men, and not all of them had alcohol as an excuse. Drunk or sober, everyone thought the Mormons to be no account, no good hoodlums at best, pure children of the devil at worst.

"Buncha suck-egg dawgs," one passenger waxed eloquent.

"I don't know if killin' them's the answer or not, but they're definitely a botheration," piped up another.

"Well, if one a Brigham's no 'count bootlickers comes on my clearin', I'd certainly introduce him to the proper end of a Winchester."

Let's make it clear right now that this is not to say that all people of the South were crude, rude, and unrefined. There were (and are) many shining examples of Southern souls just as kind and Christlike as one could ever hope to find anywhere on God's green earth, as you will see. But you could have fooled Golden by the introduction he was given on the train. If the South had been trying to make a good first impression, it definitely hadn't put its best foot forward.

Ka-lunk ka-lunk. Ka-lunk ka-lunk. The train counted off the distance like the inexorable ticking of the clock. Golden tried to concentrate on the clack of train tracks instead of the verbal abuse circulating around him and the growing pit in his stomach. He dug his finger into his collar. The further south he went, the more uncomfortable it grew. It had fit perfectly fine when he left Salt Lake, but now it was gradually turning into the world's skinniest noose. There was an awfully big part of him that wanted to jump ship and snag the first train, wagon, carriage, or horse headed back west.

When the train started out from Ogden, Golden had been part of a large group of elders, but they had slowly split up along the way, peeling off to different parts of the states and Canada. Even though a handful of elders remained with him, Golden felt isolated and, though he hated to admit it, scared. In all his years, he had never been away from home before. The South was part of the United States (again), but they may as well have been sending him to another country. Or planet.

He had been out of Utah only a few days, and already he was homesick. The sky outside the train was a beautiful blue sea speckled with cotton clouds, but he could find no joy in it. He spent most of the time staring at his hands folded in his lap. What on earth had he gotten himself into?

He fiddled with his collar again, huddling with the other elders near the back of the car, all of them quietly enduring the slander and trying their best to be invisible as the train moved ever deeper into the heart of Dixie.

CHAPTER 5

A STRANGE WELCOME

Good humor is one of the best articles of dress one can wear in society.

—*William M. Thackeray*

After seven long days, the elders arrived in Chattanooga. It occurred to Golden that it took as long for him to cross the country as it took God to make all of creation. Apparently God still has the upper hand in the getting-things-done department.

The central train depot was little more than a long building with two sets of tracks running in and out of it. Sunlight entered from large picture windows lining the span of the building. A crown of smaller windows dotting the middle of the curved roof allowed more light onto the single platform that stood tucked between both tracks. It may not have been much to look at in those days, but it was still big enough and crowded enough to overwhelm the elders clustered together on the platform like a flock of sheep trying to protect themselves from ravaging wolves.

Golden was greatly relieved to see that most people here were dressed in a civilized manner, which is to say that their clothing had at least been washed, and that the ruffians on the train appeared to be the minority. Most folks moved by the elders without so much as a glance, but Golden noticed, much to his great discomfort, that for every pair of eyes that paid no mind, there was another set that stared or, even worse, glared. The elders stood out, and none more so than Golden, his head poking out of the throng like a stalk of corn in a cotton patch. He adjusted the small frames of his glasses and played at his collar again. The once comfortable cloth felt like heavy grit sandpaper against his neck.

A Negro porter in a uniform pressed as crisply as a new dollar bill appeared out of the crowd and offered to take the elders' bags, but they politely declined. The porter excused himself with a tip of his cap and went on with his work. The elders stared after him. Utah territory has always been known for many things, but being racially diverse was not one of them. The majority of the elders had never seen a Negro before leaving Utah. They had come across them during their trip, but, sad as it is to say, the sight of a Negro, especially one in a sharply pressed uniform, was still enough of a novelty that the elders couldn't help but stare in spite of themselves. Most likely the elders would have kept staring until kingdom come if they hadn't been interrupted by someone behind them.

"Y'all gotta be Mo-muns, ain'tcha?" The voice was coated in a Southern drawl thick as molasses in January and several degrees colder. It was typical of the accent that Golden would often encounter throughout his mission, so heavy that any trace of English was almost unintelligible beneath it.

Golden turned to face a stocky man with a bushy but neatly kept beard and mustache. Dressed in a squarely cut brown suit, he was shorter than most of the elders but had the build, posture, and attitude of a bulldog. He was carefully groomed and didn't appear the slightest bit intoxicated. On the ranch Golden had worked with some of the toughest varmints who had ever lived, men who could eat barbed wire for lunch with a bowl of five-penny nails for dessert, then ask for seconds. This fellow was clearly like that. Better dressed, but every bit as tough. Golden wasn't sure what the man wanted, but from the tone of his voice and the contrary angle of his stance, he guessed it wasn't friendly conversation.

"Ain'tcha?" The man was in their faces and didn't show the merest inkling of backing off. Golden, like the others, could only gape wordlessly like a carp out of water. It may have been the first—and possibly only—time in his entire life when Golden had nothing to say.

When no one responded, the bulldog snapped at them again. "What's the matta? Devil got yuh tongue? Ain't any a yuh got a thing to say? Nothing at all?"

He placed his hands firmly on his hips and looked the group over, inspecting them like he was buying livestock. The elders might as well have been statues for all they did. After an awkward moment, the man took a step back, and his entire demeanor softened. "Well, we'll have to change that right away, won't we?"

His aggressive drawl was gone, replaced by a kind voice that carried the subtlest trace of a faded British accent. He offered an extended hand and a warm smile to the confused elders. "I'm B.H. Roberts, acting president of the mission. Welcome to the Southern States."

Golden felt his cheeks flush as he realized he'd been had. Still, it had been a daisy of a joke, and he'd fallen for it whole hog. From the stunned looks on the other elders' faces, he could tell he wasn't the only one.

Embarrassed but much relieved at the sight of a friendly face, Golden reached out and shook B.H.'s hand, "It's a good thing you told us who you were; I was about to give you a piece of my mind."

"Yes, I believe you were," B.H. chuckled. He had the laugh of a man who appreciated a good sense of humor, something that Golden took as a positive sign. President Roberts was roughly Golden's same age, a mite younger, actually, but was already earning a name for himself as one of the smartest crackers in the barrel, as far as the Church was concerned. There was hardly a soul alive who read more than B.H. Besides the scriptures and other religious texts, he also gobbled up books on history, the sciences, and philosophy. In later years the six books in his *Comprehensive History of the Church of Jesus Christ of Latter-day Saints* would come to be thought of as one of the greatest scholarly works on the Church.

B.H. greeted the elders one by one, shaking their hands and welcoming each of them personally to the mission. The genuine enthusiasm of the man did a lot to wash away the feeling of isolation and gloom that had crept like a choking vine over Golden on his journey. B.H. was a Mormon living in the South, and he wasn't dead yet. Golden figured that was a good omen.

After the proper introductions were made, B.H. helped the elders gather their few belongings and led them out of the station. Most elders carried very little. A small number of personal items were kept in a valise. Considering they'd be walking most places they went and that they'd be carrying whatever they'd brought with them, you can understand why they packed lightly.

Following B.H.'s lead, the elders stepped onto Railroad Avenue and turned to follow a narrow gully running alongside the busy road. One of the first things Golden noticed was the smell of burning coal and the plumes of chimney smoke that drifted across the sky. It was definitely an industrial city. In some parts the roads were made of cobbled brick, but most areas were still packed earth. The gravel crunched beneath the soles of Golden's new shoes as he walked along, taking in the city for the first time.

Chattanooga was born in the 1800s as a center of commerce and trade for the whole area. Just about anything that was shipped, sold, or traded flowed through it at one point or another. This distinction was further cemented by the arrival of the railroad in the 1850s. Due to its central location, both sides wanted the city something fierce during the Civil War. After a series of many bloody battles, it was eventually occupied by the

Union army as a forward depot. Very few permanent buildings survived the war, and the fighting left mostly ugly warehouses, military shops, and damaged streets in its wake.

Golden had imagined the place to be war torn and destroyed. He'd heard stories about Sherman's March and other ravages suffered by the South. He wasn't sure if Sherman had stampeded through Chattanooga or not (he hadn't), but it was nothing like he'd pictured in his mind's eye. From his experience on the train, Golden had been expecting far worse. He was sure that nothing was waiting for him but a devastated city full of crumbled buildings and drunkards ready to kill any Mormon at a moment's notice. The fact of the matter was that most folks were civilized and paid the elders little mind as they went about their own daily business.

The Southerners had not been idle or lazy, and the Reconstruction period was certainly earning its name. The streets were lined with fine, new, two-story buildings. Most of them had been built up since the war, standing as a testament to the hardiness of the people. The buildings back home in Salt Lake were built of gray granite or dusky sandstone quarried and hauled in from the local hills. Chattanooga, with its downtown of fresh, red-brick buildings, felt almost like a scene from a stage play or picture book.

Streetcars and wagons of every shape, size, and description traversed the lanes to the plodding rhythm of hooves. Some carried people while others carried freight of all types to and from the train station and beyond. Livestock, lumber, general goods, food stuffs—you name it, it all passed through the vigorous city.

Golden would definitely give the South this much, they sure knew how to raise beautiful horses. Some of the animals pulling the streetcars and wagons were as fine as cream gravy and as handsome as any he had ever seen. A Tennessee Walker with well-sloped shoulders whinnied at a long-hipped Missouri Fox Trotter and a passing Morgan. Golden's mustang back home had been excellent for cutting cattle but paled in quality and breeding to even the most average horse he saw on the road here.

B.H. led the elders along, mindful of the traffic moving down the road. Golden could feel curious eyes looking at him and the others. B.H. seemed immune to the occasional stares and hushed whispers, but Golden found it completely unsettling. He tried to remain as coolheaded as B.H., but his nerves wouldn't allow him. He had felt quite dapper when he first got all gussied up in his new suit. Now it felt all too conspicuous. Despite his promise to himself on the train, he would have loved to be in his grubby work clothes again or anything that would draw less attention to himself. He didn't know if he'd ever get used to feeling like a circus spectacle in a P.T. Barnum show.

Beyond downtown the brick structures gave way to more traditional wooden buildings and homes as the city began to spread out into the lush valleys and rolling hills of the southwestern Appalachian Mountains. To the southeast the sheer gray face of Lookout Mountain stood like a stony sentinel in its eternal vigil over the city.

Golden found, much to his relief, that as the buildings thinned out, so did the number of people. He found himself looking around more and enjoying his surroundings instead of fearing them. Despite his own qualms and the strange greeting they'd received so far, he decided that it was right pretty down here. Thick forestland covered everything like a sea of velvet green. Most of the wooden buildings, like their brick cousins downtown, were relatively new. Very few if any were more than ten years old, and everything from marbled oak to rich hickory could be seen lacing their roofs, walls, and porches.

The procession of elders rounded another corner onto a single-lane dirt road that led up a gentle rise. Ahead of them among a thatch of homes stood a beautiful chapel, built of the same new red brick as the buildings downtown. Golden was relieved to see they'd reached the mission home. It was a lovely edifice, and Golden couldn't help but imagine what it would be like to preach in such a fine building. He pictured a group of humble Saints gathered together inside. He could almost see their sweet faces, happy children and loving parents gathered to hear the good word. They smiled at him as he stepped to the pulpit, where he opened his mouth and said—

"MORMONS!"

The voice roared like thunder and damnation from the open front door of the chapel, tearing Golden violently from his daydream.

There are certain unexplained mysteries in nature, peculiarities of behavior that exist without understood reason or motivation. When startled or threatened, an opossum will play dead. Certain breeds of goat will faint, falling right to the ground. A deer will freeze in a spotlight. And Mormon elders will stop in their tracks when confronted by a Southern preacher screaming at them from a pulpit.

A meeting was in full swing, and the chapel was filled with easily over fifty people. Following the preacher's sharp finger, the entire congregation turned to stare wide-eyed with wonder and fear at the gaggle of Mormons standing immobilized just beyond the chapel doors.

"The horned demons of Satan!" the preacher yelled, still pointing. His voice scorched like acid dipped in honey. The elders might have been dumbstruck, but the preacher was fired up. "They appear as men, but do not be deceived! I have seen them! By the pale light of the full moon they reveal their true selves as Satan spawn with hooves and horns!"

Jagged lines formed as he scowled, his face contorting viciously as he pantomimed horns with a great, exaggerated motion. The heads in the congregation bobbed this way and that, jockeying for position to get a better view of the Satan spawn standing right in front of their very own church.

Golden wouldn't be preaching in this chapel any time soon. Probably not ever. His brow furrowed in disbelief, and he wished for the hundredth time that day that he could disappear, just turn invisible or vanish into thin air. He couldn't believe what he was hearing. Any thoughts that this whole mission thing might not be so bad scattered like flies chased from a carcass. Unlike flies, the good feelings wouldn't be coming back any time soon.

The preacher stepped from behind his pulpit, advancing down the aisle toward the petrified elders. He was tall and angular and cut an imposing figure, fierce as a badger by the looks of it, and twice as mean. With his striking features framed by well-groomed hair tinged with silver, he was a handsome man by any standard. The glare of his steel blue eyes pierced the elders to the core. If it were possible for a man to be reduced to ash by just a glance, Golden was sure he would have withered on the spot.

The preacher continued his diatribe, firing a verbal assault like cannon fire as he slowly advanced down the aisle. The tension was palpable. "They are a threat, not only to the flower of Southern womanhood but also to our God, to our very way of life!"

Golden felt a tug on his sleeve and looked down to see B.H. quickly motioning to the elders to follow. They withdrew without a word, tails tucked between their legs, the preacher's voice hounding them as they retreated down the street. "I warn you to stay away from our people, demon spawn, or incur the vengeful wrath of an angry God!"

As the elders beat a hasty departure down the road, Golden wondered again exactly what he had gotten himself into. He couldn't believe what he had just witnessed. Demon spawn? Hooves and horns? It was obvious nonsense, but Golden felt belittled just the same. They traveled up the road in silence for a good distance before Golden voiced the question on everyone's mind.

"Excuse me, President, but who was that?"

"That, brethren, was the good Reverend Charles A. Weatherbee." B.H. stated it as a resigned fact. "He travels about the region preaching against the 'Mo-muns.'"

"Surely the people don't believe that gibberish, do they? I mean, horns?" Golden twisted his lean face, mimicking Weatherbee's gruesome look and overdone pantomime of horns.

"You would think people would know better, but wherever he preaches, the work slows down for months." From the sound of B.H.'s voice, it was clear that he couldn't believe that anyone could swallow such poppycock either, but the fact was they did.

The scene from the chapel played over and over in Golden's mind. At first he was incredulous. Then a thought struck him. It was the kind of thought that would strike him for the rest of his life. The kind of thought that, once it occurred, would continue its natural course from his brain to his tongue and then irrevocably out of his mouth, whether he wanted it to or not.

"'Stealing the flower of Southern womanhood.'" He laughed, remembering the horrified looks on the faces of the women in the congregation. "All you had to do was look at those women and you'd know that thought would never have crossed our minds."

B.H. looked at him curiously. Golden shrugged matter-of-factly. "Even polygamists have standards."

Well, that did it. B.H. started to snicker. It started out as a smothered snort and ripped wide open into a full-fledged, hearty guffaw. The other elders figured if the president was laughing it was okay for them as well, and soon the entire group was joined together in a chorus of laughter. Golden couldn't help but feel better. The jest was small, but it was big enough to put a crack in the gloom that had been settling over him and let some sunshine in.

CHAPTER 6

HOME SWEET MISSION HOME

A poor wayfaring man of grief
Hath often crossed me on my way,
Who sued so humbly for relief
That I could never answer nay.

—*James Montgomery*

The sun had called it a day and dusk had nestled in like a blanket by the time the tired elders reached the mission home. A few fires burned in scattered windows throughout the valley, giving a dim, red glow to the thin tendrils of smoke that rose from their chimneys. They were well beyond the lights of downtown now, and Golden couldn't make out much of the street in the dark.

The home itself was a simple, two-story, wooden structure sandwiched between a small dry goods store and what looked like it might have been an unused storage depot. It was nothing so fancy as Weatherbee's chapel and in fact wasn't much bigger than Golden's barn back in Meadowville. It could have been a tin shack for all that Golden cared by this point. He'd been on the road for a week now, and they had been walking for miles. As long as there was a pillow available, it was good enough for him.

"Here we are, brethren." B.H. opened the door and ushered the elders inside. He struck a match and lit a kerosene lamp, bathing the office in a dull orange glimmer. Golden looked around as his eyes adjusted to the light. The place wasn't spacious by any means. A few simple benches stood before a solid looking desk covered with various books and papers. A cast-iron typing machine sat on a corner of the desk. All in all, the office was economical and practical, something which Golden could appreciate.

"You must all be very tired. Your room is upstairs. Feel free to head up." B.H. motioned toward a narrow staircase. "I'll be there in a moment to ensure everything's suitable."

Golden was closest to the stairs but paused before ascending. "Is there anything I can do?"

"No, thank you, Elder Kimball. Do make yourself comfortable." B.H. turned to thumb through a stack of letters on the desk. Golden's feet felt oddly heavy as he mounted the stairs, the other elders following in a line behind him. The thud of their leather shoes against the wooden steps echoed like dull drums. The soles of Golden's shoes were still new and stiff, but he suspected they wouldn't stay that way for long.

Another lamp glowed in the upstairs hall, the low flame flickering beneath the lead glass like a dying ember. In its light, the shadows of the elders moved like some sort of beast crawling through a narrow tunnel. The hall was tight as a cattle chute, even for Golden, who had to carry his valise in front of him to fit. His shoulders nearly touched both walls, and he wondered how the others would make it through.

Two matching doors lined the wall about ten feet apart. Both were made out of pine, and both were shut. Golden wasn't sure which one he was supposed to go into, but he couldn't back up either, not with the line of elders right behind him. Figuring he could move onto the second door easily enough if he were mistaken, he decided to try the first. He pushed against it, and it swung open with the slight tick of wood sliding against wood.

The burnt-amber light of the hall poured in through the door and fell across a man sitting in a wooden-framed bed. The light wasn't much, but it was enough that the man covered his eyes as he looked up at the ragtag elders peering in from the door. It was obviously the wrong door, and Golden flushed. "I'm terribly sorry."

"It's all right." The man shook his head slightly, his voice more weary sounding than any Golden had ever heard. As Golden's eyes adjusted further, he saw that the man had a large bandage wrapped around his torso and was heavily bruised about the face and neck. Off to the side there was another man lying in a second bed. Dark stains blotted the bandages that covered him from head to toe. Whatever had happened, it was apparent that he'd gotten the worst of it. There was a slight gasp from behind Golden; the other elders had seen him too.

The first man looked them over. "You fellows must be new."

Golden nodded. "What happened?"

"I ran across a mob near Lewisburg." He motioned toward the second man with his head. "That's Elder Dalton. Klan tarred and feathered him near Wytheville, burned him pretty fierce. We're both shipping home as soon as he's well enough to travel again."

Golden had heard the stories growing up. Nearly everyone in his parents' generation had suffered persecutions and almost indescribable horrors at the hands of uncivilized and ignorant men. Tarring, feathering, beating, mobbing—all these things and more had chased the Saints further and further west. Golden's own father had been run from his home five different times. Persecution wasn't part of their history, it was part of their lives. As the second generation of Mormons, nestled in the often harsh but safe embrace of the mountains, the stories had always seemed so far away, so long ago. The fulness of the elder's words pierced Golden's mind like an ice pick. They weren't just stories anymore, they were the reality into which Golden had come.

Thoughts of mission glory, of returning home with thousands

of converts at his heels, vanished like paper before a flame. Forget glory—with brutality like this going on right around him, Golden decided he'd be lucky if he got home at all.

The elder reached for a cup of water on the stand beside his bed. He fumbled it with his heavily bandaged hand, and it tumbled to the floor with a clatter, its contents spilling out and draining down the cracks between the floorboards. The elder grimaced. The look was not one of pain but of frustration. Golden quickly stepped forward and picked the cup off the floor. He refilled it from an urn, then helped the man raise the cup to his lips and drink.

"Thank you," said the elder.

"Don't mention it." Golden crouched to wipe up what little water hadn't leaked through the floor. He stood and was surprised to see B.H. standing in the doorway.

"My apologies. I didn't clarify." The president stepped inside the room, clearing the doorway for the elders. "Your room is the next door down." The elders began shuffling out, and B.H. crossed to the bedridden elder, resting a compassionate hand on his shoulder. "How are you, Henry?"

Sympathy and worry mingled freely in Golden's heart as he watched President Roberts attend to the injured elder. He spared a look at the elder who had been tarred, then followed the others out of the room.

The second room was slightly bigger than the first. It held a small dresser, a bookshelf, and three wooden bunk beds that stood lined up against the wall. His companions had fallen asleep the moment they'd doused the light, but Golden found it difficult to sleep. Not only did his feet stick out of the end of the bed, but also his mind was awash with everything he'd seen and heard. Scared, nervous, and more than a little homesick, he lay in bed, staring wide-eyed into the darkness until he finally slipped into a fitful slumber.

The next morning a hearty Southern breakfast was served at a local hotel eatery. The bacon and eggs were cooked to perfection, but Golden didn't know what to make of the grits at first. They looked like something that had been culled from some unidentified animal part. When he sniffed at them, they didn't seem to have any odor of their own. He saw some of the local gentry slather theirs with butter, so he did the same and gave it a go. To his relief they weren't half bad. In fact he decided he liked them and cleaned his whole plate.

The air was electric as they gathered back in the mission office. The elders discussed which mission conference they would be sent to with great anticipation. Golden didn't really know his Carolina from his Georgia, so it didn't make much difference to him. At this point they were all equally intimidating. President Roberts quieted them and began the meeting with a prayer.

"I know you are all very excited," he said, his own voice echoing their emotion in its lilting accent. "I have a few brief words to share with you, then we'll get down to brass tacks. I do not know what images of a mission you carry in your minds. It is likely that the South will defy most of them. I have a few guidelines that I wish you to follow while you are here. These are for your safety. Please listen attentively as what I am about to say is quite important."

Golden listened closely but wondered how he should feel when the first thing the mission president chose to speak about was safety.

"You are to avoid preaching in the cities entirely," President Roberts admonished. "Instead contain your proselytizing to the outlying areas. You will find the people there to be more humble and willing to listen to our message. Also the persecution isn't as bad there."

The mention of persecution wasn't wasted on the elders. Last night's meeting with the injured missionaries had been a harsh grounding to the seriousness of the situation.

B.H. continued, "Avoid places where there have been previous threats, places where people drink alcohol as well as any religious revival meetings, as they can stir the people to quite a fervor. As you know you will be traveling without purse or scrip, like the apostles of old, so please exercise due caution. Beyond that, be humble and submissive and stay close to the Spirit." He stopped and looked them over and then smiled warmly. "And last but not least, brethren, be of good cheer. It is the Lord's errand you are on. He will bless and watch over you."

And with that, Golden and his fellow missionaries were given their assignments and released into the proverbial wild.

CHAPTER 7

THE FIELD IS ~~WHITE~~ ~~OFF-WHITE~~ SORT OF GRAY

* * *

We were left to hustle for ourselves, and that is how I became a hustler.

—J. Golden Kimball

Missionary work in the South started as early as 1832 in parts of Kentucky and Tennessee. There wasn't much to it then, mostly just members returning home to visit families and loved ones. By 1839, missionaries were preaching in Virginia, Arkansas, Mississippi, and the Carolinas. Jedediah M. Grant (father to a fellow by the name of Heber J. Grant) was one of these first missionaries. He labored in Virginia for four and a half years, becoming one of the most effective missionaries to serve there.

As you might figure, the Civil War put an end to all missionary work in the South for a while, but the Church got back at it shortly after the war's end. The Southern States Mission was officially established in 1875. Geographically speaking, it was bigger than a Texas tall tale. If you were to take out a map of the United States and put your finger on Missouri, then draw a line straight east and one straight south, you'd get a rough idea of the size of it. At different times it covered anywhere between eleven to fifteen states, including parts of Texas, Maryland, and Ohio.

Between 1877 and 1899, two thousand eighty-seven missionaries were sent to the South, a number that made up roughly half the missionaries who served domestically. For most of these years, between one hundred and one hundred twenty-five elders were in the mission at any given time. Your typical elder was in his middle twenties. Incredibly, the youngest elder to ever serve was a mere pup at the age of thirteen while the oldest was a much more seasoned sixty-seven. Roughly 60 percent of the elders were married, and of that 60 percent, 30 percent were polygamist. The year that Golden landed, there were a thousand members of the Church, give or take, scattered throughout the entire South.

If Southerners hadn't been very fond of Northerners before the war, they were nasty as snake venom after. Some Southerners would lend anyone the shirt off their backs and probably press and starch it to boot. But plenty more were hostile, and the South quickly gained a reputation in the Church for its violence.

Threats on the missionaries were as common as fleas to a hound. They were so common, in fact, that many historians are surprised that there weren't more incidents of actual violence. Notes were often signed with inventive monikers such as Concerned Citizen, KKK, or Judge Lynch. It turns out that most violence that occurred during this time was usually led by the Ku Klux Klan, church clergy, or, oddly enough, newspaper editors.

Despite the amount and the intensity of threats, only one killing of an elder had occurred since the mission was formed. That was Joseph Standing in 1879. Tragically, he wasn't to be the last.

Golden was assigned to the Virginia Conference. The sparse population there was mostly made of coal miners and farmers—poor folk who worked hard to eke out a living from the earth.

Outside of the large cities such as Richmond and Roanoke, it remained a land of scattered farmsteads and pristine woodlands. A lacework of country roads crisscrossed the countryside like a tattered spiderweb. It was upon one such road that Golden found himself walking with his first companion, Elder Rich. The twin ruts of earth, worn low by the passing of wagon wheels, snaked their way through undergrowth thick as a lamb's wool in late winter. It was early afternoon, and the road was the only sign of humanity they had seen all livelong day. Golden was fortunate that he found the countryside pleasant and charming, for it was what he would spend most of his time looking at during his stay in the South.

Golden had gotten a good look at the richness of the area from the train, but it was still amazing how green a place could truly be. The wild growth coating the land was stark contrast to the dry desert terrain of Utah. He had always thought the fir- and aspen-covered mountains of home to be green, but even spring in the West was nothing like this place. Verdant plants covered everything that wasn't cleared by man. A canopy of oak and hickory of every kind stood over an endless covering of dogwood, rhododendron, and azaleas. Even things that weren't supposed to be green, like rocks and trunks, were covered in moss and vines. At home it was by the sweat of your brow (and often a lot of choice language) that you coerced crops to grow. Golden doubted that you could stop plants from growing in these parts even if you tried.

He had to admit that it was beautiful here. He wasn't sure if he'd ever get used to the way the humidity made his clothes stick to his scrawny frame, but he found himself enjoying the scenery. Insects and cottonseed drifted lazily in the heavy, static air. No matter which way Golden looked, all he could see was the thick emerald blanket of the Appalachian woods smothering the rounded hills that rolled into eternity. He was completely surrounded by country.

"Well, I suppose this is about as far from the city as one can get." He turned to his companion. "So what was it like growing up in Paris?"

"It's all right, I guess. The winters are long."

A glint of mischief flickered in Golden's eyes. To those who knew him well, it was a familiar look; it meant he was about to say something amusing. With a slight smile, he said, "I've always wanted to see Paris. Little did I know all I had to do was go to Idaho."

Rich missed the jest entirely. "Honestly, there isn't much to see. Just farms mostly. And I'm sure you've seen those in Utah."

Elder Rich wasn't dumb. No sir, he was just too sincere to notice the humor. He was solid Idaho farm stock, the salt of the earth. He had a genuine, down-to-earth honesty about him that Golden really respected. Of course that didn't stop him from teasing Rich a bit.

Rich thumbed the latch of his valise absently. "So, what do you think? About being a missionary?"

"I haven't been here long enough to know what to think," said Golden. "To be perfectly frank, I'm a little unsure of what exactly it is I'm supposed to be doing here."

"I know how you feel," Rich said with a sigh. It sounded so resigned that it made Golden pause. Rich was the senior companion here; he should have at least some idea of what they were doing.

Golden turned to Rich, "How long have you been out here?"

"Just two weeks."

"No, I mean your whole mission."

Rich nodded. "Two weeks."

Golden stopped in his tracks so fast his feet kicked up a puff of dust. He was flabbergasted.

"You mean they put two greenhorns together?" Golden didn't have the slightest idea how to teach, and apparently his new companion didn't either. "Just how are we to know what to preach? I've never given a sermon before! Have you?"

Rich thought it over. "Well, no."

Golden was absolutely perplexed. Other than yelling at cows, he had no training as a preacher, and anything he said to the cows probably wasn't appropriate anyhow. Golden thought of his father. On his mission to England, Heber and his companion Joseph Fielding once baptized 110 people in neighboring villages, creating four branches in only five days. Heber had been a mighty orator, able to rain fire from the pulpit. Golden suddenly wished he'd paid more attention when he was a kid.

"Maybe we could preach to the trees." Rich shrugged.

"What?" Golden highly doubted he'd heard that right.

"Maybe we could preach to the trees, just for practice?"

Yup, he'd heard it right. Trees.

"That's about the most peculiar notion I've ever heard." Golden wasn't lying. It was an odd idea, but he knew that Rich was trying to help in his own way. And since Golden couldn't think of anything better, the least he could do was take the suggestion with equal sincerity. "Let's try it."

They retired to the side of the road, approaching the first grove of trees they saw. A single oak and a few maples stood at one side of a small clearing and seemed as good an audience as any. At the very least, even if his preaching were the worst thing since curdled milk, most likely the trees wouldn't mind. Golden stood near the trees. He opened his mouth to speak, then suddenly got to feeling all sorts of foolish. He turned to Rich. "Uh, why don't you go first."

Rich shrugged an "okay, why not," and took a step toward the oak. He raised one arm in the air and raised his voice, "My dearest trees."

It looked as funny as it sounds: Elder Rich standing there addressing a bunch of trees. Golden would have burst out in laughter, but he didn't want to offend his new companion. Besides, Rich was trying and had managed to say more than Golden had dared to so far.

Rich paused. He lowered his hand and looked back at Golden. Golden was afraid that a laugh had escaped him accidentally.

"What?" asked Golden.

"I don't know what else to say." Rich shrugged.

"I don't know either. But you're doing a fine job so far." Golden didn't know who he was trying to encourage more, himself or Rich. He tried to think of something to help his companion. "Thank them." He gestured toward the trees.

"What?"

"Thank them for listening," Golden coached.

Rich turned back to his audience, "I thank you for coming out to hear us today."

He paused and looked at Golden again, "What else?"

"I don't know." Golden shrugged, thinking fast. "Tell them something about the Gospel."

"Like what?"

"Uh . . . " Long unused gears in Golden's mind began to turn, shaking off the layers of rust that covered them. "Tell them about how Christ's teachings were lost and have been restored."

"That's a great idea. I thought you said you didn't know what to say."

"I didn't. Now you're making me think about it."

"Well, you're thinking of good stuff."

"Thanks." Golden wasn't sure if what he was coming up with was good or not, but he was glad to be thinking of something. That was at least a step in the right direction.

Rich turned and began to preach about the restoration of the gospel to the attentive timber. Considering he was talking to trees, Golden thought he didn't do a half bad job. After a few minutes, Rich turned the time over to Golden. Golden felt silly as he stepped forward. He should have gone first; he'd given Rich all his best ideas. He rubbed his hand on the back of his neck trying to think of something else to talk about. The trees waited patiently.

"Baptism!" Golden snapped his fingers with excitement. That was a great idea to talk about, all right. Now, what about it?

"Baptism is, uh . . . " His tongue actually felt as if it tripped inside his mouth. "The first step! Baptism is the first step," he told the trees. No, wait, repentance was. No, that wasn't quite right either.

"Faith!" Rich whispered from behind him.

"Faith!" Golden said. That's right! "Faith is the first step. Faith in the Lord Jesus Christ." It was coming back to him now. Long discarded Sunday School lessons rose like Lazarus in his mind.

"If you can't take the first step of faith, how can you expect to take any steps further? You have to learn to walk before you can run." Golden stumbled over his words but found that the more he spoke, the easier it was becoming. Talking to trees had been a silly notion, but it was actually helping. Rich had been right.

They took turns, encouraging each other and figuring out things they might be able to talk about. The trees were a most agreeable audience, and the two elders began to feel more comfortable speaking out loud. Golden still didn't have the confidence of his father, but after a while, he was sure that if those trees could, they would have jumped up and been baptized that very minute.

When they were done preaching, it was determined that they should practice praying. In Golden's time it wasn't customary to fold your arms like it is today. When they prayed, they held their arms out, both raised to the square. It might look a little silly to us now, but they didn't think anything of it. It's just the way it was.

Golden closed his eyes and bowed his head. It was Elder Rich's turn to pray. Over the course of the day, he'd really found his voice, and his prayers had become quite protracted affairs. He used every "thee," "thou," and "thine" imaginable, pronouncing blessings, humility, and so forth and so on and on. Rich's prayer had been going on for a while now, long enough that Golden had lost track of the time. He shifted his weight, his knees growing ever more uncomfortable with each new "thee" and "thine." He wasn't sure if it was ever going to end. His legs were tingling and threatening to fall asleep by the time Rich finally ended with a solemnly pronounced, "Amen." Golden added in his "amen" and opened his eyes.

Four ragtag-looking hillbillies with rifles stood watching them. They'd evidently heard the elders from the road and had been watching them while they prayed. The one with the longest rifle and the least amount of teeth looked at them coldly. "Y'all ain't from 'round here, are ya?"

Golden had never been much of a runner, but the staccato pop of gunfire gave him wings as he and Elder Rich burned the breeze through the trees and brush. He could hear the whistle of rounds as they tore through leaves and wood. Twigs and branches grabbed at his clothes and scratched at his face. He was aware of Rich running beside him as they burst from the trees into a clearing. The tall grass was a passing blur as they dashed helter-skelter across the open field.

The sound of the guns faded behind them and then stopped altogether, but neither man dared look back until they'd crossed the field, diving behind a low stone wall so old it seemed part of the natural landscape. It wasn't much in the way of cover, but some was better than none. Squatted down behind the piled stones, Golden checked himself quickly. Everything still seemed to be intact. Rich looked all right too. That had been a close shave. Golden resolved on the spot that from this time forth in the South, he would pray with one eye open. He risked a quick glance back over the wall.

"Anyone?" Rich asked, sucking for air.

Golden couldn't see anyone. "Looks clear."

"You all right?"

"Yeah. You?"

"Yeah."

Golden leaned against the wall to catch his breath, glancing back occasionally to make sure they were still in the clear. The stone felt solid behind him, but he knew it would offer little protection if the men decided to come after them.

"Whooee! I thought we were dead!" Rich laughed.

"The day's not over yet." Golden shook his head in disbelief. He couldn't believe that someone had actually opened fire on them. "Somebody needs to tell these folks that the war's over."

With one last glance to make sure they'd really lost the hill-billies, Golden patted Rich on the arm, and they got up and left.

CHAPTER 8

SOUTHERN GENTRY

A man can't be too careful in the choice of his enemies.

—Oscar Wilde

olden and Rich followed the next road they found, walking for several hours without coming across anyone. Golden hated to admit it, but he was glad, in a way. Getting shot at was not his idea of starting a day out right. Of course, getting shot at beat actually getting shot, but still . . .

His thoughts were interrupted by a tap on the shoulder from Rich. He had stopped walking.

"What?" Golden asked. Rich looked apprehensive about something, which in turn made Golden nervous too.

Rich's voice was a breathless whisper. "There's a person."

"Where?"

Rich didn't answer; he just pointed. Golden's eyes followed his companion's finger to a small cabin planted in a patch of trees a hundred or so yards ahead. The two elders stood frozen in place like kids sizing up a haunted house. A middle-aged man stood in front of the cabin drawing water from a vine-covered well with an ancient-looking wooden bucket. His gray-flecked hair was trimmed, and the homespun cotton shirt and trousers he wore were simple but cared for.

"He doesn't look dangerous." Rich was still whispering.

"I suppose we should go talk to him," Golden said. It was, after all, why they had come here in the first place.

Rich agreed. "Right."

Neither of them moved.

"You first." Rich motioned politely.

"You're the senior companion," Golden gently reminded him. "You're older."

Touché. Golden took a deep breath. "Okay." He tried to settle his nerves and, failing to do so, stepped forward anyhow.

The man finished filling his bucket and headed for his porch. He had reached the front door by the time the elders caught up to him. In the South at the time, knocking on a door was unusual. It was more customary to walk up to the gate and shout until greeted by someone from the house, often with a "You'n's come on in." This man wasn't inside just yet, sparing them the trouble.

"G-good afternoon," Golden tipped his hat. His voice was squeaky, even by his standards. "My name is Elder Kimball, and this is my companion, Elder Rich."

The man stopped in the doorway, looking them over suspiciously. His eyes narrowed as recognition slowly crossed his mind. "Y'all're Mormons, ain'tcha?".

Suddenly unsure of how this man would react, Golden hesitated longer than he would have liked before answering. "Yes, sir."

The man slammed the door hard enough that Golden felt the wind whip across his face and rustle his hair. He looked over at Rich, whose only consolation was an I-don't-know shrug. Golden smoothed his wisp of hair back into place with his hand.

"Well, that wasn't so bad." He would take slamming doors over gunshots any day.

The sun sat like the eye of God looking down on the elders as they went about his work. The heavy stillness of the humid

midday was settling in across the countryside like a net. If you
didn't count the fact that they'd been shot at and had every door
they'd come to (which wasn't many) slammed in their faces, it
had been an uneventful day. Golden had been jumpy since the
run-in with the hillbillies, but once he'd realized most people just
said no or ignored them, it hadn't been so bad.

As they walked, Golden noticed a cloud of dust rising from
the road ahead of them. It drifted high in the breezeless air, dissipating above the tree line. After a moment it was obvious that it
was heading toward them. *Like a pillar of fire*, he thought.

Soon a wagon bearing two men came into view. Even from
this distance Golden could see that the driver was a large man.
It was hard to tell if he was taller than Golden or not, but he was
at least twice as wide and had the look of a fellow who worked
hard for a living.

The man next to the driver was something else entirely. He
was lean and dressed in black from head to toe. It was hard to get
a bead on him from this far, but he looked strangely familiar. As
the wagon drew closer, Golden adjusted his glasses, squinting for
a better look. Recognition snapped sharp in his mind. It was a
face that Golden would never forget as long as he lived.

He tapped Rich on the shoulder, motioning toward the oncoming wagon. "Isn't that the minister who preached against us?"

Rich looked and nodded. "That's Reverend Weatherbee, all
right."

Golden felt his stomach sink. The memory of the verbal
scalding Weatherbee had given Golden and the others a few days
before still echoed in his ears. There was no telling what could
happen around a man filled with that much vitriol. Rich looked
uneasy too. "I saw him a week ago at a revival I came across. He
had everybody awfully riled up. What should we do?"

The only thing that Golden could think to do was shrug. "I
don't know." Having no other plan in mind, Golden and Rich
stepped to the side of the road, hoping the wagon would simply
pass them by.

෴

Kenneth was born in the cradle of the Smokies in the area of what is now known as Rocky Grove, northeast of Gatlinburg. He grew up among the oak and the slate and loved the land and all she stood for. The South was in his blood. He defended her in the Lost Cause, and he would defend her for as long as he could draw breath.

Like many youth, he'd been full of spit and vinegar, and when the war broke out, he and his brother, against his father's wishes, had grabbed their rifles and taken off to fight for their beloved home. They had both been far too young, but they hadn't known it then. That sort of wisdom is a luxury that comes only in time, and even then, only if you're lucky. By his nineteenth birthday, the Confederacy had surrendered at Appomattox, his brother was dead, and Kenneth had seen more war and horror than he would ever care to recall. He prayed he'd never have to see anything like it again in his or his children's lifetime.

Today he wore cotton overalls and a long-sleeve shirt, like he always did, even on days when the air stuck to him like tar. On a particularly sweltering afternoon, he might roll his sleeves up as far as his elbow, but today he had them buttoned properly around his wrists. The reason for this was simple: his scar. Cords of hard-knotted flesh wrapped around the upper part of his right arm from shoulder to elbow. It was mighty impressive as scars go. Most of the healthy color had come back to it over the years, but parts of it remained discolored. It never really bothered him, but it had the tendency of making a lot of other folk uncomfortable at the sight of it. Besides, a lot of them thought he'd gotten it during the war (he hadn't), and it was easier to keep it covered than to explain it constantly.

After the war ended, he moved to Chattanooga, hoping for better, seeking employment as a laborer. He soon found that there was plenty of work to be done but very little money. Eventually he hired on as a coal miner, and it was in the dark and treacherous tunnels that he made his living still.

Reverend Weatherbee kept his chapel in Chattanooga, but he traveled all 'round bringing the word of God with him. When Kenneth learned that the reverend was going toward Kingsport, he mentioned that he would be more than happy to give the man a ride. Reverend Weatherbee had initially declined, saying he didn't want to be a burden, but Kenneth insisted. It was an honor to help out a servant of God.

He had first met Reverend Weatherbee at a revival in Chattanooga a few years back. Kenneth had been impressed by the man and liked what he had to say. The reverend preached of rebuilding a stronger South, of belief in the Bible, and of how faith was necessary to survive hardships. He preached against the evils that threatened the South in its vulnerable postwar state. He warned about Northern carpetbaggers, greedy politicians, and especially the spiritual predations of the Mormons. The reverend happened to be something of an expert when it came to their kind.

Talk of the Mormons was very popular of late. It seemed everybody wanted to hear something about them, what with them being in the papers and all. What they were doing was plain wrong. They were subverters of the Holy Bible, seducing women into their harems. He'd heard talk of families being torn apart because of womenfolk leaving husband and kin to join the elders. Many of them were shipped west and never heard from again. At least that was what he'd been told.

The South was still recovering from the blow dealt by the war, and Kenneth hated to see his fellow Southerners taken advantage of in their weakened state. He didn't know too much about Mormons himself, but he knew they'd been thrown out of every state till they finally went west. If they wanted to come preaching their blasphemy here, they could get tossed out again just the same. West was where they had run to, and west was where they should stay.

Today the reverend wasn't talking about Mormons. He was chatting broadly about the upcoming opening of the New York and Brooklyn Bridge, which he apparently had been following quite closely. It was to be the longest suspension bridge in the world and the first to use steel wires.

As with most things, the reverend knew quite a lot about it. He was a smart man; it was one of the things that Kenneth looked up to him for. Regarding the bridge, however, Kenneth couldn't see what all the hoopla was about. There were plenty of bridges in the world, even if they weren't as long as this one. He was more interested in the upcoming Preakness. Sweet Sunshine was slated to run, and it would be something else to see. The reverend was intent on talking about the bridge, however, so Kenneth mostly just listened and nodded.

Reverend Weatherbee was marveling that the towers were the tallest structures in the entire Western Hemisphere when he stopped midsentence, falling silent, which wasn't much like him at all. He was looking at something ahead of them, his eyes narrow and his mouth crinkling into a frown.

Kenneth followed his eyes to see two men stepping to the side of the road in front of them. They were both in suits, which was unusual, 'specially for folks walking in this area. He decided they were either washing machine salesmen or Mormons. From the look on the reverend's face, Kenneth assumed the latter.

The elders watched nervously as the wagon approached. Weatherbee was scowling hard enough to stump a skunk. And the man driving, good heavens, but he was a big fellow. They would most likely drive on by and that would be that, but after the things Golden had seen so far in the South, who knew what anyone in this strange place might do? As the approaching wagon drew within earshot, Weatherbee raised an accusing finger, waggling it at them like a pistol. *Here it comes*, thought Golden.

"Good morning, you sons of the devil!" Weatherbee snapped.

Golden tipped his hat graciously and returned the greeting. "Good morning, Father."

The reaction was immediate. Rich burst into laughter, clapping his hands to his mouth in a wasted effort to hold back the loud whooping that shook his frame. Weatherbee flushed with anger, his face going from self-righteous to shocked in an instant. He whirled in his seat as the wagon passed, his eyes shooting daggers into the tall, thin heathen that had dared insult a man of the cloth.

To Golden's great relief the wagon kept on moving, leaving him and Rich breathing a cloud of dust. He could feel the heat of Weatherbee's stare until the wagon was gone from sight. He supposed he should have kept his mouth shut, but the response seemed so natural that it simply came right out. After all, it was the polite thing to say, wasn't it?

As he turned to watch the wagon's dusty plume disappear into the distance, his gut instinct kicked in something fierce. He knew this wouldn't be the last he saw of Reverend Weatherbee. Not by a long shot.

CHAPTER 9

PURSE AND SCRIP

Old Man to B.H. Roberts: Where are you going to stay tonight?

B.H.: I don't know. Did you hear me tell the people I was without purse or scrip? That means without money.

Old Man: Then you won't stop at a hotel?

B.H.: I reckon not. It generally takes money to stop at a hotel.

Old Man: Well, that's too bad. But it's late and I must be getting home. Good night.

Other than the run-in with Weatherbee, the rest of the day continued like most every day of Golden's mission would. That is to say, he and his companion walked and walked, coming across and being turned down by the occasional soul. The reactions of the people ranged from polite disinterest to flat-out rude. Fortunately they were rarely as severe as the armed hillbillies from that morning, but no one was willing to listen to what the elders had to say either.

Walking was hard, but the hardest thing for Golden was feeling like he wasn't getting work accomplished. He could get rejected and insulted only so many times before things began to grow boring and monotonous. The elders were told repeatedly that polygamy was of the devil and questioned how they dared come around decent folks. When Golden reminded one person that Abraham of the Old Testament was a polygamist, he was told that "God got nothin' to do with that part of Abraham's life." One lady went so far as to tell them that polygamy would suit her husband just fine since he couldn't keep his hands off other women anyhow. They quickly became familiar with names like "cohabbing whoremonger," "polygamous adulterer," and the ever popular "Brigham's bootlickers." Whoever coined that one should have trademarked it; they would have made a fortune.

Having been born in a polygamist home and being deeply proud of his heritage, Golden found the constant disparaging difficult to take with a pinch of salt. At first he was able to restrain himself and stay calm, but it slowly ate at him till finally he swore to himself that if one more person made a crack about it, he would—well, he didn't know what he'd do, but he'd surely do something. Sure as shooting, the very next fellow they spoke to asked him if his old man was a cohab.

"My father had more than one wife, if that's what you mean," Golden answered, clenching his jaw.

"Oh, yeah? How many kids he got?" challenged the man.

The man hadn't said anything really offensive, but his tone was condescending and Golden was tired of being berated about the issue. He drew himself up to his full height and poked his chest with his thumb. "I was one of forty-six sons, and there wasn't a bootlicker among them!" he yelled.

To this day no one knows who looked more shocked, the man or Elder Rich.

The two elders walked along another lonely country road in silence. Golden swatted at a mosquito, grabbing at empty air and then checking his hand to see if he got it. He missed. Rich hadn't spoken a word since Golden's outburst, and Golden hadn't said a thing either. He figured he'd really upset Rich. He felt terrible about it but didn't know what he could say. He'd probably said too much already.

They walked on, traveling with no real aim as to direction but following where the road was taking them. The thick of the woods wrapped about them tightly, the blanket of leaves soaking up even the sound of their footsteps on the gravel sitting in the worn grooves of the road.

The only sounds were the chirps of birds and the occasional insect that buzzed past their heads. By and by the silence grew to be more than Golden could bear. He couldn't stand feeling so awful about upsetting his companion and had to get it off his chest.

"Rich, I'm sorry about airing my lungs like that, I really am. I'm just mad as, well, I'm as mad as all get out. I didn't mean to fly off the handle. I feel as if we've been barking at a knot all day. We haven't preached a thing to anyone, unless you count the trees. I suppose I'm just frustrated."

"I don't know what to tell you, Elder Kimball. I think we're trying the best we can." Much to Golden's relief, his companion didn't sound angry at all. Rich was just as much out to sea for words as himself. Preaching was tougher than either of them had thought. Some of these folk were so hardheaded that even an oak seemed flexible by comparison. No one wanted to listen and, to be honest, even if they had, Golden still didn't really know what he would say.

What he did know was that he was in an increasingly foul mood. They'd been out all day long and must have covered a good twelve miles since morning. It wasn't uncommon for the average elder to cover twenty or more miles a day, but Golden's shoes had never been broken in, and he had the blisters to prove it. He wondered why he couldn't have brought his horse; it would have made things a lot easier. The only thing louder than the barking of his feet was the growling of his belly. Now that he thought about it, he hadn't eaten anything since this morning. The sun was beginning to dip behind the horizon, and night would be upon them before long. They needed to get some food and a place to rest, and soon. Which raised the question in Golden's mind . . .

"Say, how exactly does this no purse or scrip bit work, anyhow?" Golden knew what it meant, at least on an intellectual level. It meant that you traveled without money. But now that he was confronting it face-to-face, it was suddenly becoming intense and personal.

Rich looked down a bit sheepishly. "I don't really know. I've only stayed at members' homes until now, and that was in Norton." That city was over twenty miles from where the elders now stood. "I don't know anyone who lives around here."

If they were going to get room and board tonight, they were going to have to ask total strangers for it. Judging from the warm reception the two had received thus far, Golden could only imagine the response they were sure to get. He wasn't keen on the idea of imposing on anyone, but he was even less keen about the idea of sleeping outside on the ground. He had slept on the ground plenty of times as a cowboy, but he'd at least had his bedroll then and wasn't wearing his best suit.

Rich patted him on the back. "Don't worry, I'm sure somebody will take us in for the night."

Elder Rich had one of the most optimistic outlooks of any person Golden had ever met. His positivity was boundless. It was the sort of attitude Golden wished he had himself. Rich's attitude wasn't only positive, it was genuine. Sadly in this case, it was also wrong.

Sleeping on the ground is not a comfortable experience. I'm not talking about camping-out-with-a-sleeping-bag-and-perhaps-a-tent type of sleeping on the ground. Not even a nice, soft lawn kind of ground. We're talking about pine-needles-poking-you-in-the-side-and-rocks-in-your-back sleeping on the ground. As if the rough ground wasn't bad enough, all sorts of bugs and assorted creepy-crawlies decided that night was the perfect time to buzz around Golden's head or crawl up his arms and legs. Neither elder had bathed or even been able to wash up, and they were still in the same clothes that they'd been sweating in all day.

Golden tried using his valise as a pillow, he tried bundling leaves for padding, he tried huddling in his coat for warmth. He may as well have tried keeping water in a sieve, for warmth and comfort eluded him all night. So much for Southern hospitality.

After shifting restlessly for what felt like an eternity, Golden's exhaustion finally overwhelmed his discomfort, and he fell into a shallow and haggard sleep. A few seconds later, Rich was poking him on the shoulder.

Golden blinked, bleary eyed. The sky was awful bright for the middle of the night. Golden slowly became aware that the sun was up. Judging from its angle in the sky it must have been about nine already. What felt like a few seconds had actually been hours. It didn't feel like he'd slept at all. Rich looked little worse for the wear and seemed his usual chipper self.

"How do you feel?" he asked.

"I'd say awful, but I feel much worse than that." Golden felt several things about being awake, but happy wasn't one of them. He hadn't been comfortable, but he had at least been warm and asleep and didn't appreciate being woken up just to be asked how he felt. He uncharacteristically kept his trap shut as he rose, working out the kinks that had settled in his joints and rubbing the sore spots gifted him by the hard ground. He picked up a few pinecones from where he had slept and tossed them absently.

"We are not sleeping on the ground again." Golden's promise was as much to himself as it was to Rich. He meant it with every ounce of his being. That day he and Rich did everything short of breaking the ten commandments to obtain better sleeping arrangements, but despite their best efforts, the next night found them on the ground again. So much for rash promises.

Rich appeared to have adjusted well enough; he was out cold and snoring loudly enough to wake the dead. But sleep continued to taunt Golden, who lay curled into a ball, shivering and swatting at mosquitoes. Thoughts of home came unbidden, flittering through his mind like bats in a belfry before he could chase them away. Thoughts of the ranch. Of his family and friends. He wanted nothing more than to be there, warm, in his own bed. He could picture his quilt spread over him, but all he could feel was the cold of the night and the disagreeable ground pricking at his flesh.

Doubt began to seed his mind again, taking root and spreading like a pernicious weed. Could he do it? Could he finish out his whole mission like this? He wanted to. There had been plenty of long days on the ranch, certainly days harder than this, and he'd been doing that since he was a kid. But this was a different kind of hardship, and he didn't know if he had the mettle. He was barely a few days into it, and it already felt like it was beating him. Could he really do this for several years?

He felt shameful even thinking about it. Others had done it. Quite a lot of them, in fact. All he had to do was endure to the end. But the end was so far away. He lay there willing the clock forward, picturing the end, going home. The more he thought about it, the slower time seemed to go till it nearly reached a dead standstill. How could he survive years if he couldn't even make it through tonight? He had believed he was tough enough to hack it, but here, alone in the gloom, he wasn't so sure. He tossed and turned for hours more till finally, in the stillness of the night, darkness engulfed him body and soul.

The sunshine of the following day helped chase away some of Golden's fears, but a shadow of it lingered in the back of his mind. The elders trudged along, dutifully putting one foot in front of the other but without much spirit. Neither had said much all morning. Both were unshaven and unbathed and worse for the wear.

The chill of the night had sunk into the marrow of Golden's

bones. He was white-eyed and weary to the core of his soul. His body ached, and the bags under his eyes felt large enough to hold potatoes. Worse yet he was starting to pick up a cough.

"You don't look so good." Rich sounded concerned.

Golden looked Rich over. His suit was wrinkled, his hair disheveled, and two days of stubble shaded his cheeks and jaw. A few leaves from last night's camp stuck to his back like patches.

"And I suppose you're one to talk?" Golden grinned. Suddenly both men were laughing. It might have been the joke, it might have been the lack of sleep, but either way the laughter was just the medicine they needed.

"I can't blame people for not wanting to talk to us. Look at us! Why, I'd chase myself off too if I saw me like this," Golden brushed some leaves off his companion's back. "I confess, if I'd known that without purse or scrip meant no food and no bed I might not have come."

Rich nodded with the sympathy that only someone stuck in the same predicament can have. "My father would say, 'Landon, it'll give you character.'"

"I've had about all the character I can handle—we need to scare up some chow and a pillow." Golden's stomach rumbled in agreement. "You know, if we're not eating anything, we might as well be praying too. At least then we could say we were fasting. Starving without praying is only half fast." That's a pretty funny play on words when you get right down to it, but instead of laughing as Golden hoped he would, Rich grew all excited.

"Pray! That's it! We should pray! I mean, we're teaching about prayer, we might as well apply it to ourselves!"

Sometimes some things are so obvious that you feel awfully beef-headed when they have to be pointed out to you. Like someone telling you that your glasses that you've been looking all over for are sitting on your head. The epiphany struck Golden like a brick. Rich was absolutely right.

They decided that Elder Rich would pray first. Actually Rich volunteered to go first. Golden didn't know if his knees could take one of Rich's prayers, but Rich was so eager about it that Golden agreed to let him. The two retired to the side of the road and knelt down, arms raised. Rich bowed his head and closed his eyes. Golden kept his open, glancing about. It never hurt to be too cautious. Rich thee'd and thine'd his way through the prayer, and just as Golden thought his knees might give out, Rich closed with a hearty "amen." Golden quickly shut his eyes to make sure Rich didn't see him peeking, looking up as if they'd been closed the whole time.

"Amen."

Rich slapped a hand on Golden's shoulder. The prayer had reinvigorated Rich's confidence.

"Let's go find a place," he said. The two men dusted themselves off the best they could and set about their errand.

The first place they came to was an old homestead guarded by an even older woman. She was missing as many teeth as the roof was missing shingles, and she habitually smacked her gums together as she listened to the elders' appeal. Golden wasn't excited about asking an old woman for help. He felt that he should be the one helping her somehow. She was willing to listen, at least. That is, until she realized who she was talking to.

"Y'all are Mormons?" She sounded quite surprised.

"Yes, ma'am," Golden answered.

Let me tell you a little bit about the word "humility." It comes from Latin, from the root "humilis," which means "insignificant" or "on the ground"—strangely appropriate to Golden's current sleeping arrangements. Another word that descends from this Latin term is "humiliation," which in Golden's case meant being chased off a property by an old woman wielding a broom like Excalibur.

Golden and Rich covered their heads with their hands as she herded them off, raining blows upon their backs with startling vigor for one who looked so aged. Switches of straw flew this way and that into the air. Sagely deducing that her reaction meant "no," they hurried off, catching an earful until they were beyond the throw of her voice.

❧

"Maybe I didn't pray with enough faith. You should try it this time," said Rich.

"I'm sure your faith is sufficient," Golden reassured him, "but I'd be happy to pray, if you like."

Golden's prayer was one of the most heartfelt he had ever given, even if he did have one eye open the whole time. He truly didn't want to stay outside again.

After he finished, they got up and tried again. And again. And again. But despite their best efforts, they couldn't find anyone to put them up for the night.

"Perhaps we should pray again," Rich suggested.

"No, we've prayed plenty. We just need to find a place." The words came out a little snappier than Golden intended. It's terribly hard to be enthusiastic about anything when your stomach has been snarling at you all day (and using language that even Golden found rude) and your eyelids want nothing more than to close.

"You don't think that God will help us?" Rich looked shocked, but Golden wasn't of much a mind to care at this point.

"We're going to starve to death if we keep praying. I don't think that God will help anyone who doesn't get up and hustle and move after they've prayed. We've prayed, now we need to hustle—we're riding the shank of the evening and almost out of daylight." They had asked God for help, now they had to do their part and trust him to do his. Golden kept walking, and Rich followed after.

CHAPTER 10

NO BALM IN GILEAD

If thou art called to pass through tribulation . . . if thou art accused with all manner of false accusations; if thine enemies fall upon thee . . . know thou, my son, that all these things shall give thee experience, and shall be for thy good.

—*Doctrine & Covenants 122:5–7*

It was an ancient and miserable old hovel, its moss-tinted wood panels dark and twisted with age. The whole structure was so swallowed up in vines that it appeared as if God himself had planted it there at creation. If it weren't for the fresh footprints and the glow of light in the window, Golden would have thought it abandoned.

The response to Golden's call came so slowly that the elders figured whoever was inside was going to ignore them. They were ready to walk away when the door creaked open. A worn looking, middle-aged man stood in the doorway. He was dressed in patched overalls and had a slack jaw and beady eyes buried deep beneath thick eyebrows. His hairline was so high and thin it could have been kissin' cousin to Golden's. Moving with great deliberation and no sense of expediency, the man looked the elders over for a spell before speaking.

"Whatcha-ahnt?" It was the thickest accent Golden had encountered yet, nigh unto indecipherable. He wondered again if he hadn't accidentally missed the South and ended up in a different country. He leaned over to Rich and whispered discreetly out of the corner of his mouth, "What did he say?"

Rich shrugged, clearly having no idea himself.

At that moment, another face appeared in the door. About three feet off the floor, a mop of stringy, dishwater-blonde hair framed a pair of angelic blue eyes that peered up at the strangers with curiosity. The girl was no more than five and cute as a button beneath the grime on her cheeks. She glanced at the elders, her shy smile revealing a missing tooth. Golden smiled back. He considered it lucky that children her age didn't know how enchanting they could be, for if they did, doubtless they could get away with murder.

Noticing her, the man snapped, "Lyddy! Keep indoors like Ah tol' ya!" And she was gone. He turned back to the elders, still waiting for an answer.

Rich cleared his throat. "I'm sorry to bother you, sir, but we are traveling on foot and are wondering if we might ask some accommodation for the evening."

"Wha-ut?" The man looked more wary than he had before, almost confused, like he didn't understand. What Rich had said seemed perfectly clear to Golden, and then it hit him. It wasn't what Rich had said but how he said it. It had never occurred to Golden before that here in the South he and Rich were the ones with an accent, not the other way around. Golden would find that it wasn't uncommon, especially in the more rural areas, to come across a Southerner who couldn't understand his Western tones any more than he could understand their Southern twang. The difficulties with accent went both ways.

"May we sleep here tonight?" Golden spoke as clearly as he could.

Understanding crossed the man's face, then his eyes narrowed. "Y'all Mo-muns?" Golden was almost afraid to say yes, he wanted a place to sleep so badly. But that defeated the purpose of him even being here. So he and Rich both nodded yes, fully expecting to be denied or worse.

The man deliberated for a moment. Whatever his response was going to be, he took his sweet time giving it. He sucked his teeth a few times, mulling things over. "All righ', ya kin stay. But Ah don' care fer yuh Mo-mun preachers nun. An' Ah don' wanna hear 'bout no Joe Smith or his gold bible."

Sounded good to Golden. "Deal." He stepped into the house, Rich following behind, leaving the owner standing by his lonesome on the porch.

"Reckon y'all'l be wantin' a bite a grub 'zwell?" he called into the house, then stepped inside after them.

The man's name was Horace. He wasn't the greatest host one could wish for; in fact, he spent most of the evening ridiculing and insulting the elders, but he had invited them in and he was preparing them dinner, so Golden wasn't about to complain.

The table spread was meager. The meal was some sort of mystery meat (Golden believed it was rabbit) and a morsel of dry corn bread Horace called "corn dodgers." It was far from five-star dining, but at this point it was manna to Golden. Horace set the table and offered the elders some home brewed 'shine, which smelled strong enough to polish brass. Golden and Rich politely declined.

"Too bad." Horace shrugged. "Ain't much else 'round 'cept wahta."

"Water would be wonderful. Thank you."

Horace seemed genuinely perplexed as to why anyone would prefer water over 'shine but scooped some from a bucket anyhow, dumping it in the tin cups he'd set.

They were getting ready to eat when Golden noticed the young girl peeking her head around the corner again into the room. When she saw him looking at her, she grew a little bolder and stepped out. Horace saw her as he was filling Rich's cup.

"Lyddy! Didn' Ah tell ya not ta come out when Ah've comp'ny?" He threatened her off with the scoop, sending drops of water flying about. Her expression darkened. She ducked her head and left without a word, leaving Horace shaking the empty ladle. Watching other people squabble when you are a guest in their house is a mighty uncomfortable thing, and this was no exception. Doing his best to maintain a diplomatic tone of voice, Golden asked, "Isn't your daughter going to eat with us?"

"She alreddy et," Horace stated perfunctorily, then sat down and launched abruptly into prayer. "Lord, thankee fuh this meal. Have mercy on these two sinners. Amen." He started to eat, and the elders eagerly followed suit.

A few bites into the meal, Horace paused and took a sniff at his food. Golden stopped chewing. He wasn't going to say anything, but the meat did look a bit old. If the cook wasn't eating it, he sure wasn't going to either. Refrigeration was an almost unheard of luxury in impoverished rural areas, so food either had to be eaten fresh or not at all. At the rate things were going, it would be just Golden's luck that the only home to give them shelter also gave them food poisoning.

Horace looked around, sniffing again. Then he leaned right over to Golden and took another sniff. Satisfied, he returned to his meal without skipping a beat, "Afta we done, reckon Ah'll draw some bath wahta."

Golden sheepishly finished his meal.

Golden hadn't dared push his host beyond a bed and a meal, but he certainly wasn't going to complain about a warm bath. The idea was as agreeable to him as fresh oats to a spring colt.

The bathhouse was a small shack standing a stone's throw behind the main house but on the far side from the outhouse. It was newer, not covered in vines yet, and looked like it hadn't been used much.

"Bilt this fer the missus 'fore she up'n left anyhow," Horace said as he prepared the water. It sounded as if he felt the need to explain why a man would have an honest to goodness actual bath around his home. "Ain't really made fer a fella yo size. Ah got mo' water boilin', cold water's there." He pointed to a bucket. "Holler if'n you need a thang."

Food, bath, and a place to sleep. The grungy house was a paradise. "Thank you again. This is exceedingly kind."

Horace didn't much care what exceedingly meant, he just set down the bucket and exited, closing the door behind him.

Golden eyed the steaming bath and sat on a small stool, gingerly removing his shoes. He winced a bit as he peeled off his socks revealing swollen and blistered feet. They were splotchy red, and new blisters were forming where the old ones had broken, stinging where the air touched the fresh skin. Instead of sucking air through his teeth at the sting, he broke into a fit of coughing. *Damn, but if it wasn't getting worse.*

It might have been the fatigue or having a full belly for the first time in days or the heat and steam rising off the water, but his head suddenly felt way off kilter, like a leaf in a dust devil, and he started to swoon. Everything went gray, and he caught himself against the wall until his vision cleared. He shook his head, clearing out the last of the hazy sensation, then quickly dressed down for his bath.

The tub was small, all right. It would have been a tight fit for a man of average stature, let alone Golden's lanky body. His legs hung over the lip of the thing, and the water only came up to around his navel, but it was warm and felt wonderful. Steam rose in clouds around him, and his aches began to drift away, taking Golden's thoughts with them. He closed his eyes and was beginning to be carried off himself when he heard the creak of the door. His eyes snapped open at once.

The young girl peeked inside the bathhouse. Golden jumped, attempting to cover himself as best he could, waving her off. "Shoo! Go away."

She took a step forward instead. Now she was all the way inside the door, standing there looking at him. Golden felt bad. It was obvious the girl just liked someone who gave her attention, but this was definitely not the time or place for that.

"I mean it," he stammered. "You can't be in here. Scoot." The look of rejection he'd seen at dinner shadowed her face, and she turned and walked out.

"The door—!" She'd left it open. Golden looked to make sure the coast was clear, then climbed out of the tub and closed the door to finish his bath.

Golden's head had little more than touched the pillow when he was fast asleep. The bed was only a pile of straw covered with a ragged sheet, and not much straw at that, but Golden didn't mind. For the first time in days he slumbered peacefully and deeply. So deeply that he barely registered the yelling and the sound of the shotgun cocking.

The door slammed open hard enough to shake the whole house and wake not only the dead but the two sleeping elders as well. The morning light streaming through the windows cast reaching shadows in the dust stirred up by the sweep of the door. Golden sat up as Horace crashed into the room like a man possessed, waving a shotgun from him to Rich and back again. "Which un was it? Was it this un?" He jammed the barrel in Golden's pallid face. Golden froze.

Somewhere off in the distance, Rich was yelling, "Wait!" and waving his hands. Horace shoved the gun closer. "If'n yuh touched her, so help me Ah'll kill ever' one a ya! Didja?"

Golden's nerves reconnected with his arms, which he flailed uselessly in front of him. "Hold on! Hold on a minute! What the hell is going on?"

"Didja touch her?" There was a frantic edge to Horace's anger. Lyddy stood in the doorway like a cut but tailed dog, tears covering her cheeks.

Golden's face curled in shock and horror as understanding struck his mind like a bolt. "No! As the Lord is my witness, no!" Rich looked equally alarmed.

"She tol' me yuh tried to get her inna room las' night! 'Zat true? Izzit?"

"No! She came to the bath last night—" Horace shoved the gun even closer. It pressed into the flesh of Golden's nose. He could smell the powder in the barrels. He was going to die. He flinched, blurting out the words, "I told her to leave! I told her to leave! And she left. That's it. That's all!"

Still cringing, Golden glanced up at Horace, who was staring at him down the gun, eyes wide, breathing heavily. A look of doubt mixed with his anger. He glanced quickly from elder to elder. Golden didn't know if the man was going to shoot him or Rich or both.

"Out!" Horace waved the barrel in the direction of the door. They didn't need to be told twice. Golden and Rich hastily grabbed their belongings and split the creek wide open. They half ran, half walked away from the place, pulling on their clothes as they went. Horace stood on the porch waving his shotgun and yelling. His accent was as thick as ever, but the elders understood him clear as day. "Thank the Lord she didn't let ya! Ya'd be inna pine box! Don' ever come 'round here 'gin er Ah'll fix it! Ya hear me? Ya hear?"

CHAPTER 11

GHOSTS IN
THE NIGHT

A chip on the shoulder is a sure sign of wood higher up.

—*Brigham Young*

The rest of the day was spent in a fog of gloom. They wandered aimlessly, neither elder saying much at all. Golden was in a state of shock, still trying to puzzle out what exactly had happened. He and Elder Rich were innocent of any wrongdoing, he knew that much. He would never do anything that Horace had implied, and if he ever did, he hoped that somebody *would* shoot him. How could such a sweet child tell such a heinous lie? It made no sense. It was an event that, whenever he thought of it, would plague his mind for the rest of his life.

He was coughing now in fits and starts, but Golden hardly noticed as he trudged along, lost in the melancholy of his thoughts. He barely noticed when something flew past his head, hitting the ground ahead of him with a thump. He scarcely had time to look up when another rock sailed over his shoulder. He ducked reflexively as a third hit Rich in the back.

Without even realizing it, they had wandered near a homestead. A handful of women and one young man stood in front hurling rocks and sticks at them while another woman hastily ushered several curious children inside.

"Perverts! We heard 'bout what you done to that lil' girl! Y'all should be ashamed of y'selves!" yelled one.

"Stay away from our daughters!" yelled another.

Golden ducked as a twig whirled past his head. The homes here were spread miles apart, but apparently that didn't slow the spread of the rumor that had grabbed hold like weeds in good soil. There was no point in trying to defend themselves; from the angered looks of the people, there would be no reasoning here. They just wanted the elders gone. Once more Golden and Rich hurried off without a word.

Somehow the pernicious story managed to stay just ahead of them, hounding at them constantly. Everywhere they went people chased them off with threats and curses. It felt to Golden as if the devil himself had commenced a warfare against him before he'd even begun his work. A pall had fallen over his mission, an oppressive cloud of gray through which no light could penetrate.

Before long the only thing sinking faster than Golden's spirits was the sun. Soon the long shadows of evening outweighed the light of the dusky beams jutting through the holes in the forest wall. Reluctant to ask anyone for anything at all, Golden and Rich walked further and further, procrastinating the moment for as long as they felt they could, hoping to put distance between themselves and the cancerous tale. The sun was gone by the time they reached a small farmhouse nestled among the darkened hills. They dared not wait any longer for fear that the hour would grow too late.

Lantern light flickered through the window as Golden approached the modest home. The wooden planks looked grayed with age, but that could have been just the fading light. There were no vines, and any plants around it were kept trim, most likely by grazing animals. Golden had barely called out when the door was flung open and the elders were greeted for the second time that day by a shotgun.

"What d'ya want?" The shotgun was aimed with care by a

short, older fellow. He was also balding on top, his face neatly framed by a silvered beard and mustache. He stared at them expectantly through a pair of wire-rim glasses. There was a large crack in the right lens.

Golden raised his arms defensively, looking appropriately like he was praying. He chose his next words as carefully as he could, for fear they might be his last. "We're terribly sorry to bother you, sir. We're traveling preachers looking for a place to sleep for the night."

The fellow kept the shotgun on the elders. "Y'all'd be Mormons, 'less I miss mah guess?"

Golden didn't have much time to ponder why everyone seemed to know who they were. He was more focused on the gun pointed at him. The view wasn't any more pleasant than it had been this morning. To no great surprise, this fellow didn't appear to be any more hospitable than any other they'd met thus far.

"Yes, we're Mormons." Golden wasn't sure if the man was going to speak or answer with the shotgun. He kept on staring them down over the gun barrel with a contemplative look on his face. Maybe the fellow didn't know, himself. After a tense moment, his features softened.

"You boys look hungry." He lowered the shotgun and walked back into the house, leaving the door open as an invitation to follow.

Golden breathed a sigh of relief. Guns were getting old fast. He'd never seen so many in one day, and he'd grown up in the Wild, Wild West. Exchanging a glance with Rich, he followed the man inside.

Their host introduced himself as Jesse and apologized for the rough way he answered the door. "A man can't be too cautious these days."

Golden supposed he was right. Jesse seated the elders at a simple wooden table. Like most everything inside the one-room farmhouse, it was handmade and well used.

"I was born here, worked this patch a earth my whole life,"

Jesse explained in response to a question from Golden. "I was right fortunate durin' the war, I reckon. I had opportunity to house soldiers from both sides of the Mason-Dixon—usually by my own choice." He chuckled, indicating that the choice hadn't always been his.

"I never got caught in the thick of it. My crops got trod on a time or two an' most a my livestock disappeared, but I figger it a small price t' pay compared to some."

He set a freshly chopped onion with a pitcher of milk and some bread. "I 'pologize for not having much, but Ah'll be able to gather some fresh milk 'n' eggs come morning," he said.

Golden couldn't properly express his gratitude as he began to eat.

"We had us a minister come through here." Jesse joined them at the table. "Said to watch out for your kind. That the Mormons were here to steal our daughters."

Golden realized that maybe he'd gotten comfortable too soon. He finished his bite of bread with a gulp, looking up at Jesse.

"And do you believe that?" he asked.

Their host sat back in his seat and shrugged. "Ah ain't got any daughters." Then he laughed at his own joke. Relieved, the elders chuckled a little themselves.

You may recall me saying that there were good and honest folk in the South, some just as kind as angels. Well, it turns out that this man Jesse was one of them. Oh, he teased the elders a bit, but it wasn't at all mean-spirited, and dinner, as simple as it was, proved to be a pleasant affair. Even more than the meal, Golden and Rich were grateful for some decent human company. It was turning out to be a rare thing indeed. As scarce as hen's teeth.

After they had eaten, Jesse led them out to the barn. The house had only a single room, so this was as close to a guest room as he could come by. He swung the large door open and, stepping inside, hung the lantern he carried on a rail spike sticking out of the central post. Jesse kept it clean, but it still smelled of animals. This may be offensive to our delicate modern-day noses, but Golden was a cowboy and Rich was from farm country, so it didn't bother them. Besides, they were so tired it wouldn't have mattered either way. Golden and Rich helped Jesse spread out some old blankets over a fresh pile of hay.

"It ain't the best bed," Jesse apologized again.

Golden tested it with his hand, "I doubt the Queen of England has any finer. Thank you again."

"If y'all need anything else, lemme know," Jesse excused himself and headed back toward the house.

Only the angels who record all that transpires below know how grateful Golden was to sleep that night. He thanked the Lord with all his heart for the kindness their host had showed them and sincerely hoped that he might somehow be able to return the favor. With these thoughts in mind, he drifted off, warm and comfortable.

The moon was high when Golden was awakened by Jesse bursting into the barn. "Boys! Boys!" Golden stirred heavily. His mind was groggy, and his body did not want to wake up. The sharp urgency in Jesse's voice finally registered somewhere in the recesses of his mind, and he snapped awake. There was real fear in Jesse's eyes, and he kept looking back over his shoulder as he pushed the elders out of their makeshift bed.

"Get up! Get up! They're coming!"

"Who?" Golden had no more than voiced his question when he heard faint shouts and the braying of hounds.

The South during the Reconstruction was a convoluted mixture of different forces. Most people were simply working to rebuild and recover from the war. They just wanted to pick up the pieces and get on with their lives. But there were other social undercurrents that opposed the new way of life, resisting change and the progressive movement, often violently.

The Ku Klux Klan represented the worst, most extreme effort of resistance to the new South. They attempted to preserve things as they had stood before the war at any cost. Their ideology, if it could truly be called such, was narrow-minded at best. They terrorized and killed Negroes, Catholics, Jews, and Republicans alike. Anything that didn't walk or crawl around in a white sheet was potentially fair game for the Klan. They certainly didn't hesitate to extend their brand of hospitality to any Mormon elders they happened across.

Jesse threw Golden's belongings into his hands and pushed him and Rich out the door. From the sound of the dogs, the Klansmen weren't far off now. Jesse pointed into the darkness behind the barn. "There's a hill on the far side of my field. Head that way. I'll keep 'em diverted long as Ah can."

"They're here for us," Golden said. He knew it was a bad situation, but he was concerned about his host. "We should go out there so they'll leave you alone."

"They'll kill you sure as shootin', an' Ah'll get whatever's comin' to me anyhow. Ah'll brook no argument. Git." He shoved Golden out of the barn, sending the elders packing as fast as their legs would carry them. The sound was louder now, closer.

Angry mobs were the stuff of storybooks and campfire tales, not something that existed in terms of a modern, civilized world. But the sound of the dogs was real enough. Maybe the world wasn't as modern and civilized as it believed itself to be. Men were really coming to hurt them. The thought that he could actually die here pricked Golden's mind, and a cold sheen of sweat covered his brow.

Sticking to the shadows, he and Rich sneaked out the side of the barn. From there they quickly scampered across Jesse's field, finally taking cover behind a small hill on the far side. Safely hidden, Golden crawled on his belly to peek over the crest, watching helpless and frightened from beneath the cover of some low-hanging branches.

Seconds later he caught his first glimpse of them: men clad

in white moving between the trees like ghosts illuminated by the flicker of torches. About ten of them stepped from the woods, carrying rifles and clubs. They were dressed from head to toe in white robes and sheets, some with elaborate patches and decorations sewn onto them, like homemade military uniforms for a school play. In a letter home, Golden would later note that each man wore a hood that had a point to it, "which is more than could be said for their beliefs."

The mob gathered in front of the farmhouse, the hounds barking with excitement. One of the men wore robes dyed a green so dark that it appeared almost black by the light of the torches. He gestured toward the house, and several of the men charged up and kicked down the door, running inside.

Jesse appeared from the barn, running to meet them as they emerged from the house. The men grabbed him by the arms. Words were exchanged, and he was thrown to the ground. Too far to hear much more than the barking of dogs, Golden watched in horror as the nightmarish scene played out before him.

The dark-robed figure asked Jesse something, and the old man pointed up the road in the opposite direction of the elders. The Klansman didn't like the answer. One of the others butt-stroked Jesse, and the old man was held down at gunpoint. The lead Klansman pointed toward the barn, and the rest of the mob closed in around it. Golden could faintly hear him yelling something about Mormons as he shook his fist in the air.

Golden jumped as several of the men opened fire into the barn. The crack of the rifles hit his ears like the sound of the heavens splitting open. The report hadn't even faded before men were nailing the barn closed and hooded figures began jamming torches into its sides. The wood was old, and the fire found quick purchase in the scattered hay. The barn went up like old parchment, the intense flames silhouetting the mob like imps dancing to the sound of howling dogs and dying livestock.

The next morning tendrils of smoke mingled with the mist, clinging to the ground like a shroud. It swirled around Golden's feet as he and Rich returned to the farm. The fire had utterly devoured the barn; only a few blackened pieces of wood remained. It had burned late into the night, the mob standing vigil until the last ember had faded. Satisfied that nothing inside had survived, they left, but only after gifting their host with several more bruises as a caution against any further empathy toward the enemies of the South.

Jesse sat slouched on the ground among the smoldering ashes of his livelihood, listlessly twirling the bent frames of his glasses in his fingers. Both lenses were broken out entirely. He was looking off at some point in the distance, never looking at the elders.

Golden was glad that no permanent harm had come to the man. He had no words to describe how awful he felt. The indignities he had suffered personally were bad enough, but now they were spreading out, harming others around him just for showing a little kindness. He was still searching for the words when Jesse spoke first.

"Boys, you need ta understand somethin'," he said, "The war did somethin' ta these people. They've seen horrible things, the likes a which you and I can't hardly imagine. Many a them came home to nothin'. Their houses were destroyed, their families scattered or killed." He continued playing with his glasses. "They need something to hate. You give them something to hate."

Jesse was apologizing . . . to them. Golden couldn't believe it. It should have been the other way around. It was Rich who finally gave words to his feelings. "I don't know what to say."

Hearing Rich's voice perked Golden's mind just enough to speak. "What about the law?" he asked. "Surely somebody must be able to do something."

Jesse looked up at him. A wistful smile flickered across his face, and he shook his head slowly. "You don't get it, do you? 'Round here them ruffians are the law. Or at least there's nobody that's going to do a thing about it."

Most Klan mobs were usually made up of locals from whatever area they were in. It was rare for mob members to travel very
far from where they lived. If the masks from the night before
were removed, it would be no surprise to find that some of them
were local civic leaders or prominent citizens. Likely as not they
were from this very neighborhood and Jesse would know some
if not all of them. Jesse looked back down. "Ya'll'd better go."
There was no anger in his words, only resignation. "Be careful
now."

Golden couldn't understand it. It wasn't right. They'd finally
come across a respectable man who had treated them kindly, and
it had cost him everything. The injustice of it was overwhelming,
but there was nothing to be done. Burdened by the outrage and
frustration of the night but powerless to do anything about it,
Golden nodded, and he and Rich took their leave.

CHAPTER 12

SICK AND TIRED

I am not learned, but I have as good feelings as any man.

—Joseph Smith Jr.

Golden and Rich continued to work, but a shadow hung over their efforts. Week after week, month after month of wandering in the face of constant rejection began running together into a dull blur. There were other good folks around, and the missionaries were given places to stay and fed enough that they didn't starve to death, but they found little success in sharing their message. Golden felt more like a vagabond beggar than a missionary.

He kept hoping his spirits would lift, but he got to feeling worse and worse each passing day. He had often been prone to bouts of depression, but this was far more awful than he had ever experienced. Every time he felt as if it were going to lighten, the despair would return darker than before. His cough was worse than ever, his body growing dragged out and sluggish, with his mind following closely behind.

Finally, after yet another day of nothing but the cold shoulder, the two elders found themselves talking to a young couple they happened upon near a crossroads. The discussion, as if often did, turned to polygamy. It was clear that the husband had no interest in the gospel but was enjoying the discussion from a purely intellectual point of view. His wife, however, would have nothing to do with it and was becoming quite agitated that her husband would even entertain the thought of speaking with Mormons, especially on such an uncivilized subject. The missionaries soon found themselves left out entirely as the discussion turned into a full-blown squabble between the couple.

"It makes sense," the man said.

"No, it does not make sense," his wife snapped. "I can't believe you're agreeing with them."

"Honey, I'm not saying I believe what they're saying. I'm only saying that I *understand* what they're saying."

"Well, that's the same thing."

"No, it's not the same thing."

They were well practiced at disagreement for such a young couple, carrying on as if they had forgotten the elders were even there. They could probably go on for days. Golden could only watch, unsure of how to change the subject or excuse himself or even get a word in edgewise. After a few minutes, he felt as if he were watching the argument from afar, like looking through a telescope. He could see their lips moving, but their words began to blur together, fading into an incomprehensible buzz. It sounded like cicadas gone mad. His mind was drifting now, and he had the most peculiar sensation of becoming detached from his body. The forest around him seemed to bend inward, curving impossibly like a bowl, and the edges of his vision went gray. Suddenly his knees buckled and he sank to the ground. The couple stopped bickering, looking at him as if noticing him for the first time.

At least that finally shut them up, he thought. Then Rich was kneeling over him, "Elder Kimball. Elder Kimball. Are you all right?"

Golden tried to answer, but the words never made it past his throat. The world went dark, and he passed out entirely.

The light at the end of the tunnel came slowly into focus. The bright blur floating above his head gradually shifted into the shape of wooden planks. He was looking at unfinished wood. The thick fog of disorientation faded, leaving only a slight haze, and Golden realized he was staring at a ceiling. He was lying in cotton sheets in a deliciously soft bed. Could he have died and gone to heaven? No, heaven couldn't be this cold. And they probably had better ceilings. His sheets were soaked with sweat, and he was shivering despite the heavy blanket covering him.

"Hello there."

Golden turned to see who was speaking, and his head spun. As his vision returned to center, he saw President Roberts standing beside him. He was back in the mission home. He tried to speak, but his voice cracked and he couldn't get any breath out. He couldn't seem to get enough air in either. He was gasping like he'd just lost the race at the county fair. He lay there for a moment just trying to breathe. By and by his breathing regulated somewhat, but it was still very weak.

"How'd I get here?" Speaking took much more effort than he expected. It felt like someone had set an anvil on his chest.

"Elder Rich brought you."

"Where . . . "

"Where is he?" B.H. finished his sentence. "Back out in the field. He didn't want to leave. I promised him I'd take care of you the best I could." He sat down by the bed. "I'm not going to beat about the proverbial bush, Elder Kimball. You look gravely ill."

Golden caught a glimpse of himself in the small mirror over the dresser. He was thinner than ever, almost skeletal, and his skin hung loosely about him like a mealy yellow sack. He looked back at the president. "Hell, I've always looked this way."

B.H. smiled despite himself, then his expression became somber. His voice was full of concern. "I'm very serious. You've contracted malaria. I'd like to send you home."

Home. Never had any place sounded so wonderful to Golden. If the president sent him home he'd be there in a week, back among the mountains and the Saints and away from the ridicule of indifferent people and homicidal mobs. He'd gone into the field and had done the best he knew how, he truly had. And here was an opportunity for him to leave this miserable place. He was legitimately ill. He didn't know much about malaria, but he now knew all too well how it felt. It was a hard thing that had come upon him. He could hang up his saddle and no one would blame him or think the worse of him if he chose to go home.

No one except for himself.

He would never forgive himself if he didn't at least try to stick it out. He knew he could lick the malaria. Well, he didn't know he could for sure, but he planned on trying. Still, here was a glaring chance for him to go home, an open invitation to leave all this trouble and care behind. All he had to do was say yes. Just one little word. Instead he looked up and said, "I appreciate your concern, but I'd prefer to stay."

B.H. cleared his throat lightly. "To be honest, Elder Kimball, it's an economic consideration. If we send you home alive, it will cost us fifty-three dollars. Should you die, it will cost several hundred."

Golden reached out weakly. He placed a shaking, pale hand on B.H.'s arm. "I want to stay, President. If I die, I'll pay the difference."

The words were meant as a joke, but B.H. could see he was serious.

"I'd at least like to get you to a doctor."

"I don't want a doctor. I want you to give me a blessing." Golden gripped down as tightly as he could, which, in his weakened state, wasn't very tight at all. The words took a great deal of effort, but he was going to have his say, "I've been as faithful and true as I know how and made great sacrifices to be here. I need to test God out—if he can't take care of me now, then he is not the God of my fathers."

B.H. nodded. Without another word, he stood and placed his hands on Golden's head.

∾

If you stared at them long enough, you came to realize that the unfinished planks in the ceiling were actually quite beautiful. The wavy pattern of the grain looked like a river flowing across the ceiling, forming eddies around random knots. If you looked even closer, you could see shapes. A wild bronco galloped in the corner closest to the window, its long mane flowing behind it. A fox chased a hare across the middle, the hare diving for cover in a dark crack in the wood.

Golden had looked long enough to not only see the shapes but also memorize them. He knew there were exactly forty-three planks and four crossbeams. He knew that in the evening, when the sun was low, the beam nearest the front window drew a shadow across the ceiling like the black sail of a pirate ship. Most of all he knew that he was tired of looking at the ceiling and was ready to be out of this bed. He'd lost track of time, but it had been at least a month since he'd been brought to the mission home. Maybe two.

His skin had mostly returned to its natural color, and he'd even gained a few important pounds back. He still looked like the barber's cat, but he was greatly improved. He moved his covers aside, carefully getting out of bed and walking to the window. The sunlight coming through was almost blinding, but the warmth felt good against his thin frame. He was certainly in much better shape than he'd been when he was brought here, but the feeling of depression that had enveloped him still persisted.

"How are you feeling?"

Golden turned from the window. B.H. stood in the doorway, bringing Golden his daily treatment of quinine and hot lemonade.

"Better, I suppose." By now Golden had drunk so much of the president's concoction that he wasn't sure if his yellow color was from the fever or the lemonade.

B.H. was dressed immaculately, as always. He may not have

worn the fanciest or most expensive clothes around, but the clothes he had he wore properly. He wasn't a vain man; he just understood the importance of appearance.

"Well, you're standing. That's a good sign." He set the tray down on the bed stand.

"Yeah." Golden's voice lacked any hint of vitality. The words seemed to drag out of him.

"Are you sure you're all right?"

"I'm fine." Golden was positive that the president could tell otherwise, but he was too polite to force the issue, bless his soul. B.H. moved to excuse himself when Golden spoke up again. "President Roberts?"

"Yes?" B.H. stepped back into the room.

Golden didn't know how to voice what he was feeling. He finally blurted it out as straight as he could. "I'm not sure what I'm doing here."

B.H. took the words with his usual calm and understanding manner. "I thought you said you wanted to stay."

Golden smiled wryly. "I was a little delirious at the time."

B.H. crossed the room, joining Golden at the window. "Do you not want to stay? The choice is completely up to you."

"I want to stay." Golden sighed. "But I don't feel like I'm doing a bit of good for anyone. I've been out trying to teach people about the gospel, and I . . . well, I don't really know the first thing about it myself." He sat down on the bed.

Golden continued, "When I first got here, I thought that Epistles were the wives of apostles. That's how little I knew. I tell you, the gospel has to be true or ignoramus missionaries like myself would have ruined it long ago."

B.H. smiled at Golden's jest, but it was clear he understood the hurt behind the words as well. B.H. sat beside Golden on the bed. He was silent for a minute, collecting his thoughts. When he spoke again his voice was as solemn as any Golden had ever heard.

"Elder Kimball, I'm going to tell you something, and this

may be the only thing about the gospel that I truly, truly know—the gospel isn't about how many scriptures you can quote or how hard you pound the pulpit; it's about what's in here." He pointed at Golden's heart. "Do you know what the first two great commandments are?"

Golden had to shake his head. He had no idea.

"The first is 'thou shalt love the Lord thy God with all thy heart' and the second is 'thou shalt love thy neighbor as thyself.'" He held up two fingers as he listed them. "Love God, love your neighbor as yourself. Everything else—everything—rests upon these two commandments." He shifted his weight. "Do you remember the first night you arrived in the mission? How you helped Henry Shepherd with his glass of water?"

Golden nodded. How could he forget? The poor man had been beaten so severely that he couldn't even get a drink of water by himself.

B.H. continued, "Nobody asked you to do that; you just did it."

"That wasn't anything. Just a glass of water," Golden deferred.

"'I was thirsty and you gave me drink.'" B.H. smiled. "Don't discount yourself. You might not be able to quote the commandments by heart, but I think you know far more about the gospel than you realize. It's evident in how you behave, it's evident in how you treat others, even when you think no one else is watching. Do you understand what it is I'm trying to say?"

Golden nodded, and B.H. patted him on the back. "As for the rest, since you're stuck here with me till you're fully well, you and I can study together. How does that sound?"

Golden brightened considerably. B.H. was sharp as an Arkansas toothpick and knew more at thirty than most men ever would should they live to be one hundred. The idea of being able to study under his guidance excited Golden plenty. "I'd be honored to study with you, President."

"Call me B.H."

"That certainly beats being called BS, doesn't it?"

A strange expression crossed B.H.'s face, and Golden froze. His spirits were higher than they'd been in a long time, and the words just popped out. He feared he'd overstepped his bounds. Much to Golden's relief, B.H. began to laugh. "Yes, I suppose it does." He patted Golden gently on the leg and rose to leave. "I'd better let you rest."

Golden interrupted him before he reached the door. "B.H.?"

"Yes?"

"Thank you."

"You're most welcome."

Thus commenced the spiritual education of J. Golden Kimball. Having been raised in a Mormon household, he knew the basic teachings of the Church. Fact is, Golden already had a good understanding of the gospel, just as B.H. had said. It wasn't a scholarly knowledge; that would come in time. But he knew it was true in his heart.

As his body mended and grew stronger, so did his mind and spirit. B.H. proved to be a mighty sharp teacher and, as time would prove, friend. Though Golden was healing from sickness and still struggled with recurring bouts of melancholia, the spell of time he spent studying with B.H. was one of the most joyous of his life.

CHAPTER 13

CANE CREEK

One of the most striking differences between a cat and a lie is that a cat has only nine lives.

—*Mark Twain*

The letter, purportedly written by one Bishop West from Juab County, was pure sedition and brimming with treachery against the United States government. It called for the vengeance of God to fall upon it and its representatives holding federal office in Utah. Among other things, it rallied for the assassination of the non-Mormon governor of the state and general civil upheaval against any and all forms of federal interference with the Church.

Men who were considered authorities on the subject declared it a genuine document "with a few trifling exceptions." It was later proven that the "trifling exceptions" were one: Bishop West didn't exist and two: no such address had ever been given in Juab County, or anywhere else, for that matter. In other words, the letter was a fake. A forgery. A complete and blatant lie.

Unfortunately truth has never stood in the way of a good scandal. The letter was quickly passed around by anti-Mormon forces in Utah. When the national news got wind of it, they printed it up in papers across the country, including those in the Tennessee Valley area. When the letter was proven to be hogwash, letters of retraction were printed, but not with equal enthusiasm and often near the back pages, where few would ever be read. No matter how many apologies were issued, the cat was out of the bag.

"Here's another renunciation of that foul letter." B.H. set the paper down and turned to Golden. "Too little, too late I'm afraid. It will take one hundred years of truth to repair this one minute's worth of lie." Golden knew that B.H. was right. But neither of them knew how great that damage would be.

The shroud of late summer settled heavily into the South. The heat cranked up its last offensive before the onslaught of fall, reaching a crescendo of muggy oppression that weighed on everything like a pressure cooker. Under the right circumstances, high temperature and pressure can create diamonds; under different circumstances they are just as likely to cause an explosion.

Despite the sultriness, it was a beautiful Sabbath morning. After nearly five months serving in the area, the road that Elder Jones walked was familiar territory. The quietly gurgling water of Cane Creek greeted him like an old friend as he followed its meandering path, where it flowed in and out of the shadows of trees, freely sharing its waters with the forest and fields alike. On a day like this, Jones would have liked nothing more than to jump in and enjoy the refreshing water, but he was dressed in his Sunday best and, if he didn't hurry, was going to be late for services.

He and his companion, Elder Thompson, and the two other missionaries serving in the area, Elders Gibbs and Berry, had stayed the previous night at the home of Mister Thomas Garrett, who lived a few miles from the James Condor home, where the meeting was to be held. The other three elders were already at the Condors's place, having left a few hours earlier. Jones had stayed behind to finish a copy of the *Deseret News*, saying that he'd catch up with them when he was finished.

The members of the Condor family were some of the oldest converts in Cane Creek. James and Rachel had two boys, J.R. and Martin. J.R.'s last name was actually Hudson and was Rachel's boy from an earlier marriage. He was twenty-four, roughly the same age as the elders. Martin, the younger at nineteen, was from their current marriage.

Elderly and known for his gruff but kind manner, James had opened their home for Sunday meetings after the building they had used previously had been burned to the ground. The cause of the fire was never determined, and though it was generally believed to be arson, no suspects were ever found. Of course, it doesn't appear that the local authorities ever put much effort into finding any either.

Jones enjoyed serving here. The other elders were honorable, hardworking men, and they had been able to enjoy some success in their preaching and the company of good, honest folk, like Mister Garrett. Possessed of an agreeable temperament and a well-developed belly that he referred to as his "table muscle," Mister Garrett wasn't a member of the Church, but he was an upright soul with a generous manner and got along well with Mormon and gentile alike. The elders always knew they had a friend when they were in the area.

Gibbs and Thompson were both from Utah and roughly Jones's age. Berry was older and, although his family lived in Utah now, was a Tennessee native. He spoke with a slow, thoughtful, but always kind manner. As the father of no less than fifteen children, he had made great sacrifices to return to his home state and had thus far been blessed in his efforts.

Just ahead, past a field of yellowing corn, Elder Jones could see the large cotton tree that had been chopped down and trimmed to serve as a bridge across the clear waters of the creek. He turned from the road onto the well-worn footpath that ran through the thick underbrush to the crossing. He was halfway toward the bridge when there was a clamor from his right. He scarcely had time to turn when he was lit on by a group of armed Klansmen who rushed from where they had been concealed in the corn.

"One lil' peep outta you an' yer a dead man." The Klansman waggled his gun for emphasis. His eyes flitted about quickly beneath his mask. When he didn't see what he was looking for, he leaned in close enough that Jones could smell the liquor on his breath. "Where're the others? Where are they?"

Jones knew what it was like to look danger in the eye. He had met rough types during his time in the South, just as all the elders had. But that never made it any easier. He knew that the mob wanted the other elders, not just him. Knowing what it might cost him but refusing to endanger his fellow missionaries, he steadied himself and looked his assailant in the eyes. "I'm not sure where they are." Somewhere deep inside, Jones figured the Lord would forgive him for the lie. He wasn't so sure about the Klansmen.

"Bet they's at Condor's place alreddy," one of the other robed men piped up.

Jones hung his head as the Klansmen bound his wrists together with a length of cord; his ruse had done no good. He could only hope that perhaps the others weren't at the Condor's for some reason or that these men might have a change of heart.

"If he tries to escape, shoot him," the leader ordered one of the men, pointing at Jones. It didn't sound like a change of heart was on the menu. The leader waved the others to follow him. "C'mon."

As quickly as they'd appeared, the men disappeared, leaving only a single guard. Jones caught one last glimpse of their sheets and hoods as they crossed the bridge, then they turned up the path on the far side and vanished into the undergrowth.

The Cane Creek branch was one of the oldest in the region, but it was still small enough to fit into a farmhouse. The Condor home was a modest, two-story plank and log abode that stood on a bluff overlooking the creek. Men, women, and children in their Sunday best milled about the well-tended yard and in the orchard spread out behind it. The Saints greeted each other with smiles and handshakes, socializing and catching up on the latest news with each other. Children behaved as children will whether it's the Sabbath or not—running about and eluding their mothers, who chided them in vain to not dirty their clothes. Inside, Elder Gibbs sat with his companions, thumbing through his scriptures in search of a text for the morning's discourse.

It was about time for the meeting to begin, and Brother Condor was on his way in to check on the elders. He was just passing the gate to the front of the house when the Klansmen poured out of the woods, descending full split on the house like a pack of wild dogs.

It took a moment for people to realize what was happening. For one surreal instant, the congregation stood frozen in shock, watching the costumed barbarians close in. The mobbers reached the fence before someone finally screamed. Panic arced its way through the crowd, and the storm broke loose with full fury. People scattered like gazelle before a bunch of hyenas.

"Boys! Get your guns!" Brother Condor cried the alarm.

"Hold up, old man!" The mob seized him, several men holding him fast while the rest continued their rush on the house.

Their father's yell carried over the house loud and clear. J.R. and Martin ran, leaping over the fence, around the trees, and into the back door. Southern bred, they were well accustomed to the hardships of backwoods life; the notion of defending their home by force came naturally.

J.R. rushed up the stairs to the living quarters, with Martin entering seconds later, arriving at the same time as the mob reached the house. Martin made a beeline for the Kentucky rifle hanging above the fireplace. It was loaded and ready to go. Seeing him, the mob leader raced him across the room, both grabbing the rifle at the same time, wrestling furiously for control.

Though only nineteen, Martin was a farm boy, strong for his age, and he held his own against the mobber. Back and forth the two men strained, locked in their death match. Martin pushed. Pulled. Grunted and strained. Slowly, he forced the Klansman

back. He was gaining the upper hand when the hooded Klansman drew a pistol. He shoved it in Martin's face and fired point
blank.

Click.

It was a dud. Martin flinched, jumping back reflexively,
and the white-sheeted man seized control of the rifle. Instead of
using it on Martin, the man turned, bringing the rifle to bear on
Elder Gibbs. They must have been after him the whole time. The
Klansman pulled the trigger. This one wasn't a dud.

The chaos of gunfire and yells carried down the bluff to where
Jones and his guard stood, both staring in dismay in the direction of the maelstrom. Jones was tearful with panic. His guard
seemed to forget all about him as the horrific sounds reached
them. The man's eyes darted back and forth between the direction of the farm and Jones, growing visibly more agitated with
each scream and gunshot.

"My God! They're shootin' among the women and children."
He sounded almost as upset as Jones. He dropped his gun to his
side.

Perhaps the man had a conscience after all. Jones grabbed
desperately at the opportunity. "Please, you must let me go. There
will be wounded, someone must get help."

His plea was cut off by a large volley of gunfire, followed
by more terrified shrieks and wails. Jones looked at his captor,
unsure of what to expect. The man hedged, indecisive, then
began frantically untying Jones's wrists.

"Get straight up this road." The guard spoke quickly as he
worked at the knot. His voice was shaky and tense. "Don' stop,
keep straight. It'll bring yuh to the depot. That'll getcha out safe.
An' don't come back, no matter what, ya hear? Go!"

Jones turned and showed his heels. He expected to be shot in
the back any second. But the shot never came. He focused on his
feet, the pumping of his legs. He never looked back to see what

became of his guard. Everything was moving past him in a daze. Eventually the only sound he could hear were the buzz of cicadas and the harsh rasping of his own breath. Ignoring the pain in his legs and the fire burning in his lungs, Elder Jones ran and ran.

CHAPTER 14

WORD REACHES CHATTANOOGA

What we have done for ourselves alone dies with us;
what we have done for others and the world remains and
is immortal.

—Albert Pike

The world has hardly seen a more ragged, exhausted soul than that of Elder Jones as he burst through the door of the mission office. He looked like Job himself. Drenched in sweat, with thick saliva crusting the edge of his lips, Jones had reached his Marathon. According to legend, the Greek messenger had died of a heart attack; Jones looked like he might follow suit. Gasping for breath, he looked wildly around the room. "President Roberts! President Roberts!" There was no answer. He hauled himself up the stairs, trying the first door, then bursting through the second. "President Roberts!"

Golden bolted upright in bed, upset at being awakened. "He's not here, dammit." He took one look at Jones and stopped. Something was terribly wrong. Golden leaped from his bed. "Are you all right?"

"I'm fine, I'm fine. They . . . " Jones choked up, struggling with heavy emotion and lack of air. He'd been trying to outrun the truth, but now it caught up to him with a vengeance.

"Who? What's wrong"

"The Klan . . . yesterday . . . "

Golden tensed. His reaction was visceral.

Jones continued, forcing the words out between gasps of air. "They attacked the church meeting at Cane Creek."

Golden's jaw dropped in horror as comprehension plowed into him like a steam train. A church meeting. It couldn't be. He felt like he'd been physically hit. He sank back down, sitting on the bed. The obvious question rose in his mind. He didn't want to ask it. He was afraid to hear the answer. "Is anyone hurt?"

"I . . . I don't know." Physically and emotionally worn, Jones was past all endurance. He broke down, almost wailing, "I was ambushed about a quarter mile away. My guard let me go. I don't know. I didn't see. There were shots and screams. I don't know."

Golden could see that Jones was unraveling fast. He was being pushed further than should ever be expected of anyone. He would need time to get over it, but the time was not now. Golden needed him to keep it together just a little longer. He grabbed the tattered man's shoulders. "We've got to find out. Come on."

The horses' hooves thundered out a steady rhythm as they kicked up a trail of dirt behind them. The dust settled in a thick layer on Golden and Jones where they sat in a small surrey. Golden could feel the grit in his teeth. Over and over his mind kept running through different scenarios, all of them bad. B.H. was several hours away in Alabama, visiting with some of the elders there. Golden had dashed off a telegram wire to him before lighting out of town with Jones.

Golden drove the team hard. His years as a mule skinner paid off in spades. He knew how to coax the horses to give him their all without driving them past their limits. They were in a hurry, but it wouldn't do anyone any good to bake their horses.

Elder Jones sat nearly comatose in the seat next to him,

looking very nearly like a corpse himself. Golden's heart went out to the man, but other than to verify directions, he didn't say much to him.

They were making good time, having covered over ten miles or so, when they spied another wagon approaching rapidly from the opposite direction. As they drew closer together, Elder Jones sprung to life, grabbing Golden's arm. "Stop! That's Elder Thompson with Mister Garrett!"

Sure enough, Mister Garrett was approaching, his runabout drawn by a handsome Missouri Fox Trotter. Jones waved and was quickly answered by Thompson, who waved back. Thompson looked to be in about the same shape as Jones. Golden brought up the reins, pulling his team to the side of the road as Mister Garrett brought his wagon alongside them. Jones and Thompson both jumped from their seats to embrace each other.

"Jones! You're alive!" Thompson cried, rejoicing. He held Jones by the shoulders. "When we couldn't find you we feared the worst."

"I'm fine. Where are Berry and Gibbs?"

The smile faded from Thompson's face, and he looked down. His silence was answer enough.

The four men returned to the mission home, and B.H. soon arrived from Alabama, where he'd left posthaste upon receipt of Golden's telegram. After attending to Jones and Thompson to make sure they were without harm, B.H. gathered them all together upstairs.

The mood was somber as B.H. led with a short prayer that they might have the fortitude and the wisdom to do what must be done. It was as sober an occasion as any that Golden could remember in his whole life. It felt like his father's funeral.

Heber had died at the apex of summer. Golden could still see rows of mourners dressed in black, filing in and out of the Salt Lake assembly hall. He recalled the brightly colored flowers around the casket and thinking how out of place they seemed. The bereaved had come and gone, patting him on the shoulder and telling him what a brave young man he was, but he hadn't felt very brave at all. His father was dead. He felt pretty useless.

The casket was carried up the hill to the cemetery in a wagon, the drape covering it fluttering in the wind while the congregation sang a hymn. He couldn't remember what they had sung. It didn't matter. There would be no hymns sung today.

No one was in any mood to talk, but things needed to be sorted out quickly. By this time Golden had already heard most of the story from the elders, but fresh disbelief filled him all over as they went over everything again with B.H. The story was almost worse to hear the second time around as the initial shock of it settled into cold reality.

Elder Thompson related his part first. His voice was numb from the shock that had sunk back in after the excitement of seeing Jones had subsided. B.H. took pen and paper from his desk and was taking careful notes, his normally practiced handwriting an almost illegible scribble as he tried to keep pace with Thompson's words and his own racing emotions. It was a mission president's worst nightmare.

"Before I knew what was happening, both Martin and J.R. rushed in, arriving about the same time as the mobsters." Thompson spoke as if in a trance. "Martin grabbed for his rifle above the fireplace, but one of the mob grabbed it and wrestled it loose, turning it on Gibbs. He shot him there in cold blood."

Thompson was staring at a spot somewhere beyond the wall, lost in his memory. His eyes never moved from it while he spoke. "Martin came down then and shot the mob leader. The mob retaliated, and Martin was cut down where he stood. I had a rifle turned on me, but Berry held it fast with both hands and yelled for me to run." He paused, his emotions finally breaking through the wall of shock, pinching his voice, tears flowing heavily now. "He gave his life for me." He paused to collect himself. No one rushed him. Other than the scratching of the quill on paper and a few sniffles, the room was gravely silent.

"After that, I hid in the woods till Mister Garrett found me," Thompson finished, with a grateful nod in Mister Garrett's direction.

Golden could feel an explosion of anger and tears welling inside him, but there was nothing to be done. He stood quietly leaning against the far wall, struggling against the pit in his stomach that grew deeper and blacker the longer the tale bore out. He could hardly bear to listen to it. He didn't know how Thompson had the strength to continue speaking. Golden wasn't normally prone to crying, he had too much cowboy in him for that, but drops of moisture were somehow escaping his eyes. He wasn't the only one. He noticed teardrops blotting B.H.'s notes as he dutifully wrote out the last of Thompson's words. Some men might see crying as weakness, but Golden knew it was a testament to the kind of man B.H. was. If a man could endure such a sorrowful tale and not shed a tear, he probably wasn't much of a man at all.

B.H. looked to Mister Garrett then to hear his part of the story. It was clear to all that this was taxing B.H. heavily.

"Mister Roberts, we can finish this later," said Mister Garrett.

B.H. looked at him with gratitude in his eyes for the man's generosity and care. "No, if it's all right with everyone, I need to get this to Salt Lake."

Mister Garrett nodded. He clamped a supporting hand on Thompson's shoulder, then picked up the story where the elder had left off. "I wasn't there myself, of course. But here's what I gathered. After the point that Mister Thompson here left off, J.R. came downstairs with his own rifle. He fired and killed the leader of the mob, which turned out to be David Hinson. Hinson was one of the local citizenship, if you can believe that. His place isn't much further from the Condor's than mine." He shook his head. "As soon as they saw Hinson fall, the mob retaliated, firing back into the house. J.R. was killed then, and Missus Condor was wounded in the hip. She'll be all right, I understand, but she's in a great deal of pain and will be bedridden for a good while yet.

After that, they ran off, firing at random as they left, injuring several others."

"Savages." B.H. shook his head in disbelief, his hand trembling as he finished jotting down the last few notes. He set down his pen and took a moment to collect himself and his thoughts. No one dared disturb the silence.

Helplessness is an awful feeling. As upset as Golden was, he couldn't think of anything he could do except continue holding up the wall he was leaning against. Innocent men had been murdered, and nothing would change that.

He would probably help B.H. to draft his letter, then send the terrible news off to Salt Lake first thing tomorrow. He could see no further course of action and sadly thought that would be the end of it. Then the President stood, resolutely wiping his tears.

"We have to get the bodies of those elders out of there. We have to send them home to their families."

His declaration caught them all by surprise. It was a dangerous proposition, and everyone knew it. Mister Garrett jumped to his feet, his voice filled with concern.

"It's a noble thought, Mister Roberts, but that mob is still out there. They've threatened to kill any Mormon elder they find. And they're not alone. Hinson has a large number of friends in the area, and there are a lot of people out there that resent you all. Even if they're not up to joining the mobs directly, they'd tattle on you gladly. No, it wouldn't be safe at all."

As president, B.H. had spent a lot of time in Cane Creek visiting with the elders and the Saints. He knew many of the people, including Mister Garrett, and just as many people knew him. It would be impossible for him to step foot in the area without being recognized.

"What about the state authorities?" Golden asked.

B.H. shook his head. "I've already petitioned the governor and the adjutant general this afternoon. They are either unable or unwilling to help us."

Just like before, when the mob had burned down Jesse's barn back in Virginia, there were legal recourses they could take, but realistically they didn't amount to much help at all. Even if they pursued the legal route, their case would most likely be ignored or mired in apathy. It looked like the elders were on their own with this one. Well, almost alone.

"I'll go," Mister Garrett volunteered. "I'm no Mormon. They won't bother me."

B.H. clapped him on the arm, "Thank you, Mister Garrett. That is a great help."

Mister Garrett nodded. Golden relaxed slightly; the matter was settled then. Or so he thought.

"I'm going with you," B.H. announced, taking the group by surprise yet again.

"No, you can't," Golden blurted with a start.

Mister Garrett was equally alarmed. "He's right, Mister Roberts. Let me tell you, you're still a young man; you got only one life, and if you go, you will be killed. Let me beg you, do not go. They will kill you."

"I will do what is most prudent, I promise you," B.H. was trying to reassure them, but Mister Garrett shook his head. He'd have none of it. The risk was simply far too high.

"Then I gotta take back my offer. I ain't gonna be party to your death," he said. He wasn't going to budge. B.H. saw it and nodded reluctantly.

"All right. I shall find someone else." He glanced at Golden, then turned his attention to Jones and Thompson. "I'm very grateful to have both of you alive and in one piece. We should let you sleep." They definitely needed rest; they looked liable to keel over where they sat. B.H. motioned to the door, and Golden followed Mister Garrett out of the room. B.H. exited after, closing the door behind them.

Golden moved down the hall, his spirit as heavy as his feet. As tired as he was, Golden's head was abuzz with conflicting thoughts and emotions. What strength he'd gotten back convalescing here in the mission home seemed to dissipate in the face of the day's atrocities. Would these things ever end? Hadn't enough blood been shed in the world? You'd think a people just recovering from a war would know better by now.

He'd caught the look that B.H. had sent him. The prospect of facing murderous mobs again, and on purpose this time, made his blood run cold. It was a hard thing to ask of him. The last time he had faced a mob of masked men it had been tucked behind the safety of a hill at night. That had been harrowing enough. He had no desire to repeat the experience up close. But if it was God's will, it was God's will. Golden resolved that he wouldn't shirk his duty no matter how much it might frighten him.

They moved down the stairwell, out of earshot from the elders. Not that it mattered; they were probably out cold already. They looked ready to pass out before Golden had even blown out the lamp. At the bottom, Mister Garrett grew even more serious. He drew a bundled handkerchief from his coat and forced it into B.H.'s hands. From the way B.H.'s hand dipped, Golden could tell that whatever was inside, it was heavy. B.H. peeled back the handkerchief. Golden was surprised to see the metal of a loaded pistol gleaming in the light of the lamp.

B.H. handed it back, but Mister Garrett refused. "Take it. No telling what might happen. You may need it." B.H. didn't look crazy about the idea, but Mister Garrett was so insistent that he tucked it reluctantly into his coat. Mister Garrett crossed to the door. "Good night, Mister Roberts. It's nice to see you again, though I wish it could be under different circumstances."

"Likewise to you. Would you care to stay here tonight, Mister Garrett?"

"Thank you, but if it's all the same, I think I'll head into town, see if I hear anything. I'll be by come first light."

Mister Garrett excused himself, and B.H. closed the door. Golden looked at the stocky Englishman and raised his skinny frame with as much determination as he could muster. "All right,

B.H., if you think I should go, I am willing."

B.H. looked confused, then understanding dawned on him. He smiled warmly and shook his head. "You're a good man, Golden. Generous and sincere. I know you would go. But I'm not asking you. I myself am going."

Golden was caught off guard. "You have to ask me—I finally talked myself into it! Besides, you can't go. You said you weren't going to. You heard it tonight—it's far too dangerous."

"And no less dangerous for you. No, I'm the president of this mission. These brethren are my responsibility, dead though they are. And you are my responsibility as well. It must be me."

In the months he'd spent with President Roberts, Golden learned quickly that the president could teach a Missouri mule a thing or two about being stubborn when he set his mind to it. And B.H. definitely had it set. Golden knew there would be no argument.

B.H. removed the gun from his jacket and handed it to Golden. As a cowboy, Golden had carried a pistol for much of his life. But that one had always been loaded with shot for killing snakes. This one was loaded for a different purpose, and frankly, he didn't care for the weight of it, even if it was only for self-defense.

He opened up the trunk by the president's desk and unceremoniously dumped the pistol inside, burying it beneath a stack of papers. Shutting the lid, he piled a stack of books on top for good measure. "If anybody can come here and look at me as sick as I am and then make an attack upon me, I'll let him do it."

The mood was still heavy, but B.H. managed to crack a weak smile.

"Bless you, Golden."

Golden was glad to see him smile, but the thought of him going to Cane Creek still concerned him. He pointed out the obvious to B.H. "They'll know you from the moment you step foot in the county," Golden said.

B.H. sat down, his brow creasing. "You're right about that.

I'll have to think of something different." He leaned back in his chair, stroking his beard and thinking. Golden sat down across from him to see if he could think of anything. He had no beard but stroked his chin anyhow. He reasoned that if it helped B.H. to think, perhaps it might help him as well. B.H. was intent on going himself, that was clear. Maybe if enough elders went with him their numbers would be enough to scare off any mobs long enough to get the job done. But it would take too long to gather the elders together. There had to be another way. Before Golden could think of anything else, B.H. snapped his fingers and stood up. "I have an idea."

CHAPTER 15

CLETUS

Take time to deliberate; but when the time for action arrives, stop thinking and go on.

—Andrew Jackson

Early the next morning, Mister Garrett returned to the mission home to find Golden waiting out front standing next to a rugged-looking man. He was a prime example of the poorer sort of rough-hewn man found throughout the region.

"Good morning, Mister Garrett." Golden shook Mister Garrett's hand. He had the firm grip of a man used to working the earth for a living. It was a handshake Golden could respect plenty.

"Morning. Where are Mister Jones and Mister Thompson?" Mister Garrett asked, looking around.

"Upstairs," Golden pointed a thumb at the mission home, "I thought it best to let them sleep."

Mister Garrett nodded his agreement.

"President Roberts asked me to apologize on his behalf, but he left earlier for Nashville to try and petition the governor again." Golden spoke in a loud clear voice. It was certainly louder than was his normal custom, but Mister Garrett didn't seem to notice.

"Thank heavens he's come to his senses," said Mister Garrett, relieved. "I hope he can get something worked out."

Golden took a folded letter from his jacket and handed it to

Mister Garrett. B.H. had written and signed it himself. "Here's a letter authorizing Mister Cletus here to retrieve the bodies in his stead." Golden motioned to the fellow standing next to him.

"How do?" Cletus nodded, brushing the brim of his hat with his fingers.

Mister Garrett gave Cletus a once over. He was a gruff-looking fellow. From his slouched hat to his rough, cowhide boots, his unkempt clothes looked as if they'd been salvaged from a discard pile. Some kind of grime covered his hands and baby-faced cheeks. Mister Garrett didn't want to know what it was. This was obviously not a very hygienic man. Mister Garrett couldn't help but wonder how on earth Mister Roberts had ever found such a man or why he would consider hiring him. But he'd have to do. On the upside, it was going to be dirty work, and the man looked well suited for it.

It was clear from Mister Garrett's expression that his opinion of the fellow wasn't a very good one. Golden couldn't argue with him either. He didn't care much for the idea of this particular fellow going to get the bodies, although it was for entirely different reasons than Mister Garrett was harboring. But beggars can't be choosers. Time had been short and the hour had been late.

Mister Garrett took the letter, reading it as he walked back to his wagon. When he was out of earshot, Golden leaned over to Cletus and whispered quickly, "This isn't going to work."

"You just take care of the shipping with the railroad and the other arrangements as I've asked." Cletus whispered back. His thick Southern accent was suddenly replaced by B.H.'s subtle English tones. B.H. sounded as resolute as ever, but Golden could see a flicker of fear in his eyes. Who could blame the man? B.H. was as brave as any, but even the bravest men know fear. He wasn't sure if this was going to work either.

They had spent several hours of the night shaving B.H.'s beard and mustache. Golden was no barber but did a decent job, all things considered. B.H. then scrounged up some ragged clothes that more or less fit him. Dressed in these, shortly before

Mister Garrett's arrival in the morning, B.H. had smeared grease over his hands and face in the effort to make himself further unrecognizable.

"I still think it should be me," said Golden.

B.H. glanced at his beanpole frame. "Golden, your long, lean greyhound figure would make effective disguise impossible. I'm the president. The Lord will protect me. If you doubt it, feel free to go ask him."

Before Golden could argue any further, Mister Garrett beckoned him over with a wave. He was making a great show of checking his animal's harness, securing each buckle and adjusting the fit. When Golden drew close enough, Mister Garrett glanced back at Cletus. "You really think we can trust this Cletus feller?" he whispered.

Golden looked at him in disbelief. Could he really not know? The dog and pony show he had been putting on, the letter and all that, had been for anyone who might have been eavesdropping or otherwise spying on the morning's procedures. But Golden thought Mister Garrett at least would have known. Apparently B.H.'s disguise was working. That was a good sign. Golden hoped the charade would be as effective with everyone else they came across. They had a lot of mileage to cover before this was over.

Golden nodded reassuringly. "Oh, I'm pretty sure we can trust him."

"All right. If you say so." Mister Garrett beckoned B.H. over. "Well, come on, Cletus."

B.H. crossed over from the porch and swung easily up into the passenger seat of the wagon. Mister Garrett, a little older and not quite so nimble, climbed stiffly up his side and picked up the reins.

Golden barely had time to utter one last "Be careful," and they were gone. He let out a deep sigh and turned back toward the mission home. He had work to do as well.

One of the first things B.H. had done when wiring the news to Salt Lake was request the funds necessary for shipping the bodies of the slain elders home. However, those funds would take a while to arrive. In order to cover things in the meantime, B.H. asked Golden to pay a visit to Bernard Moses, a local merchant tailor in Chattanooga, to ask if they could curry a favor and borrow the money.

The thought of asking strangers for a bite to eat still made Golden nervous, let alone asking for a great sum of money. He felt ashamed about feeling nervous since his errands in town were nothing compared to what B.H. was about to undertake. To Golden's relief and the eternal credit of Mister Moses, upon hearing their plight, the kind merchant generously agreed to lend them as much as they needed without asking for so much as a letter of promise as collateral. A right generous and trusting fellow, that Mister Moses. It's unfortunate there aren't more folks like that around these days.

The railroad company made it abundantly clear that in order to ship the bodies, they had to be closed up in airtight containers so as not to expose anyone on the train to anything unpleasant. With Mister Moses's help, Golden purchased two specially crafted metallic caskets from the undertaker, which B.H. and Mister Garrett would pick up from Shady Grove depot on their way to Cane Creek.

When B.H. had told Golden it would be costly to return him to Utah if he'd died, he hadn't been joking. By the time Golden had made the final shipping arrangements, including caskets, permits, and ticketing, the total cost reached nearly one thousand dollars. It was no small sum, and Golden was almost as embarrassed to ask for it as he was astounded by Mister Moses's willingness to give it. The man's charity left a deep impression on Golden. It was reassuring to know that there were people like the good merchant and Mister Garrett here in the South after all. He knew there were good folks, but he'd met so many of the other variety that it was easy to forget. Golden resolved that, should he ever be in the position of such wealth himself, he would use it as generously as Mister Moses.

His duties finished for the time being, he returned to the mission home. The late afternoon sun poured through the front window and reflected off the walls and floor, giving the office a soft yellow glow. Any other time Golden would have been warmed by the beauty of it, but today his soul was too burdened to notice. Running errands and making arrangements had been good, for it had kept him busy and his mind free from worry. Now that he was back in the mission home with little to keep him occupied, time ground to a standstill, leaving his imagination to conjure up the worst.

Back on the ranch, if a cow ever needed roping or branding, Golden would rope or brand it. It was as simple as that. That was his nature. He'd done all that B.H. had asked of him, and there was nothing else to do but sit around and feel useless. It was as frustrating as all get out. The clock mocked him with every tick. He filed papers. He studied his scriptures. He even made a modest effort at tidying up around the mission home, not that the place needed much. He tried to nap but found it impossible to sleep. Mostly he paced and paced and did the hardest thing of all. He waited.

CHAPTER 16

INTO THE MAW OF MADNESS

You will never do anything in this world without courage. It is the greatest quality of the mind next to honor.

—Aristotle

A s he said, B.H. had indeed petitioned the state authorities, hoping for assistance that never was to come. His efforts to retrieve the bodies received no official sanction, but that's not to say they went unnoticed. Word that he intended to retrieve the bodies quickly made it back to the mob forces. They in turn had responded by blockading and patrolling every road into the county from the direction of Chattanooga. It was made clear that if he dare step foot in Lewis County, they intended one Brigham H. Roberts a serious amount of bodily harm. B.H. would be a liar if he said he weren't frightened, but the Spirit had told him that he was the one who should go, so here he was.

Keeping up his Southern drawl, B.H. talked at length with Mister Garrett as they rode, trying to determine as much as he could about the circumstances of the shooting and more specifically about the where the graves were located. Mister Garrett was cordial enough, but he didn't seem his usual self and his responses felt guarded. They had been traveling for some time when they came to a dip in the road where the underbrush and trees were dense and they were quite hidden. B.H. looked quizzically at his companion. He dropped his Southern accent and whispered, "Mister Garrett. You don't seem to know me."

Mister Garrett did a double take, then took a hard look at the ruffian who had been asking so many questions. Recognition dawned in his eyes, and he raised his hands in surprise.

"Mister Roberts! Are you here?" Realizing he'd spoken out loud, he clamped his hand over his mouth, quickly looking around. No one was there. His surprise was total and unfeigned. He really hadn't recognized B.H.

"Yes, it's me," B.H. assured him.

"Stars and garters! I . . ." he stammered, "I even shook your hand!" He slapped his leg, then looked at B.H. again, shaking his head in disbelief.

"Are you here?" he repeated, mostly to himself. He continued shaking his head as he snapped the reigns lightly and the horses resumed their pace. Mister Garrett was glad to see B.H. but at the same time unhappy that he'd risked his life by coming to Cane Creek after all. But it was too late to turn back now.

The first stop was to pick up the caskets that Golden had ordered. They had been delivered by train to Shady Grove, the closest depot. After Shady Grove, they stopped briefly at Mister Garrett's house to pick up some digging tools. They climbed back into the wagon and drove the few miles to Cane Creek.

B.H. began to recognize some of the houses and landmarks. They were getting close. He doubled his efforts to remain nonchalant in appearance. At least the hot weather gave him an excuse for the sweat that began to sheen his brow.

They rode past the log footbridge below the Condor place. Boot marks could still be seen clear as day in the earth between it and in the cornfield. Hearing of the event had been bad enough. Seeing it was another, and it was only going to get worse. B.H. felt a swell of emotion then. Sadness hit him like a wave, but another emotion, every bit as human and primal, lurked beneath the surface. His heart rate picked up, and he felt his first real tingle of fear. Contrary to reports, they didn't run across any mobs along the road during their journey. Maybe they hadn't been there or maybe he and Mister Garrett had been lucky. But the killers were here. He could feel it.

Mister Garrett led the wagon up the steep path to the roadway, running by the gate of the Condors. Martin and J.R. had been buried in the orchard out back. B.H. could only imagine the sorrow inhabiting the walls of the house. Brother Condor was on the far side of the yard chopping wood, but B.H. could see his vacant stare from where he sat on the wagon. He had the look of a ghost, going through the motions of life but not really living. B.H. knew that Sister Condor was inside, bedridden by her wounds, the pain of her hip surely outmatched by the ache in her heart. The grief of a mother for one child could not be imagined. The loss of two in the same hour was unfathomable.

B.H. wanted to go to them, to throw off his disguise and see if he couldn't somehow administer some comfort to them. But he knew it was impossible. He forced his emotions into check, concentrating on the task that loomed ahead.

Mister Garrett led the team a little further to a point beside the road where, under the direction of the county coroner, the elders had been buried. The road ran along a fence that followed the ridge parallel to the creek below. The graves themselves lay no more than a foot or so removed from the edge of the road. They were covered with unusual markings, which, upon closer inspection and much to his horror, B.H. saw to be wagon tracks. He couldn't tell if they had been created by natural traffic flow or if they had been run over intentionally as a sign of disrespect, but if the graves weren't moved, they would be obliterated by road traffic in no time at all.

He had hoped that the area would be vacant. So far, other than Brother Condor, he hadn't seen a living soul, but he knew his luck wasn't likely to hold.

When they got closer, the only thing that surprised him about

finding people in the area around the graves was how many of
them there were. Men and women were gathered around, standing in small clusters, mostly across the road, sitting by the fence.
Some were crying, but no one was talking. Silence was the rule of
the day. B.H. recognized some of them as local Church members
and friends, many of whom had doubtlessly been at the Condors's during the shooting. Why on earth they were hanging out
here, he couldn't comprehend. Perhaps it was shock; they simply
didn't know what else to do. *Go to the Condors*, he thought. *They
need you.* But he could say nothing.

He felt a tap on his foot. Mister Garrett was getting his attention with his boot. He whispered out of the side of his mouth,
"Some who did the shooting are here." He discreetly motioned
in the direction of nine or so men standing only twenty yards
away. They made no attempt to conceal the fact that they were
armed. They were very bold about their presence. In fact, they
had shown up claiming they were there to ensure that nothing
illegal or queer went on, as if they were doing the world some
great service. The rest of the citizenry gave them wide berth.

The gathered Church members looked at the new arrivals
with equal apprehension as they drove up. They quickly recognized Mister Garrett and relaxed a bit, although they continued
to eye B.H. warily. One of them approached the wagon as Mister
Garrett drew to a stop.

"Mister Garrett! So glad it's you." It was Brother Hemsley.
He addressed Mister Garrett but was looking at the strange man
accompanying him in his wagon. B.H. hesitated a moment,
unsure if his disguise would hold. Brother Hemsley quickly
glanced away and took the reins, helping the older Mister Garrett step down. So far so good, but B.H. could feel the eyes of
the Saints upon him. They didn't know what to make of this
frightening-looking stranger who had entered their midst. He
was with Mister Garrett, who was a trusted friend, but he looked
coarser and more fearsome than most of the mobbers. Mister
Garrett saw their unease and quickly made an introduction.

"This is Mister Cletus. He has been hired by Mister Roberts in Chattanooga to come and collect the bodies." He made the announcement loud enough that everyone, including the mob members, could hear. The Church members looked relieved if still a bit cautious. Mister Garrett then turned in the direction of the mobbers. "You boys may as well head home. I know who you're looking for. He's smarter than to show up here."

The mobbers said nothing but kept their place. One of them spit, continuing to chaw his tobacco, eyeing Cletus closely. It was clear they had no intention of leaving. They continued to glower at the gathered people, especially the two newcomers.

B.H. felt as if they were looking right through his disguise. He was certain that they would see through his act and it would be all over for him. It occurred to him that if he were discovered, he was a danger to Mister Garrett and the Saints as well. Resolutely he climbed down from the wagon. He could see the fear in the eyes of the Saints and struggled to remain in character. The desire to comfort the Saints rose again, but he knew the mobbers were watching him closely, and he forced it back down.

As if in confirmation of his fear, at that moment he heard one of the mobbers ask, "Do you believe that's Roberts?" B.H.'s blood froze in his veins. It was all he could do to maintain a calm demeanor. It was just an idle question but enough to turn the eyes of the mob on him. He was no coward, the fact that he was here at all proved it. But the instinct to flee rose up in him like a cyclone, mixing with the other emotions of the day. It was a foolish thought, and he knew it. Running would only prove his identity and ensure his doom. He forced his feet to walk normally as he turned and began removing the picks and shovels from the back of the wagon. The metal instruments chattered together for a moment. He willed his trembling hands to be still until they quieted.

"No. It ain't him. He wouldn't dare come 'round here." The answer, given so surely by another mobber, allowed B.H. to breathe a small sigh of relief. He knew that he was still in danger, but if he could maintain his pretense, he would be fine. Still, there was a lot of work to be done and a great deal of road to travel before he was safe again.

He rounded the wagon and tossed a shovel to Mister Garrett. "Here ya go." His voice sounded so callous it surprised even him. He almost didn't recognize it himself. He was just a hired hand here to do some dirty work. So be it. He put the head of the shovel under his boot and began to dig.

The soil was still loose, not packed in. That was good, at least. It would save them some time and backache. Mister Garrett was insistent on helping, but B.H. knew he'd be doing the brunt of the work. In his youth, B.H. had worked as a miner. Laboring his way through rock and earth was nothing new to him, but that had been years ago, and he'd been much younger then. Despite the softness of the dirt, he hadn't dug more than a few feet down before he felt the first twinges of complaint in his lower back. A few more feet, and fatigue seeped into his arms and legs. He definitely wasn't the young buck he once was. By the end of this, his body would be screaming in protest. Let it scream. He had work to do. He would allow no rest until it was done. It was simply a luxury he didn't have.

He expected no help from the mobbers, and in this he wasn't disappointed. The self-appointed so-called peace keepers did little more than stand idly, chewing and spitting. It was fine if they didn't help as long as they didn't interfere either.

To his surprise, the members didn't volunteer much help either. They were probably too frightened. B.H. supposed that his own appearance didn't help in this regard. It was probably just as well. Being in the presence of an armed mob was bad enough. There was no need to endanger anyone further.

And so the task was left to B.H. and Mister Garrett. The day grew steadily hotter. By early afternoon, the humidity pressed heavily across the land, crushing everything beneath its weight. It lay like a curse on the shoulders of the two men as they labored in the forge of the late summer sun. The others, members and mobbers alike, had all retreated to the shade of the nearby trees, relinquishing the two men to their work. Everything was quiet and still except for the steady *chunk* of the shovels against the dirt.

Broken blisters marked B.H.'s progress. They had formed quickly, stinging like the devil when they first broke, mixing with sweat and dirt. That had been hours ago. Now they were just a dull irritation that he hardly felt at all. He'd long since shed his jacket and vest. The rest of his clothes were soaked from head to foot with enough sweat that mud formed on his sleeves where they touched the rich earth.

The cool gurgling of the creek could be heard below them like a mocking bird. He wanted little more than to run and fall into its soothing waters, to float downstream, to let it carry him away from this scene of madness and inhuman cruelty. But time was growing ever shorter, and he had to concentrate on digging. He was pushing his luck as it was.

A handful more mobbers had gathered over the last few hours. Some had started pouring booze in their faces, and they were growing restless. Boredom and alcohol were a dangerous combination, especially when mixed in men already prone to violence.

Despite his efforts to focus, he was daydreaming again of the cool waters below when his shovel struck something solid with a hollow *thunk*. They had reached the coffins at last. B.H. felt a bit of vigor return to him. There was still a lot of digging left, but they were closer to the end now.

After the massacre, the members who had fled into the woods had returned to the Condor residence and the bodies of the elders had been placed in plain coffins made of poplar lumber. They were then removed from the property and buried here, side by side together in the earth in the best possible manner under the circumstances.

The lids of the coffins were almost completely cleared now. It would take them another good hour to finish uncovering them and to remove enough dirt from around them that they could be lifted from the earth. The digging had been grueling despite the soft soil. B.H. knew that the worst part still lay ahead but forcefully shoved the thought to the back of his mind and continued clearing.

When the coffins were finally unearthed, B.H. and Mister Garrett passed lengths of thick rope under each end in order to lift them out. This step would take more than the two of them. Even though he didn't want any of the members involved, B.H. and Mister Garrett needed their help. He crawled out of the grave and glanced at the members still under the tree across the road.

"Hey!" He barked. They had been working in wordless silence for hours now, and the sound of his own voice startled him. "It'd be mighty 'preciated if'n y'all'd lend a hand."

The mob, as he'd hoped and expected, simply ignored him. The members looked at him like dumb cattle. If he was disappointed by their hesitation, it at least reassured him that his disguise was still working. Mister Garrett climbed out beside him and called over to the Saints. "Y'all had best come help. We could use a hand or two here."

At first no one moved. B.H. thought he might have to go and drag them over. By this point in the day, it was something he was willing to do. After a moment's deliberation, a few men came over, looking down to avoid any eye contact with the mob. Each man took up an end of the rope and on Mister Garrett's mark began to heft the first coffin out. The weight of it was surprising. It took eight grown men straining and heaving to raise it from the grave.

As it settled with a solid thump beside the excavated ground, B.H. caught the first wafts of smell. It was awful. It hadn't been noticeable below ground. The movement must have stirred it up. Dread of the part yet to come leaped to the forefront of his mind, and he shoved it back again. *Get the other coffin out first. Don't think about anything else*, he told himself.

The ropes were drawn under the second coffin, and the

strenuous process was repeated, setting this one down next to the first. The lids had been nailed firmly shut, but the boxes were far from airtight. With both coffins above ground, the smell was impossible to ignore any longer. Once the coffin was securely down, the men backed away as quickly as they could, covering their noses. One man turned green and had to retreat to the trees, much to the amusement of the mob. Their laughter angered B.H. immensely. How could they be so unfeeling?

B.H. asked the men to retrieve the caskets from the back of the wagon, and they hustled to it, eager to get away from the smell of the grave. They placed the metal caskets beside the coffins, and B.H. groaned in disappointment. He had hoped to place the coffins directly into the caskets and seal them that way. Looking at them now, side by side, it was clear they would never fit. The coffins were far too large. It was as he had feared: they were going to have to open the coffins and transfer the bodies directly. It would be a gruesome task. There was nothing he could think of that he wanted to do less. But the task was his. The only thing he could do was get it done.

It seemed like they would never finish. B.H. focused on the next step and then the next, never allowing his mind to wander any further. After both coffins were opened, the bodies were wrapped in white sheets some of the members had generously provided. The bedding was carefully tucked around the deceased so that they had the appearance of being completely swathed in pure white. They were then placed in the metal caskets.

According to the instructions, B.H. spread oil paste over the lower flange of the container and then, mercifully, the lids were placed on them, the airtight seal preventing any further fumes from escaping. Even with the caskets sealed, the foul odor hung in the stagnant air like a ghost. There had been no breeze to cool them all day, and there was none to clean the air now. The smell had permeated his clothes and lined his nose and throat so thickly he could taste it. He tried very hard not to think about that.

The lids were secured by small bolts running an inch apart along the length of both flanges. Tightening them all was tedious work and slow going, much slower than B.H. had anticipated. Working at a steady pace, it took the two men until twilight before the last bolts were tightened. His fingers ached. They were stiff, almost refusing to move anymore. He had earned himself several more blisters, but at long last, the caskets were ready to be loaded back into the wagon.

By this time even more mobbers had arrived on the scene, and the general unease among the bystanders was growing. Several of the remaining members were again called over to help load the caskets into the wagon. As the last casket was secured into place, B.H. took a moment to rest his head against it. The heat of the day still radiated from its metal. He couldn't recall a time he'd ever been more physically tired or emotionally worn.

"What were these men killed for?" B.H. asked. It was question to which he expected no real answer. He wasn't even sure he'd said it aloud until one of the members clapped a gentle hand on his shoulder.

"God only knows. I don't." It was Brother Hemsley. He sounded as perplexed as B.H. felt. "Thank you for your work here today."

It was the end of the day, but B.H. was pleased to know that at least one of the membership was willing to reach out to the ragged stranger that he appeared to be.

"Don't mention it," B.H. replied.

With a few brisk thanks to those who had helped, Mister Garrett and B.H. climbed aboard the wagon. B.H. looked back at Brother Hemsley and the small group of Saints huddled together, bidding them farewell. As weary as he was, the desire to leap from his seat and administer to them arose again, stronger than ever, but he could feel the eyes of the mob upon him. They were still on alert, and despite not receiving any interference from them during the day, who knew if nightfall might embolden them? He dared not risk it or all of the day's work would be lost.

"Are you ready?" Mister Garrett asked.

B.H. could only nod.

"Let's get out of here. Haw!" Mister Garrett snapped the reins, and the wagon drove off into the sinking dark of night.

CHAPTER 17

AFTERMATH

In great deeds, something abides.

—Joshua L. Chamberlain

The front door scraped open, and Golden jerked upright. His head bore red marks on his forehead and cheeks from where it rested on his wrists, which were tingling and numb. Pinpricks danced up and down his fingers. He had no idea he'd even fallen asleep. He'd practically worn out a groove in the floor, pacing around the office until the small hours of the night, sick with worry. The last thing he remembered was thinking he should check the oil in the lamp to make sure it would still be burning if—not if, when—B.H. got back.

Now the soft light of a gray morning was filtering in through the window and he had a crick in his neck from passing out sitting at the desk. B.H. stood in the doorway looking more ragged than he had the day before. Yesterday's haggard look had been a costume; today it was the real thing. The grease he smeared on himself was mixed thickly with dirt and sweat. His pants and boots were caked with mud, as were his sleeves up to his elbows. And his eyes . . .

During his years in the South, Golden would come to recognize that look. He would see it time and time again in the eyes of people who had been exposed to the worst horrors of the war and lived. It was a distant, haunted look that hinted at incomprehensible grief. Nearly a century later, when war had become almost a science and a constant way of life in the world, medical types would give it a name: post-traumatic stress disorder, as if calling it by some fancy name would somehow lessen the damage. Soldiers would call it something more direct: shell shock. It was the look of someone who has been through hell and some irreplaceable part of them never made it back.

B.H. had that look now. Golden couldn't imagine what he must have been through. Part of him didn't want to know. The pain was evident enough in B.H.'s eyes, but beneath the shock and sorrow burned a steely resolve. B.H. had stepped into the fires of hell and come through, not unscathed, but forged stronger than ever before. The B.H. that stood in the doorway was tattered and worn, but Golden had never seen anyone more regal in all his born days. The power and authority flowing from him was an almost tangible force. Kings would have bowed before him in that moment. There was no doubt he had been on God's errand.

He looked at Golden, answering the unspoken question. "We've got them."

There was nothing more to say.

Relief and sorrow mingled upon the faces of the two men as they quietly watched the caskets being loaded onto the train. Lamplight glinted off the steel surfaces like shooting stars, beautiful and short lived. Neither had spoken much all day other than what was necessary for conveying the bodies home.

B.H. had bathed and was properly dressed again. He looked like an entirely different man with no beard, but that tenacious look never left his eyes, even now as his tears flowed freely. Over time the haunted look would fade, but the fierce resolve would remain as bright as ever until his dying day.

Golden could feel his own tears running their course down his cheeks. The contrast of emotion he felt was so great he was surprised that his heart could handle it all at the same time. On one hand, he was almost overcome with joy that B.H. had returned safely. He had succeeded in his purpose, and no one else had been harmed. He should have been killed. It was a miracle he hadn't been, it really was. On the other hand, Golden's sorrow for the needless tragedy felt heavy enough to crush him. These elders had died in the service of God and would surely find their final reward all the greater because of it. But such thoughts would be small consolation to their families when their sons returned home in coffins. He felt every bit as bad, if not worse, for the living.

Mister Garrett had helped them most of the day in making final preparations for shipping the bodies, until B.H. had sent him home in the early afternoon. Mister Garrett had wanted to stay, but B.H. insisted that he had done more than enough already and that he should get back to his family before night fell again. Mister Garrett had reluctantly agreed and promised that he would check on the members at Cane Creek as well.

It was around midnight when the doors of the freight car were finally closed. With a mournful whistle, the engine began churning its pistons. Metal squealed against metal as the wheels struggled for traction. It was as if their cargo was made heavier by the weight of the tragedy. With a final shuddering heave, the train pulled forward and inched its way from the station for the long ride west.

Golden and B.H. watched as it chugged its way up the valley and disappeared into darkness. They left the station without a word.

Each man walked along, lost in his own thoughts. High above them the stars burned crisp pinholes into the heavens. The night was still, filled with the strange quiet that seems to occur only after a major calamity.

"Do you know when it was that I first met Elder Gibbs?"

After hours of near silence, Golden was startled by B.H.'s voice but was glad to hear the sound of it. As for how B.H. met

Elder Gibbs, Golden had never thought about it. He assumed it was in the field like everyone else. Perhaps in Salt Lake. He shook his head.

"I was five years old," B.H. said wistfully. "It was on the ship crossing from England to America."

Along with one of his sisters, B.H. had left hearth and home in England, sailing for the United States in 1866. They were traveling to join their mother, who had immigrated to Utah just ahead of them. Eventually they met up with a wagon train departing out of Nebraska, walking barefoot for most of the journey to Utah.

B.H. continued, "He and I got into fisticuffs over a game of marbles. Marbles, Golden. And for the life of me, I can't remember why."

The two men fell silent again for the rest of the walk home.

Dawn was breaking by the time Golden and B.H. dragged themselves back to the mission home. The blanket of dew was beginning to lift under the growing heat of the morning sun, melting into thin clouds that drifted across the valley floor.

Golden was glad to see the coming of the light. It had been one of the darkest nights of his life, and the sunlight stretching across the morning sky was a blessed sight. On the other hand, he and B.H. were both spent. Golden had passed out a few times from sheer exhaustion, but he hadn't really slept at all in the last three days. B.H. had rested even less. As grateful as he was to see the sun, Golden intended to be fast asleep before it climbed much further. He could already feel the cool cotton of the sheets and the gentle caress of the pillow about his head.

Golden was so preoccupied with thoughts of slumber that he didn't see the piece of paper on the door until B.H. reached for it. It was a small piece of rough parchment stuck fast with a penknife. B.H. dislodged the knife and took the paper. He read it quickly, his brow knitting together as he did. He didn't look pleased.

"What is it?" asked Golden. He wasn't really sure he wanted to know, but he asked anyhow. B.H. handed it over.

The parchment was wrinkled and splotted with grease. Written in crude charcoal letters, the note read:

Leav The state in Twenty-fore hours. If you do not you will certenly go The way The rest of The mormon elders are going.

Thoughts of sleep vanished from Golden's mind. A knot started in his belly; he felt it grip his stomach, drawing tighter and tighter till his entire frame was trembling like the earth beneath a stampede. It took a lot for Golden to completely lose his temper. This had been more than a lot, and he lost it something fierce. He was madder than an old, wet hen. Crumpling the paper in his fist, he threw it down with all his might.

"You damn cowards!" He yelled at the vacant street, shaking his fist at no one and everyone all at once, daring the perpetrators to show themselves. "If a fight's what you want, then by hell, I'll give you one!"

It was more than anyone should have to bear. That human beings, God's children, could treat each other like this was an outrage. Golden couldn't recall a time he'd ever been more upset. Of course, he was too angry to recall much of anything at all.

"Golden," B.H. grabbed him firmly by the shoulder. Golden shook himself loose of his grip, and B.H. grabbed him again, holding him fast this time. "It's a letter. A silly, trite letter. Nothing but bosh. Calm down."

"No, I tell you, it's the last straw! The devil has laid claim to the South, and by hell he can have it!" Golden wouldn't be sedated.

"You're right!" B.H. yelled back, the sudden edge to his voice outdone only by the sharpness in his eyes. "Who cares about these people? So what if they're the ones who need the gospel of peace more than anyone else on earth? Let's just give up!"

B.H. may as well have slapped him. The words struck home, upsetting Golden even worse. He was upset because of the note. He was upset because B.H. was yelling at him. He was upset because he knew B.H. was right and he was wrong. Mostly he was upset because he knew that in losing his temper, he'd wounded his own pride. He kicked the ground, sending up a spray of dirt, then manned up and forced himself to calm down.

"You're right." His voice still quivered with frustration. "You're right. We should get back to work." He glanced at B.H. with a look of repentant chagrin. "But I'd still rather bushwhack the bootlickers."

B.H. patted him on the shoulder with an understanding nod. Golden knew that B.H. was as frustrated as he was but wasn't about to let his emotions have the run of him. In that moment Golden was more glad than ever for the company of such a righteous man. Whereas he might have acted rashly, doing more damage than good, B.H. had chosen the better course.

He found it surprisingly easy to calm down as his body decided its weariness greatly outweighed its anger. He stooped and picked up the note, uncrumpling it. "Ignoramuses can't even spell right."

B.H. led the way into the mission home. Golden followed, once again looking forward to some much-needed sleep.

Following the tragedy at Cane Creek, mission activity declined sharply. Members, missionaries, and investigators alike were scared, and B.H. called for a temporary halt to all proselytizing activity. The missionaries were to sit tight until things got sorted out.

At the request of Church leaders, B.H. returned to Salt Lake to discuss the fate of the mission. Many of the Saints in Utah felt that the Church had done everything possible for the South and that sending more elders into the region would only place more lives in needless danger.

Once again Golden was forced to stay behind and wait. The fate of the mission hung by a thread, and the suspense was tearing at him like a thorn. The only upside this time was that he didn't have to worry about B.H. getting himself killed. He also had more to do this time than pace the office. A great number of the Saints from the Cane Creek area began emigrating west, forced to leave their homes by continuing mob threats and violence. Golden was kept plenty busy making transportation arrangements and helping groups get ready for their journey.

Most of the Saints would relocate to settlements in Utah and Colorado such as Richfield, Manassa, and Ephraim. It wasn't just the Saints. Local intolerance extended to anyone friendly to the Mormons as well. After repeated threats on his life, Mister Garrett moved to Bond County, Illinois. The Condor family elected to remain in Tennessee but moved to the western part, settling along the Buffalo River.

Back in Salt Lake, the debate whether to keep the mission open or not dragged on. It wasn't an easy decision. The Cane Creek massacre was an atrocity beyond question. Pulling the elders out of the region would certainly keep it from happening again. It wouldn't be the first time Mormon elders had packed up and left an area in order to live and preach another day. In a long series of meetings and councils, many logical arguments were presented for and against keeping it open. In the end, it came down to one thing: After much prayer and fasting, the decision was given by the prophet himself. All other reasoning aside, it was the will of the Lord that the mission should remain open. And so it did.

B.H. returned to Tennessee after a two-month absence, pleased with the verdict. He had been a proponent of keeping the mission open from the start, despite the difficulties. Nevertheless, if President Taylor had called for the mission to be closed, B.H. would have supported him fully. He was grateful it hadn't come to that. He firmly believed there was much work yet to be done in the South.

He wasn't the only one. Despite everything that had happened thus far, Golden was happy to receive word that the mission would stay open. He hadn't fully paid his dues to the Lord yet, if such a thing was possible, and he was eager for another crack at it.

CHAPTER 18

THE HANGING

Don't pray for lighter burdens, but for stronger backs.

—Unknown

Polygamous adulterers!" The door slammed in their faces.

"Well, that's a relief. I've been sick so long I was afraid these people had forgotten who I was."

After a few days spent recouping and getting the mission up and running again, Golden and B.H. had left Chattanooga to proselytize together in the surrounding area. They were encountering roughly the same amount of success they had before, which is to say very little. To his delight, Golden found that this no longer surprised him or lowered his spirits. In fact, he found himself enjoying his time traveling with B.H., and they approached the work with renewed vigor.

It was afternoon when they found themselves on another ubiquitous rural lane winding its way between settlements in the Tennessee backcountry. The weather had cooled, and the day was a pleasant one. Golden and B.H. were involved in a lively discussion regarding the nature of celestial marriage, more commonly known as polygamy. B.H. had been studying the topic extensively and was pondering the necessity of taking a second wife while Golden expressed his interest in being able to take a wife at all. The conversation was interrupted when they spotted several men coming toward them up the road.

As they drew closer, they saw that the men were armed with rifles and lashes of bundled sticks. Golden doubted they were out hunting pheasants. He nudged B.H., and they turned back, only to stop dead in their tracks. Several more similarly dressed and armed men were coming up behind them. They were surrounded. *Here we go again.* Still recovering, Golden was definitely not up to outrunning anyone, and B.H. wasn't about to abandon him. They turned to face the closest group.

The men approached with the cocky swagger of hunters who have finally tracked and trapped their prey. They stopped about ten feet away, and the one who appeared to be the biggest toad in the puddle stepped forward, grinnin' like a baked possum but with fewer teeth. He lay his rifle across his shoulders and looked at his catch. "'Less Ah miss mah guess, you fellers'd be Mormon elduhs."

Had this been his first day in the field, Golden would have most likely soiled his britches. He had come to the South with the intent to preach the gospel and had his will shaken by trial and tribulation. But he wasn't a greenhorn anymore; he'd had his baptism by fire, and he'd realized something. The South was a mess, yes. The devil was definitely here and spoiling for trouble. Well, if trouble was what he wanted, then Golden was much obliged to give it to him. He'd had enough of standing back frightened and watching things happen. Besides, he'd come here to test out the Lord. And if you had the Lord on your side, who could stand against you? Emboldened by his newfound resolve, he looked the man right in the eyes and answered, "Yes, that's right. We're Mormons."

"Y'all got guts bein' 'round these parts after what happened up to Cane Creek," he said, sizing the elders up. He was gloating, proud as a peacock, as if he had something to do with it. Considering how far away they were, it wasn't likely.

A second fellow piped up, "Ya know, we could jes' kill the

both a ya, and no one'd do a thing a-tall."

"Apparently the sixth commandment doesn't apply at this latitude," Golden observed. His tongue was getting the better of him, but he refused to take their abuse lying down.

A curious expression crossed the first man's face and held there like a mask. He looked up, thinking. He and the second man both began counting on their fingers, their faces screwed up in marvelously ponderous expressions as if the sudden cogitation pained their craniums. With considerable effort, the first got to about three, then gave up, shaking his head with a frustrated grunt. He jammed his rifle in Golden's face. "Shut up, you."

Golden didn't know if it was possible to ever grow completely numb to being threatened at gunpoint, but he was certainly getting close to it. Still, no point in risking it. "Silence is Golden," he acquiesced and raised his hands.

Satisfied that the Mormons had been tempered properly, the men turned to each other as the rest of them arrived from behind.

"Looks like we got 'em," they observed.

"We sho do."

"We gonna lynch 'em or jess shoot 'em here?" asked one.

"I say we whup 'em," voted a muscular fourth man. He was tapping a harsh-looking lash of sticks in his hand. Golden guessed he really liked whupping.

Apparently the exact fate of the two elders hadn't been decided yet. These fellows reminded Golden of a hound dog chasing a bird who, once he's actually caught it, hasn't the slightest notion of what to do next. Golden had a few suggestions of his own but doubted they'd be highly appreciated.

"Less jess shoot 'em." The debate continued. Golden didn't like that one.

"Less whup 'em." Golden didn't like that one either, but it was better than the first.

"Naw, less jess lynch 'em." That one was worse. Given his druthers, he'd rather be shot—it was quicker. But neither option sounded all that swell to him. He was positive that not everyone in the South sat around all day discussing ways to kill Mormons, but it seemed a most popular topic whenever he was around.

The second man was still counting on his fingers. He looked quite proud of himself. He'd made it all the way to two. The debate was getting balled up and confusing. This one really wanted a shooting, that one really wanted a lynching, and the fellow with the lash really, really wanted a whupping. Men were talking over each other like children arguing over which piece of cake they got. Finally the first man interrupted them all. "Quiet! Quiet! Shut up alla yah! I gotta idea."

Golden couldn't wait to hear it.

What such a large iron cage was doing here and why it was hanging from a tree no man could remember. Yet here it was, its iron bars patched with rust, suspended a few feet off the forest floor by a heavy chain attached to a massive branch of an ancient oak. One thing about the South: it definitely kept you guessing. The door squawked loudly in protest as it was opened, rust crumbling like soot from its thick hinges, painting blood-red speckles on the earth below.

"Get in," the man ushered Golden and B.H. inside with the butt of his rifle. As iron cages go, it was big, but even so it was scarcely big enough for both of them to fit. B.H. was barely able to stand up fully. There was no such hope for Golden, who stood hunched over, the exposed skin of his head pressed against the roof of the cage. The hinges protested again as the door was closed with a loud *kerrang* of ringing metal. One thing the mob agreed on was that the elders should be kept in the cage until they could decide for sure what to do with them.

"Y'all sit tight now," the first man said as he secured the lock, which was every bit as old and rusted as the rest of it. Golden hoped he had the key.

"Looks like we got ahselves a couple a songbirds," the man said, showing off the gaps in his smile. "We'll be back for ya come mornin', hear what kind a song you got fuh us."

It looked like they were going to be spending the night here. Golden quickly noted that the floor was too small for either of them to be able to stretch out completely. This was going to be rough. So what was new? About the only thing in the South that would surprise him anymore would be getting a good night's rest.

With that, the group of men took their leave, leaving the two birds swinging gently from their tree. At least it wasn't by their necks. Golden could hear the men still arguing among themselves as they walked off.

As soon as they were alone, Golden and B.H. tested the lock. They tried to pry it loose, to break it, to wiggle it. It rattled and shook. Something was loose inside, but the latch held tight. They even tried to pick it with Golden's glasses but had no luck there either.

One corner of the cage had rusted through, but the bars were too thick to bend and the gap was only large enough for maybe a cat to squeeze through. There was no way it would accommodate a grown man, even one so thin as Golden.

When it was clear that they wouldn't be able to get out, they sat down and settled in as comfortably as they could manage, which wasn't very comfortably at all. It was going to be a long night.

"I confess, when I said we should get back to work, this isn't quite what I had in mind." B.H. sighed with resignation.

Golden shrugged. "It beats sleeping on the ground."

The thick, leafy branches of the oak obscured most of the night sky, but the little they could see twinkled with countless stars. The tree caught the slight breeze, rocking the cage gently back and forth like a cradle, which was fitting because Golden had to curl up like a baby to fit. Not surprisingly, he couldn't sleep well. The bars bit into his shoulder and hips, cutting off the circulation.

Hints of his illness were coming back, as they would for years whenever he got tired or worn down. He wasn't aware of it, but he must have been wheezing or coughing a bit because B.H. asked if he was feeling all right. Golden didn't realize B.H. was still awake, but he wasn't surprised either. B.H. must have been every bit as cramped.

"It's just a bit of this malaria come back on me," Golden said. "I'll live, unless it kills me first."

B.H. took off his coat and covered Golden with it. B.H. was shorter than Golden, but with Golden curled up, the coat covered most of his shoulders and torso. It didn't help all that much, but Golden was grateful for the gesture.

"I've seen all sorts of things during my time here," B.H. spoke quietly, his voice stark against the night. "I've been threatened more times than I can remember, and I'm still frightened half to death. You don't even seem the slightest bit nervous."

Golden rolled over to face B.H. "Oh, I'm plenty scared. This to me is a picture of hell on earth."

Both men fell silent for a moment. There was no need to rush the conversation. Neither of them was going anywhere. By and by, B.H. spoke again.

"You know, on the way back from Cane Creek, once we'd retrieved the bodies, Mister Garrett and I were planning on catching the train at Carpenter's Station, but we got lost and ended up going twelve miles past it, to Mount Pleasant. It wasn't until later, after I'd arrived back in Chattanooga, that I learned that a mob had gathered at Carpenter's Station, waiting to intercept us. Mount Pleasant wasn't the road we'd planned on taking, it was longer and harder, but ultimately that road saved our lives."

Golden hadn't known that. Still, he had to laugh a bit. "Are you trying to say that hanging out in a cage might save our bacon?"

"No," B.H. said, chuckling, "simply that we don't know why

we get detoured sometimes. I think we have to accept things as they are and try to make the best of them that we can."

Golden couldn't argue with that. In fact, making the best of a difficult situation seemed like a really terrific idea. The only trouble was that he had no idea how to make the best of this particular situation. "So what do you suggest for making the best of this? I can't think of a damn thing."

"Me either." B.H. shook his head.

"I was sort of hoping for something a bit more inspirational than that."

B.H. smiled. "Well, what do you think we should do?"

Golden thought a bit longer. At first he drew only a blank. Then a seemingly unrelated thought popped into his mind. A memory from childhood, something he hadn't thought about in many years. He smiled despite himself.

"My father, before coming to Utah, was driven from his home by mobs on five different occasions. Once, when he was asked to pray for his enemies, he said, 'Sure, I'll pray for our enemies. I pray they may all go to hell.'"

B.H. looked amused. "Heber C. Kimball said that?"

Golden nodded. "I think he was only half joking." Golden smiled, but it wasn't very enthusiastic. "I've never known anybody who could pray like my father. There seemed to be a friendliness between him and God. When you heard him pray, you would think the Lord was right there and that Father was talking to him. I have been sorry many times that I can't pray like my father did."

"You think we should pray?" B.H. asked. It was more of a statement than a question.

Golden shrugged. "I can't think of anything else."

"It sounds like a magnificent idea to me," B.H. said, and both men rose to their knees.

The bars hurt under his knees, so Golden folded his jacket and placed it under him. He handed B.H.'s coat back so he could do the same.

"Will you say it?" B.H. asked.

Golden bowed his head. He opened his mouth to speak and realized he still had his eyes open.

"I guess no one is going to sneak up on us this time," he said, laughing to himself. B.H. looked at him quizzically, but before he could ask, Golden closed his eyes and began to pray.

CHAPTER 19

THE SONG BIRDS SING

Success usually comes to those who are too busy to be looking for it.

—*Henry David Thoreau*

Golden was in the midst of a great party, surrounded by a host of people. They were all involved in conversation. "Izzat them?" they whispered. "You think they's still alive? They look half dead." He couldn't see them very well, but they could see him. That's what they were here for. "They just sleeping." He was the center of attention, the life of the party. "Should we wake 'em?" "You do it." "No, you." One of them was close. Golden wanted to move, but he couldn't. Someone reached out and poked him in the shoulder. That was rude. Golden swatted their hand away. They poked him again, harder this time.

"Y'alive?"

Golden felt a stab in his shoulder. "What the hell do you want?" He woke, disoriented. Then it all came back to him in a rush. He was still in the cage, face-to-face with a young boy, roughly twelve or so, who stood poking a stick through the bars. Barefoot and in overalls a few sizes too large for him, he jumped back quickly when Golden sat up.

Golden's eyes adjusted, and he looked about in amazement. In the clearing around the tree, there stood about twenty people gawking with fascination at the caged curiosities. At the sight of Golden waking, a ripple of excitement went through the crowd. Still keeping their distance, they crowded into each other to get a better look. So this is what it was like to be in a zoo. Except that the animals in a zoo got fed, and Golden's belly was empty. He nudged B.H., who sat up, staring at the crowd with equal wonder.

Word had gotten out that a couple of Mormons were stewing in the old cage, and curious men, women, and children of all ages had come to see for themselves. Old men with corncob pipes and women in dresses with laced collars and pewter brooches stood side by side, staring with fascination.

"Ah heard if Ah came 'round Ah could see a real-life Mo-mun." The boy with the stick brushed a shaggy brown lock of hair out of his eyes.

"Is that so?" Golden asked.

"Yassuh."

The boy seemed genuine enough. He had a lot of spunk for a youngster, something that Golden could appreciate. He wasn't here to throw rocks at the elders; he only wanted to see what the commotion was all about. Well, if a Mo-mun was what these people had come out to see, a Mo-mun is what they'd get.

"You want to see a Mormon, do you?"

"Yassuh."

Golden stood up as best he could. He straightened his coat, smoothed what little hair he had left, and presented himself to the audience. To his side, B.H. did the same.

"Well, what do you think?" asked Golden.

The youth gave him a dubious once over, looking strangely let down. "You ain't no Mo-mun."

"I'm not?" That surprised Golden.

"No, suh." The boy shook his head. "Ah heard Mo-muns got horns."

"You did, did you?"

"Yassuh. And neither y'all got any."

"I assure you, my companion and I are both Mormons."

The boy still looked doubtful. Maybe even a bit disappointed. He was really expecting horns. Golden hated to disappoint anyone, especially a youth with so much pluck. He knelt down. "All right. Would you like to feel my horns?"

Another murmur rippled through the crowd. The boy looked at him warily. B.H. looked at him funny too. A few people in the crowd backed up, but most pressed closer, trying to see better. One or two nodded with satisfaction. They had known it was true all along.

"Go ahead." Golden pointed to his balding pate. "It's all right."

The boy wasn't quite sure what to think. He was leery, but he wasn't about to be no chicken. He reached out slowly. You could hear the crowd gasp and hold its breath. The boy's tentative hand passed through the bars and carefully came to rest on top of Golden's head. The gasp from the crowd was audible. One woman fainted and was caught and gently lowered to the ground.

"Do you feel anything?" Golden glanced up at the boy, who still had his hand on his head.

"Uh-uh."

"Keep trying," Golden encouraged. The young man felt his hand over the Mo-mun's head. "Do you feel anything now?"

"Ah don't feel a thing."

Golden looked at him, grinning wryly, "Not even a little bit stupid?"

The boy realized he'd taken the bait hook, line, and sinker. He stepped back, embarrassed but smiling.

"Shoot, Ah knew y'all didn' have no horns."

Golden grinned at the boy, and the crowd began to laugh, the boy laughing right along with them. Golden was proud of the kid. It takes a big person to laugh at himself. Amid the laughter, someone suddenly yelled, "Hey, y'all are preachers! Give us a sermon!"

Golden exchanged a disbelieving look with B.H. They had to be joking, caught up in the lightheartedness of the moment. Unbelievably another took up the cry. "Yeah! Preach us som'thin'!"

Well, even if the crowd was joking, why not? Golden motioned to B.H. as if to turn the time over to him. But the crowd would have none of it. "No, we want to hear from the tall, skinny feller!"

Golden pointed at himself. *Me?* As if there were any other tall, skinny Mormons around.

"What should I say?" Golden asked.

B.H. smiled. He had confidence in Golden. "Whatever you feel you should."

Golden took a deep breath and faced his audience again. He thought of what B.H. had said: "They're the ones who need the gospel of peace more than anyone else on earth." Sometimes, with all the hostility surrounding them, it was easy to forget that these were his brothers and sisters. They were children of God, just like himself, who had wandered from the path or never known it in the first place. Seeing them in this whole new light, he was suddenly filled with brotherly love for each and every one of them. He opened his mouth and began to preach.

"My brothers and sisters, you have come here to get a look at a real, live Mormon. Well, you shall have a chance to not only see what we look like but to hear what we sound like as well. I am not here to provoke trouble but to teach the gospel of our Lord and Savior Jesus Christ."

To his great astonishment, the audience listened.

The debate whether it would be a whuppin', a lynchin', a shootin', or all three had raged on late into the night. That and copious amounts of moonshine had ensured that the original group of roughnecks who had thrown the elders into the cage didn't show up until quite some time after Golden had begun his sermon.

The mob had finally reached a verdict among themselves and had arrived on the scene excited to carry their plan out. You can imagine their surprise to find their prisoners surrounded by more than fifty people, all listening to the caged men sermonize. In fact, several hours had passed, and Golden and B.H. had traded off turns speaking a couple of times now.

"How many of us think of God thirty minutes out of twenty-four hours?" Golden's high voice carried across the clearing. "There is not one out of five hundred that actually thinks of God and his Son thirty minutes a day. I do, but the first thing I know, my mind wanders off on something else." Some in the audience laughed, and some shouted "Amen!" Golden was caught up in teaching and didn't recognize the new arrivals as his captors. The audience was entertained and didn't pay them much notice either.

"Oh, this ain't gonna do a-tall." The fourth roughneck, the one who was just a bit too excited about whuppin' the elders, took a step forward, but the leader put out his arm, stopping him.

"Now, hold on, Ah ain't evah heard these fellers preach before."

The whuppin' roughneck didn't know what "incredulous" meant, but that's still the look he gave. "Yuh joshin'?"

"Shut your bazoo," the first fellow shushed him and stood listening. The rest of the men shrugged and joined him.

"There is no fault in the gospel of Christ," Golden continued, "If lived up to, it makes you better. It makes you good in your home, makes you good to your wife and good to your children. It makes you honest. It makes you kind and generous."

As he had been all morning, Golden was met with more hearty "amens!" The crowd was enjoying it. Even the woman who had fainted had come around again and sat listening in the shade against the tree trunk. Golden glanced back over at B.H., who smiled and nodded approvingly.

It was afternoon when most of the crowd began melting away. Their curiosity sated, they had more important things like farmwork or lunch to attend to.

Golden was surprised he had been able to preach for as long as he did. Some of what B.H. had taught him must have sunk in after all. He had spoken on repentance, on baptism, on the Apostasy and the Restoration. He had talked of the need for continued revelation, of the bravery of the pioneers. He had spoken and testified until he thought he'd run out of things to say, and then he testified some more.

It was one of the most thrilling experiences of his life, except he was still locked in a cage and the men who had done it were here waiting for them. Eventually the last of the crowd left, leaving only the roughnecks. Golden felt a thrill of nerves again as they approached the cage. With morbid curiosity, he wondered what fate they had decided for him and B.H.

"You sho fired hot shell at us today with them words yuh spoke," said the first fellow. He had his rifle slung over his elbow.

"Yeah, you preached a right fine sermon," the second piped in.

"Thank you." It seemed to Golden the only proper thing to say. The man with the lashes was strangely silent. Golden guessed he'd been outvoted.

The first man scratched the side of his nose with his thumb, glancing about as if what he was about to say would injure his pride. "We, uh, we gonna let y'all go this time 'round." He paused like he couldn't really believe he was saying what he was saying. "But don' come preachin' 'round these parts again, understan'?" he said, trying to sound tough. He had an image to maintain, after all.

"Yeah," the second man pitched in again like a small pup acting big while shielded behind a bulldog, "'Cuz necks time we might not be so gen'rous."

The first man produced the key. Golden figured with his luck the old, rusty lock would freeze up and they'd really be stuck, but it opened with only a little protest from the rusted mechanisms. He decided he should be less pessimistic and just be grateful.

Golden and B.H. both stepped out. The ground didn't seem as solid as he remembered, and it took Golden a second to find his land legs again. He took a big stretch to work the kinks out of his legs and back.

"So, uh, y'all best get along now," the roughneck shooed them off.

"Yeah, careful now, y'hear?"

Both elders were wiser than to push their luck any further than it had been already. Grateful for their freedom and their lives, they tipped their hats and hurried off down the road before any of the men could change their minds.

The roughnecks stood alone by the deserted cage, watching the elders hustle off.

"I still say we shoulda whupped 'em."

The others looked blankly at the big fellow.

"Jus' a little." He shrugged sheepishly.

They closed the cage behind them and left.

Golden and B.H. made tracks, cutting and running as fast as their legs could carry them, putting as much distance between themselves and their captors as possible. They didn't look back until they had several bends in the road, three hills, and two small creeks behind them.

"All right, they're gone," B.H. said.

Golden stopped to catch his breath, resting his hands on his knees. "Can you believe it? I thought we'd had it for sure."

"Come now, Elder Kimball," B.H. teased, "where's your faith?"

"I think it's lodged in my throat."

Golden was tired, but his heart was still pumping fast.

Spiritually, he was nothing short of ecstatic. He and B.H. had preached to a crowd that not only was willing to listen but had actually asked them to preach too. Even if they had been joking at first, they still stayed and listened for hours.

They hadn't been able to stick around to see it, but he knew that their words had reached at least some of those people. Even if there were no converts, many of those good people would be more receptive to the gospel down the road. At the very least they would be more tolerant of any "Mo-mun" missionaries they might come across in the future.

It could have been a disaster. By good rights, they should've been beaten or worse. Instead it was the highlight of Golden's career so far in the South. He hoped there would be more to come. Highlights, that is, not rusty cages.

"That is without a doubt the largest congregation I have ever preached to. And the most receptive." Golden was exultant. "You ought to consider putting all the elders in cages."

B.H. laughed, stroking his chin as if pondering it. "That's not a bad idea."

When they both laughed, it felt as if all the fear and tension from the night was evaporating into the air. B.H. clapped Golden heartily on the back. "You preached a fine sermon today. You did a marvelous job."

Golden tucked the compliment away in his memory. B.H. would never know how much praise from him meant to the skinny cowboy.

"Thanks, B.H. I had a great teacher." It was a humble demurring, but it was also true.

At B.H.'s suggestion, they gave a quick prayer of thanks. A longer one would be given later, but for now they thought it best to keep traveling. They turned up the road again, talking and laughing as they went. Golden was fired up about the work. He finally understood what people meant when they spoke of the joy of serving. The Spirit had been with them today, there was no denying it, and Golden relished the feeling like no other.

He looked at the road they were on, following it as far as he could see. It wound its way through the rolling hills and into the unknown distance. He had seen views like this countless times before, but today it looked different. It was as if the entire South had opened up to him like an emerald sea of possibilities. It would still be hard, he knew, but for the first time since he'd arrived in the field, he finally felt as though he was up to the challenge.

CHAPTER 20

SILENCE WAS GOLDEN

Speak your mind, but ride a fast horse.

—*Cowboy Proverb*

It was Golden's great privilege to work side by side with B.H. over the next handful of months. Golden helped out with mission duties, which taught him a lot about how things were run around the home, but the part he loved the best was when he and B.H. got to preach together. Under B.H.'s patient teaching and guidance, Golden kept right on learning and growing by leaps and bounds. He now knew his Epistles from his apostles and his Leviticus from his Numbers. He was learning so much that he almost felt guilty about it. Here he was, called to teach the people of the South, but he was the one doing all the learning.

Before long it was springtime in the South again. The abundant foliage regained its greenery, and the insects wasted no time in making their presence known. It was iris time in Tennessee, as the locals say, and the vast green canvas was sprinkled with bright splashes of color as the rhododendron and azaleas blossomed like nature's fireworks. Their scent permeated the air, lending their perfume to the smell of charcoal and hickory-tinged chimney smoke.

The weather was warm without being hot, and yesterday's rain had cleared out the valley, leaving a rare cloudless day in its wash. B.H. sat at his desk. His mustache had grown back in, though he'd decided to forego his beard this time around. The bar handles curved down to his chin, the thick growth extending his lip almost to the tip of his nose. Golden thought the mustache was more overgrown than kudzu in a gully but never mentioned that particular notion to B.H.

The work was progressing—slowly as always, but slow progress was better than none. As converts were found, they were gathered and helped move west into Utah, as was the policy of the time. Not all Saints emigrated, but many did. Usually they moved because they wanted to, but just as often they didn't have much choice, like the Saints in Cane Creek. But overall, things were back to normal: mob threats continued and so did the work. And while there were still occasional run-ins with violence, no one else had been seriously injured, for which everyone was most grateful indeed.

The silhouette of the mailman crossed the curtains, moving toward the door. B.H. pushed himself away from his desk and retrieved the mail from where it dropped through the mail slot onto the floor with a thump. He returned to his seat, flipping casually through the pile of letters. Most of the daily mail consisted of letters for elders and correspondence from Salt Lake, with the occasional bill thrown in the mix.

On a good day he would receive a letter or two from home. It was always a special treat to hear from Sarah. She wrote faithfully and often, but that regularity never diminished the happiness he felt each time a letter came. Not being so fortunate today, he opened the first letter from Salt Lake instead. It bore the official seal of the first presidency. Mission business then. Correspondence from Salt Lake was common enough. Usually they were just checking in or addressing some issue of policy. This letter was different. Halfway through, he lowered it, leaning back in his chair, his expression thoughtful. After a moment he stood and went upstairs.

"They can't send me home now!" Golden protested.

The letter was an honorable release, signed by the first presidency. He'd done it; he'd fulfilled a mission. Like all missionaries, Golden had looked forward to going home for a long time. It felt like he'd never last that long. In fact, there were several occasions when he doubted that he'd make it home at all, at least not still in one piece. Yet now that the moment had finally come, he felt blindsided. He knew that his time in the South was coming to an end; he just hadn't expected it so soon. There was so much more work to be done, so much that remained yet to do. How could he just leave?

"I just figured out what the blazes I'm supposed to be doing here." He paused as a thought flashed across his mind. "I sure hope I don't say that on my deathbed."

B.H. shrugged. "It's just time."

"It's three weeks shy of two years." In those days there was no set period of time for mission service. Though most elders served for roughly two years, it wasn't uncommon to serve between three to five. Golden knew that many elders had served much longer, and he didn't want to be the one to not fulfill the measure of his duty.

B.H. smiled. Golden had become quite the missionary, fearless and hardworking. And a true friend. Golden often spoke of how much he had learned from him, but B.H. knew that he'd learned just as much from Golden. He was a solid example of rugged determination and tenacity even in the face of adversity. His loyalty and faithfulness were unquestionable. And perhaps most important of all, Golden made him laugh. It was so easy to get caught up in everything. A man like Golden helped keep things in perspective. For that B.H. would always be grateful. Golden would be missed here in the Southern States, but it was time he moved on.

"Consider it your last mission assignment to go home and get caught up on your rest. You need to get fully healed up and then get on with your life." B.H. said as encouragingly as possible. "Maybe find yourself a wife and get married."

As usual, B.H. knew just what to say. Golden's ears perked right up. Missionary work sounded good. Finding a wife sounded even better. "You're right, B.H. I mean it's only three weeks shy of two years!"

And that's how Golden found himself back on Union Pacific #9, traveling westward from the land of cotton, through amber waves of grain, beneath spacious skies, through the fruited plain and back toward the purple mountain majesties of home.

As Chattanooga disappeared rapidly behind him, Golden watched the lush greenery pass by outside the window. Thoughts of his time in the South flickered through his mind as quickly as the trees passing the train. Looking back, it all seemed to have gone by so fast. He could hardly believe how blessed he had been. The task had seemed daunting, almost insurmountable, but here he was on the other side of it. He had come through mostly unscathed and had grown in ways he never would have imagined.

He was so lost in his thoughts that he didn't notice that the conversation of the passengers around him had once again turned to disparaging remarks about the Mormons. It wasn't until the man sitting right next to him pitched in his two cents' worth that Golden became aware of it.

"What's worse is these Mormon elduhs practice the arts of seduction."

People expressed their shock and horror at the pronouncement. The conversation had attracted the attention of nearly everyone in the car. From their reactions, it was clear that Mormons were downright unacceptable as human beings. Much to Golden's distaste, their reactions seemed to only encourage the fellow, who apparently considered himself quite knowledgeable on the subject of Mormons even though he failed to recognize the fact that he was sitting right next to one.

"It's the truth! Seducers, every last one of them. They learn it from their leaders like Brigham Young. And they're everywhere these days. I've seen them preachin' as far as Bristol." The other passengers nodded. Apparently that meant that the Mormons were far spread indeed. Golden wanted to tell him they preached in Hawthorne, Richton, and as far as Creeds as well but kept his tongue.

The expert sat back, crossing his arms, resting his case. Golden found he had little tolerance for this sort of discussion anymore and hoped that would be the end of it. No such luck. The man fired off his final round. "Makes me want to go further east, just to escape the Mormons."

Another fellow had a brilliant solution. "You could go north to get away from the Mormons."

"You could go further south," pitched in another.

"You could go to hell." Golden suggested helpfully. He hadn't spoken very loudly, but his high-pitched voice was more than enough to draw everyone's attention. The expert looked at him, not believing he'd heard right.

"Excuse me, young man, what did you say?"

"I said you can all go to hell, for I know there are no Mormons there!" Golden shouted, his voice carrying sharp and clear through the entire car.

He was met with stunned silence. The passengers could only stare, mouths agape. If they sat like that long enough they were sure to swallow a bug or something, Golden thought. That was the end of the discussion. Confounded by the boldness of the tall, thin man sitting among them, the entire car fell quiet.

Golden leaned back in his seat contentedly. The rest of his trip home went without a hitch.

CHAPTER 21

INTER-MISSION

We feel that we are kind of half comfortable in these valleys of the mountains, but the devil is not dead yet.

—John Taylor

Golden returned home—back to Utah, to his cherished Rocky Mountains and beloved family. He was still in one piece too. Not too shabby an accomplishment, all things considered. He'd learned a lot and really come a long way spiritually. Now it was time to get back to the business of living, something that he did with real gusto. He even got to following B.H.'s last advice to find a wife for himself, not that he needed much encouragement in that area.

Now, getting married and having children are a pretty significant part of any person's life, and Golden was no exception. In fact, Golden's marriage would affect his life like few other things ever would. However—and I feel I've got to do a bit of apologizing here—I'm not going to be spending a lot of words about his marriage, at least not on these pages, because this story isn't about that particular aspect of his life. Golden's marriage is a great story, mind you, and one that certainly deserves a good telling. And I reckon it will be told someday, just not in this volume, I'm sorry to say.

Be that as it may, I'd be greatly remiss if I didn't tell you at least briefly what happened after Golden's return from the South. So bear with me here while I sort of gloss over the highlights.

It wasn't too long after Golden got home that he stumbled across a schoolteacher in Kaysville named Jennie Knowlton. Born and raised in Tooele County, Jennie was the daughter of John Q. and Ellen Smith Knowlton, the scion of a prominent pioneer family. Winsome, full of energy, and possessed with an artistic temperament, Jennie was constantly busy with her love of literature, music, and the arts. She also loved flowers and took great pride in the gardens she would plant around her home. Like Golden, she was fiery and free-spirited. She didn't take any manure from anyone, and if she did, she used it as fertilizer for her roses.

Golden fell for her like a featherless bird and, after a brief courtship, asked her to marry him, even though she'd graduated from the University of Utah. And Jennie agreed to marry him, even though he'd graduated from the Brigham Young Academy. That might not mean a lot to folks from outside of Utah, but that's akin to a cat exchanging vows with a dog. They decided to jump the broom and were married in the Salt Lake Temple in 1887 and shortly thereafter relocated to Logan.

That same year President Taylor passed away at age seventy-eight, and the Apostle Wilford Woodruff was sustained as prophet, seer, and revelator in his place as the fourth president of the Church. A few years later, in 1890, President Woodruff would issue the Manifesto on polygamy, which ended the Church's official support of the practice. Church members were no longer to enter in polygamous marriages but instead enter only into marriages recognized by laws of the land. And with that, Mormons were no longer polygamists. Still, try telling that to the rest of the world.

About this time, Golden and Elias decided to trade off the ranch and try their hand at the farm machinery business in hopes of a better life, or at least an easier living. Appropriately named "Kimball Brothers," they opened two stores, one in Logan and another in Montpelier, Idaho. They also began to invest heavily in real estate, signing notes for properties around Logan and a large tract of land in Canada through the Alberta Land and Colonization Company, which was founded by John Taylor, Jr., the son of the late prophet.

Yes, sir, things were on the up and up for Golden, and he was looking forward to settling down and enjoying life. But God had other plans.

Golden had been home for six years when a letter arrived. It had come one afternoon while Golden was tending to the store. Brother Lindquist, the postman, had brought it.

"Letter for you, Golden, from Salt Lake," he said, as if it were important. Not that he really had any idea, and neither did Golden, even once he'd read it. It gave no details save President Woodruff wanted to see Golden in his office at his earliest convenience.

Not wanting to keep the president waiting, Golden made arrangements with Elias regarding the store and packed his saddlebags. The very next day, he threw the saddle on his Bay, told three-year-old Jack to take care of his sister and mother, and kissed Jennie good-bye.

The horse ride from Logan to Salt Lake gave Golden plenty of time to ponder what it could be about. He'd paid his tithing, what little there had been to pay so far. He'd done his best to be active in his ward. He'd been serving as the superintendent of the Bear Lake Stake Mutual Improvement Association. His best guess was that it had something to do with that, but he still had no real idea by the time he hitched his horse in front of the president's office.

Wearing a proper suit this time, Golden knocked lightly on the office door.

"Please come in," the president's voice called from the other side, and Golden stepped inside.

With a spry step belying his age, the prophet walked around his desk to greet Golden. President Woodruff was eighty-three years old. He was more robust-looking than President Taylor had been and had a more rugged build. Like Golden, he was of tough pioneer and cowboy stock. In fact, he had been an original member of the first pioneer party to enter the Salt Lake Basin. He had a much gruffer air about him than President Taylor but was every bit as warm and kind.

"Brother Kimball, come in, come in. Please, have a seat." He motioned toward a high-backed chair, then stepped back to his seat behind the desk.

"Thank you, President." Golden sat in the chair, most likely the very one he'd sat in before when he'd met with President Taylor and received his call to the Southern States. As much as he'd enjoyed speaking with the prophet then, and as much as he'd learned and grown from the experience that followed, he was mighty glad to have it all behind him. It hadn't been all that long ago, but somehow it seemed like another lifetime. Maybe even a dream.

The office was more or less the same as Golden remembered it from the last time he'd been here. The furniture was mostly in the same arrangement. Some personal items had been traded out, and there were definitely more books on the shelves than there had been previously, a testament to President Woodruff having served as Church historian for roughly thirty-five years.

The prophet leaned forward. "I understand you served your mission in the Southern States." Light from the window sparkled in his eyes. He was obviously very interested in the subject.

"Yes, sir." A twinge of nervousness fired itself like an ice cube being dragged from Golden's neck to the base of his spine. He shifted in his seat.

"Did you know that I served there myself?" asked President Woodruff.

"No, I didn't know that."

"It was a long time ago, years before the war." Leaving from

Kirtland, Ohio, in 1835, President Woodruff had been one of the earliest missionaries into the South. He had served a successful mission and helped lay the foundation of missionary work in the region.

"Tell me, how are the people of the South faring since the war? I understand it's extracted a terrible toll on them." He smiled expectantly, eager to hear what Golden had to say.

The question placed Golden in a bit of a dilemma. President Woodruff was a compassionate man, filled with love for all of God's children. And it was clear that this included the people of the South. Golden's experience there had been quite a bit different, and so were his feelings on the matter. He thought about buttering up his answer, maybe softening it a bit. On the other hand, Golden wasn't inclined to lie to anyone about anything, and he certainly wasn't going to start with the prophet.

"President, if I had my way, I'd drown them all and do baptismal work for the dead," he answered.

The strangest expression creased the elderly man's forehead. It was an astounded look of concern mixed with a liberal dose of worry. The prophet was quiet. Golden was quiet too. The last thing on earth Golden wanted to do was offend the prophet, but from the look on President Woodruff's face, it appeared he had. It was clearly not the answer the prophet had been expecting to hear. Maybe honesty wasn't the best policy after all. Perhaps tact would have been better, but it was too late to turn back now.

"Well, I don't really know what to say to that." There was no way to miss the anxiousness in the prophet's voice when he spoke. He clasped his hands together in front of him. "Brother Kimball, you've been called to replace Brother Spry as president to the Southern States Mission."

Now it was Golden's turn to be shocked. No one had asked. There had been no discussion or interviews or mention of any of this. It was completely out of the blue.

The memory of being charged by the swan-diving bull so many years ago sprung to his mind. When he was thrown from his horse, the wind had been knocked from him with such force that it had taken him several minutes to get his air back. He knew he wasn't going to die, but it had sure felt like it. President Woodruff's words knocked the wind from him every bit as hard as if he'd been bucked all over again. The difference was that, unlike getting the wind knocked out of him, the South might actually kill him. He still counted himself blessed to have made it home in one piece the first time around, and he was awful hesitant to push his luck.

The expression on his face must have been something else, because now President Woodruff looked concerned for a completely different reason. "You understand that we wouldn't be calling you unless the Lord felt you were the right man for the job."

Golden was far from excited. The timing could hardly have been worse. He and Jennie were expecting their third child, and the farm implement business was still in the rocky beginning stage. It's not that he didn't trust Elias; he trusted him plenty. Golden just hated to dump the entire burden on his brother. He had every reason to be hesitant, reason even to say no, but one thing Golden had gained in the South, one thing that he would forever be grateful for, was a testimony of the gospel and the work. He knew that if it were the Lord's will, he would go, no questions asked. It was the right thing to do. But that still didn't make it any easier.

He looked down, picking at his fingers, rubbing his hands together slowly, mustering his bravado and decorum. After what must have seemed a long time to President Woodruff, Golden raised his head and nodded.

"I'll go." His voice was quiet as he answered. "If the Lord wants me to go, I'll go, even if I am brought back in a casket."

"Splendid. You leave in a week."

Why was it always a week? Golden had no idea how he was supposed to get all of his affairs in order in so short a time. Even worse, how was he supposed to break the news to Jennie? As unhappy as he was about leaving, he knew that it would be much harder on her. Having your husband leave for an undetermined length of time to live in a region known for its violent hostility is not a pleasant thought for any wife, especially one with two children under the age of five and a third well on the way.

Despite the long ride home, Golden couldn't think of any way to break the news gently. So he just sat Jennie down and told her. It was evening, and the children were fast asleep in bed. The sun was down below the rim of the mountains, but the last bit of its glow filtered softly through the windows. A single candle burned in the lantern on the kitchen table in anticipation of the coming night. Its meager glow was the only bright spot in the room as he gave Jennie the news.

Jennie took the news as well as could be expected. Golden could see tears pooling in her eyes, but she refused to let them spill over. She knew how loyal Golden was to the Church. It was one of the reasons she'd married him. She wasn't happy, but she was bound and determined to be the best wife and mother she knew how to be. She was such a strong woman. His heart filled with love and admiration for her all over again.

He reached across the table and took her petite hands into his long fingers. He loved the feel of her hands. They were so soft and smooth compared to his calloused cowboy hands. Everything was better when she was with him. Which made everything so much worse when they were apart.

"I guess I didn't get it right the first time around," He felt horrible about leaving her. No amount of remorse or apology would make any of this easier for either of them, "I have faith enough to go, but I confess I'm not very excited about it. It's hell down there."

Jennie remained silent for a long while. It would be hard, and she knew it. But it was only for a few years, she told herself. She could handle that somehow. The hardest part would be the children. It may be only a few years to her, but it would be a very long time for a small child. She knew that children were adaptable, but still, there was no replacement for having a father around the house. Or a husband in your arms.

She understood her husband well enough to know that he was struggling with the calling, divided between duty to his family and duty to God. It was clear from his eyes that he was plenty torn up inside. It wasn't fair that he had to go. Surely there were others who could go in his place. She wanted to beg him not to go, to keep him here. But it was hard enough for him already. She didn't want to make things any worse. She fought back the rising tears again, trying to be strong for both of them.

"If it's hell, then you must bring them heaven," she said, "even if you have to force it down their throats like stuffing a goose for baking." It was a silly image, and a slight smile cracked through the mask of sadness on her face.

Golden returned her smile and squeezed her hand. Jennie was strong, and he knew she could survive the toughest of times. It was one of the reasons he'd married her. However, being capable of surviving tough times doesn't mean you have to like them. The South was risky, and it would be hard on him, but things would be difficult for her as well. No one got off easy. He shook his head gently, as if trying to shake his doubts.

"I feel sad and all broken up in leaving you." He placed a gentle hand on her protruding belly. It would be only a few more months till the baby would come. He would be long gone by then.

Jennie rested her hands on his. "We've got some money from your investments, cows for milk, and flour for bread. That will do for the time being. But please be careful, Golden. I have no replacement for you."

She knew the danger. She knew the stories. They were entertaining before; amusing anecdotes that Golden would tell at dinner or around the hearth fire. But now they were horrifying.

To send her husband or anyone's husband into conditions such as that seemed almost cruel, unjust somehow.

She leaned in and placed a kiss lightly on his cheek. His whiskers were rough, scratchy against her lips. How she would miss that. Finally a single tear spilled from her eye. It left a thin trail of reflected candlelight as it moved down her cheek. Golden wiped it gently with his finger. Then he excused himself, stepping outside of the house to shed tears of his own.

CHAPTER 22

THE MORE THINGS CHANGE

If you get thrown from a horse, you have to get up and get back on, unless you landed on a cactus; then you have to roll around and scream in pain.

—*Cowboy Proverb*

Nothing had changed. Standing on the front step of the mission home, Golden swore that even the weeds and anthills were in the same place as they had been before. It was as if everything had frozen in time the instant he'd left, only to resume the moment he'd returned. The street was the same. The dirt was the same. Even the wagon tracks looked the same. The only thing missing from the image in Golden's mind was a lonely tumbleweed rolling across the road. He'd have to make do with a few floating wisps from the cottonwoods.

The notch from the penknife that had pinned the threat to the front door after Cane Creek was still there. He ran his fingers over its scar. Surely the Lord must have a reason that he was here again, but for the life of him, Golden couldn't figure out what it was. With a drawn-out sigh, he pushed the door open.

And scared the bejeebies out of the fellow on the other side, who nearly jumped out of his skin.

"President Spry?" Golden asked. He set down his bag and removed his hat.

"Yes?" The jittery fellow decided he wasn't being attacked, calmed himself, and shook Golden's hand enthusiastically. "You must be President Kimball. So glad to meet you."

President Spry seemed genuinely glad to see Golden. Golden suspected it was because his appearance meant that Spry could finally leave. He struck Golden as a nervous sort of fellow. Of course, the South could do that to a person.

Spry was in the final stages of packing his bags, fussing over them like someone trying to catch the last train out of Dodge. He rifled through his desk and produced some keys and a thin book from the top drawer.

"Okay, keys." He handed them to Golden, then opened the book. "Here is the money ledger." He ran a finger over the hand-written figures, double-checking something he already knew. "Budget . . . let me see, yes, you've thirty-five dollars." He closed the book and handed everything over to Golden.

"Thirty-five dollars? Is that it?" Golden flipped the book open, scanning over the numbers himself. Not that Spry was lying. Just sometimes you have to see something for yourself and hope that you heard wrong. Golden hadn't heard wrong.

"Yes, that's what the book said." President Spry looked at the book over Golden's shoulder to triple check himself anyhow. He nodded with a satisfied conclusion. "Thirty-five dollars, yes."

Now, thirty-five dollars was a lot more money then than it is now, it's true, but it still wasn't much. Anyone could have told you it took more than thirty-five dollars to run a whole mission. Golden knew he'd have to get more funding as soon as he could. Which raised the question . . .

"How do you receive money around here?" he asked.

Spry paused, looking at Golden as if it was the most obvious thing in the world. "Why, we go to the Lord and ask him."

Golden scowled at the ledger again. "Well, I don't think he's very liberal." He was hoping for a bit more of a practical answer.

He knew things were tight in Salt Lake. Things were tight all over right now. Several major railroads and banks had recently collapsed, and the fallout had started a nationwide land panic. The economy of the entire country was in the dumps. Golden knew he was going to have to make do with what he had.

President Spry didn't carry much, but he was most meticulous about the way his bags were packed. His clothes were rolled and folded just so and placed in the bags in an organized fashion. Golden sat down, watching him, waiting for any further instructions and guidance. He figured that Spry would talk to him once he was done packing. Instead the man closed up his bags, put on his coat, and opened the door to leave.

"Uh, President, is there any advice you wish to give me?" Golden asked before Spry bolted from the door. Spry looked up, startled, as if he'd forgotten that Golden was sitting there.

"Oh, uh, yes." He fidgeted with his hat. "Only fully converted members should emigrate west to gather with the Saints. Everything else I leave to your discretion. Good luck." He tucked his hat neatly on his head and stepped out the door, leaving Golden abruptly alone.

Golden took a slow look around the inside of the office. It was still the same size as it had been before, but it had never felt quite so big back then. Or so empty. A few small changes had been made, most noticeably the formerly stark walls had been papered, but everything was pretty much the same as it had been.

With a sigh, he stepped to the desk, running his fingers over its surface. It was well used, and the finish was worn through to the wood in places. It had been here long before Golden, and chances were it would be here long after. He sat down, trying out the chair. He'd sat here plenty of times in the past, but the soft cushion had never felt like a hot seat before. He shuffled through a few letters and papers without reading any of them. The emptiness was intimidating.

Up till now he'd always had a companion for support and guidance, but B.H. was no longer here, and Jennie and the kids were thousands of miles away. It was just him. Sure, he'd learned a lot his first time out here, but he was still just an ignoramus cowboy at heart. He could preach a sermon or two, but that didn't really prepare him to be a mission president. He tried to think of what B.H. would do if he were sitting here now. Something intelligent and presidential, no doubt, but Golden had no idea what that might be.

He was still thinking it over when he was interrupted by the *thump* of something hitting the wooden ceiling. Golden had thought he was alone, but apparently he had company. Thinking it was best to go see who it was, he rose and climbed the familiar wooden stairs.

The hall was still as narrow as ever. He didn't expect it to be any different, but it struck him with wonder again at how cramped it was. He opened the first door and peeked inside. The sound had been directly over his head, so whoever it was had to be in here. The furniture had been rearranged, but otherwise this room too was the same as it had been. And just like before, an injured missionary lay on the first bed in front of him. He was lying on his belly, and from the amount of blood staining the wrappings on his back, Golden guessed that it wasn't by choice. One arm and hand were also heavily bandaged.

The elder looked up out of the corner of his eye. "Who are you?"

"I'm J. Golden Kimball, the new president. I just got in. I didn't know anyone else was here."

"President Spry?" asked the elder.

"He just left."

"Lucky him."

It didn't take a vision to know that the poor fellow was dispirited and down in the mouth. From the look of things, Golden couldn't blame him. Golden sat down so the elder didn't have to turn his head quite so far to see him when he spoke. In his condition, it had to be painful.

"It looks like you've really been through the mill," Golden

said. He noticed there were splints underneath the wrapping on the elder's arm. "What happened?"

"Mob gave me twenty-two lashes with a bullwhacker. Broke my arm."

Golden grimaced with empathy. He felt a strange sense of disappointment, although he didn't know why he should. Nothing else had changed down here, why should this be any different?

"I was hoping this sort of thing would have vanished by now."

"Well, it hasn't." The elder didn't sound upset, just resigned to the fact. He wore a look that Golden recognized well. It was the sad, tired look of someone who has given their best effort but still come up shy. He had worn it himself not so long ago. The elder looked at him again. Golden could tell he had something on his mind but was reluctant to say it. Golden waited patiently, giving him time to collect his thoughts.

"President?" he finally asked. He looked down as he spoke, "I . . . I want to go home." A look of shame and hurt flashed across his face.

Golden was no stranger to how the elder felt. Being in the mission home again and looking at the elder, thoughts of his own struggle and doubt during his mission came rushing to his mind. He clearly remembered the sting of persecution and the crushing sense of inadequacy that had nearly overcome him. He'd never been more miserable in his entire life. "I can't say I blame you." And he really didn't. He wanted to be home right now himself.

"Don't think me completely yellow." There were tears lurking in the elder's eyes now, but he wouldn't let them flow. "I want to work. I just can't take any more of this."

The elder seemed like a good enough fellow. Chances are he wanted to do what was right, but it was just so confounded tough sometimes. With the level of adversity that was far too common in the South, it could be almost insurmountable. Golden knew he was going through an unquestionably hard time. It made Golden wonder how the other missionaries in the field were faring.

"Tell me, how do the other elders feel right now?" Golden asked.

"I can't speak for everyone," the elder answered, "but it's pretty awful out there." Now that the subject had been breached and the new president appeared willing to listen, he seemed more comfortable discussing it. He went on to explain a lot of what Golden already knew and feared. Threats, violence, and bigotry were still common as snakes on a hot rock, and morale was running low. It was unfortunate to hear, but Golden was glad to at least know the general temperament of the mission. The question now was what was he going to do about it? He'd have to figure that out. But first things first.

The elder's intentions seemed good, and Golden respected his feelings; he had been through more than anyone should have to bear. Still, Golden tried to imagine how it would have been for him if he'd gone home when he had felt like it instead of sticking it out. He would have missed out on so much and doubtless would have regretted it to this day.

Golden rested a hand on the elder's unbandaged shoulder. "I'll make you a deal," he said. "You keep resting and get healed up. When you're well enough, if you still want to go home, we'll get you that ticket directly, no questions asked. But until then, think it over, okay?"

The elder nodded. Then he held out his good hand for Golden to shake. "My name's Davidson."

"Pleased to meet you." Golden smiled, taking the elder's hand carefully. As he did, he noticed a figure lurking at the edge of his vision. Someone was right behind him. He jumped as high as a frog that's been jabbed in the back end with a hot poker, whirling to face another elder who was sitting properly in a chair behind the door. The elder looked back at Golden attentively through a pair of glasses. Apparently Golden had hidden him when he opened the door to enter the room.

"Perdition!" Golden said, trying to calm his nerves. "You scared the dickens out of me! Have you been here the whole time?"

"Yes, sir. I'm sorry about that." He sat with both hands resting on his valise, which he held on his lap.

"It's all right. I'm a little high strung, that's all." Golden couldn't help but notice how young both the elders seemed. They hadn't been that young when he was a missionary, had they?

This particular elder was relatively tall and thin, though not as tall or thin as Golden himself. His features weren't particularly strong in appearance, but there was something about the set of his mouth and the calm of his eyes that reminded Golden that a man's true strength wasn't always apparent from the outside. The other thing that struck Golden was that the elder's suit was brand-spanking new. The stitching was still intact, and there was no wear or tear on his knees or elbows. That would change soon enough.

"You must be a greenhorn," Golden observed.

"Yes." The elder looked surprised. "How can you tell?"

"Oh, I can tell. What's your name?" The elder stood and shook Golden's hand. His grip was stronger than expected, confirming Golden's impression to not judge by appearance.

"I'm George Albert Smith," he said.

"A Smith, huh? Who's your father?"

"John Henry, sir."

The son of John Henry Smith. Golden noticed that George Albert had humbly omitted the word "apostle." Not only was his father currently serving in the Quorum of the Twelve, but also his grandfather had been counselor to Brigham Young. Not too shabby a pedigree as far as Mormonism went.

Whether they deserved it or not, particular names have always carried a certain weight in LDS society. As a Kimball, Golden understood that well enough. With a name like Smith it would be easy to ride slack on the coattails of his forebears. But it was apparent from George Albert's manner that he would do no such thing. He would stand on his own feet or not at all. That was good.

"Well, Elder Smith, welcome to the Southern States."

Golden looked about the room. There was a small brass candelabra sitting on the dresser, which he grabbed and handed to

Davidson. "I'm going to head back downstairs to get settled in a bit. If you need anything, thump on the floor with that. I'll come a-running."

Davidson actually smiled at that. "Thank you, President."

Golden exited. George Albert followed.

The conversation with Davidson worried Golden. He was concerned about the state of the mission. More to the point, he was worried about his missionaries. He knew Davidson was feeling down. Who wouldn't be in his shoes? But if the mission in general was feeling as discouraged as he'd indicated, then Golden had a real problem on his hands.

When he got to the bottom floor, he turned to George Albert and motioned upstairs. "I suppose you heard all that about the mobs?"

George Albert nodded. "Don't worry, I'm here to stay." He knew what Golden was concerned about.

"Me too," said Golden. To his own surprise, he meant it. "But I sure know how he feels. Have you ever been depressed, Elder Smith?"

"Not like that, no."

Golden had. He knew all too well how awful it could be. "Let me tell you, it makes it damn near impossible to feel the Spirit."

"I suppose it would," George Albert agreed.

"I've got to do something." Golden was talking to himself as much as to George Albert at this point. "Somehow I've got to pick these elders up by their bootstraps."

"What do you have in mind?" George Albert looked at him expectantly, waiting for the mission president to say something. It took a second for Golden to realize that meant him. That was going to take some getting used to. Golden wanted to tell George Albert that if he was looking to him for true leadership that he'd be looking for a very long time. George Albert was waiting for an idea from his mission president. Golden was waiting for any idea at all.

When it became apparent that no sudden revelation was going to strike out of the blue, he slapped his hands on his knees and crossed to the desk. "Well, at the very least I suppose I ought to meet everybody." He looked up at George Albert. "Do you type?"

"A bit."

"Splendid. You're hereby called as mission secretary."

George Albert was shocked. "You must be joking." George Albert was not the kind of person to ever speak out of place or question his elders, especially his mission president. He was so surprised by the calling that it just slipped out, and he quickly apologized.

"Do you not want the calling?" Golden was all too familiar with how it felt to receive a calling out of the blue. He supposed there were other ways that callings were given, but that was the only way he was familiar with. Besides, it wasn't as if he'd asked the young man to leave his family behind or sell his horse or anything.

"I'm fully willing, but surely there are others who have served longer?"

"That's true," Golden conceded, "but you're the closest one who can type. Have a seat." He motioned toward the desk and the heavy cast-iron typewriter resting on it. George Albert sat down and located some typing paper in the drawer. He loaded it, then looked up, ready. Golden began to speak, and the keys clacked crisply as George Albert typed.

"To all elders of the Southern States Mission. Greetings from your new president, J. Golden Kimball. It is my honor and privilege to serve with you. I will be touring the conferences of the mission in order to become acquainted with each of you and also to reacquaint myself with the region . . . "

Golden traveled from state to state meeting with his missionaries, testing the waters, so to speak. It wasn't much of a plan, but it was all he had. Most of his travel was done by train or a buggy that was rented or borrowed. Sometimes local members or elders would pick him up, but just as often, he was flat footing it. He made an earnest effort to get to know each and every man serving with him. Many of the elders were from towns back in Utah, and he had known some of their families or had at least heard of them.

To his great relief, not everyone was as bad off as Davidson had been. The elders were still willing to work, God bless them. But they were discouraged, and morale was as low as he had feared. Most weren't asking to be sent home, but he knew some of them would take the chance if it were given. Since Cane Creek, there hadn't been any more killings, thankfully, but the sheer number of mob threats and violence had increased dramatically since Golden had been a missionary, a fact that concerned him greatly.

Golden knew the sort of hardships they were up against. It could be flat-out awful at times. He'd been so miserable himself he was ready to die, or at least he wouldn't have complained if he had. When Golden told the elders he understood what they were going through, they could tell that he really did. The troubles he had gone through the first time around had been worth that much, at least.

He knew that these elders, his elders, needed something to pick them up. He could give them a pep talk, sure, but he knew they'd already heard plenty of words. They needed something more. All it would take was one good stroke, some solid action by a confident leader to change the whole thing around. But what? These missionaries were looking to him just the way he had looked to B.H., who had always made it look so easy. But B.H. wasn't here now. It was just Golden. It was worse than the blind leading the blind; Golden felt deaf and dumb as well.

The day found him walking along yet another rural roadway, valise in hand and expression of consternation fixed to his face. Even the weather seemed to reflect his mood. The heavens were covered by a gray haze, edging the light with a gloomy quality.

The train had been delayed getting to Arkadelphia. The whole works had been gummed up by a single cow for nearly an hour, and now he was running late for his appointment with the elders down near Gum Springs. He hadn't been able to procure a wagon either and was forced to hoof it. He could still make it to the meeting as planned if he hurried, but he couldn't convince his feet to move any faster—the worry in his mind was spilling over, affecting him physically.

The road that lay before him was two lines of pebbled earth surrounded by green-covered land. It wasn't any different than any other road he had traveled before, but today it felt as daunting as any a man has ever faced. The gloom only thickened as he walked, his body growing heavier with every step.

Finally he stopped walking altogether. He shook his head, trying to shed the doubt that gripped him, but the feeling refused to leave him in peace. All these men. Struggling so hard. Looking to him for leadership. The responsibility was too great. He felt he would buckle at any moment, crushed beneath the weight of it. Succumbing to the depths and drowning in his sorrow, Golden sank to his knees beneath a large and twisted oak, its branches so thick and gnarled that they hid the sky entirely. All of his doubts, all the fears of his inadequacy and shortcomings came together. He shouldn't be here. There had to be some sort of mistake. He wasn't the man for the job.

"Father, I can't do it. I can't lead these men." He didn't raise his arms. He didn't even bother looking to see if anyone was watching. He sat on his knees and poured out his soul. "I'm over head and ears here. I don't have the spirit of the appointment, and I feel awfully uninspired."

He wasn't blaming God at all. He was begging. He wanted to get this right. He had to get this right. These were the souls of men he was concerned about. Could the stakes ever be higher?

"Father, please help me."

Suddenly everything was quiet.

Golden stopped midsentence. The chaos eating up his mind was gone. An undeniable sense of calm spread through him. It started small, deep in the middle of his being, and slowly expanded till it warmed every facet of him like honey on a waffle. It spread so wide that the hint of a smile threatened to break through his face. He realized he had been wrong. It wasn't just him here. It was him and the Lord.

There had been no other change. He didn't see a vision. He hadn't been struck by lightning. The secret of how he should help his elders hadn't been miraculously revealed to him. As far as that went, his mind was still a blank slate. But he knew he wasn't alone. And that made all the difference in the world.

He stood, dusted himself off, grabbed his valise, and began to walk with renewed vigor, moving faster than he had all day. He had ground to make up; his elders were waiting for him.

After a moment, he became aware of a new sound. He couldn't place it at first. Then to his own astonishment, he discovered that he was whistling. By his nature, Golden wasn't a whistler. He'd never done it before, and years later he'd look back and realize he'd never done it again after. But song was bursting from him today. He couldn't contain it if he tried. Whistling as he walked, he headed for his meeting.

CHAPTER 23

GUNFLINGER

Wherever our life touches yours, we help or hinder . . . wherever your life touches ours, you make us stronger or weaker. There is no escape—man drags man down, or man lifts man up.

—*Booker T. Washington*

The gospel had first been taught in the backwoods of Arkansas nearly fifty years earlier. Progress had been slow, but the seeds sewn by those early labors were gradually coming to fruition. Over the years, the branch here had grown to include a small handful of families.

Golden had always admired converts, especially in the South. The Saints here were not only faithful but also courageous. They had to be; they knew what they were getting into before they joined. To be baptized in the face of that kind of adversity was nothing short of awe inspiring.

Still whistling, Golden had met up with the elders with time to spare. Now they were walking together to the chapel where the meeting was to be held. The tiny branch had finally outgrown the house they had been meeting in, and the members had been renting a small Baptist church for a few months now.

Golden was genuinely enjoying getting to know his missionaries. He found the elders' company to be delightful and was fond of spending time with them. His association with them would spark a lifelong love of mingling with the Saints.

Broad-shouldered Elder Fisher's family was from Grantsville, and Golden was actually acquainted with Elder Peterson's father, having done some business with him in the Montpelier store. Both elders were doing what they could in difficult circumstances, but discouragement was visible in their faces and unmistakable in their speech.

"Brethren, let me ask you about your feelings on things. I understand you're having a tough time out here." Golden breached the subject.

The elders agreed that things were pretty rough.

"Let me ask you, what do you think I can do to help things out around here?" Golden asked.

"You could get rid of the mobs," said Elder Fisher. He was only half joking. He paused, giving the question some serious thought. "I think just having you here helps, President, honestly. When we told the members that the new president was coming to visit, they were all excited and, uh . . . " He stopped.

They had come around a thicket of scrub oak into a clearing. A modest wooden chapel stood at the center of it. The sky had cleared, and the sun shone down through the trees, casting mottled shadows across the ground while birds and insects sung their praises to the glory of nature. Golden's first impression was that it was like a photograph or a painting, a jewel hidden in the woods.

All in all it would have been a perfect scene except for the handful of armed men barricading the entrance to the building, marring the picture like a cow pie thrown against the canvas. They were the crude sort of fellows that Golden had become all too familiar with in the South. They were dressed in plain clothes, not in Klan robes, thank heavens, but from the look of them, they meant business. Golden turned to the elders and nodded toward the hooligans.

"I take it the fellows with the guns aren't the members you were talking about."

They certainly weren't. The members they had been talking about were still huddled in their wagons at the far side of the clearing, as far away from the mobbers as they could get.

Chester ended yesterday like most every day, swinging by Henry's place for a drink, maybe some whittlin' and chawin' on the porch. He hadn't been there more than two shakes, not even enough time to finish his first cup, when Henry asked him if he'd heard the news about Reverend Atkins's church.

"What 'bout it?" Chester'd asked.

"Hearsay is the Mo-muns been usin' it fuh meetings of late."

"Izzat so?"

"Matter a fact, I heard there's a meeting takin' place there tomorrow. Purty big one," Henry continued.

Chester had been out to the chapel a time or two, whenever the missus had been pushing on him about churching it up, which thankfully weren't often. Atkins was good people, and it weren't no ill will against him, but the fact that Mormons was using the place didn't bode well. It was a right defilation of the chapel, if you asked Chester. If they had taken a shine to using that chapel, it wouldn't be long afore they felt right at home in these parts, and that just wouldn't do at all. In fact, Chester P. Harrington of Pulaski County would be darned like a sock if those Mormons were getting in that chapel tomorrow or ever again.

He stood up without even finishing his drink, which Henry noted as highly unusual behavior. Where was Chester going in such an all-fired hurry?

"Devil set fire to yuh britches?" he asked.

"Henry, them Mo-muns is taking over that chapel. Cursin' it, is what they doing. As God-fearin' men, we've got to put a stop to it right now."

Henry never mistook Chester for a God-fearing man, but he had a point.

"'Kay. What yuh got in mind?"

"Let's get some a the boys. Tell 'em there's a church needs defendin'."

Henry wasn't particularly thrilled about the notion, but when Chester got a burr up his hindquarters, there was a snowball's chance of stopping him. And whenever Chester did something, the rest of the boys followed suit. Now Chester got it in his mind to defend the church. So that's what they did.

Golden and the elders crossed to the members, skirting the edge of the copse. The Saints looked relieved to see the missionaries. A stout, older fellow climbed off his wagon and greeted them with hushed excitement.

"Elders!"

"Brother Holman, is everything all right?" Elder Fisher addressed him. "Is anyone hurt?"

"No one's hurt, but those men won't let anyone in. We didn't know what to do, so we just waited for you." He looked over at Golden. Elder Fisher took the cue and quickly made introductions.

"Brother Holman, this is President Kimball."

"President Kimball! I'm so glad you're here!" His face lit up, and he took Golden's hand, shaking it eagerly. Then he grew serious. "What should we do?"

It was the million-dollar question of the day, the one on everyone's mind. Golden suddenly felt the eyes of all the Saints on him. He knew these good people had sacrificed a lot to be here. It would be a shame to let it be in vain.

He glanced over at the mob. They carried pistols, and several had knives tucked in their pants to boot. They were doing their best to look tough and were succeeding admirably, acting as if they owned the place. The members, on the other hand, were succeeding only in looking scared. Golden suddenly burned with righteous indignation, which is to say he got mighty ticked off. What right did these goons have?

Acting on gut instinct, Golden turned to Brother Holman. "Follow me." He spoke before he thought about what he was doing, which, in this case, was probably a good thing, for if he'd thought about what he was going to do, he wouldn't have done it. But as it turns out, he did do it. And what he did was this:

He marched straight up to the front of the church. The members hesitated at first, exchanging dubious looks, then fell in step behind him. They figured the new president knew what he was doing, a thought that Golden would have laughed at, no doubt.

The Saints outnumbered the mobbers, but their number included women and children, and the mob was armed. The mob tightened their ranks in front of the door, sizing up the oncoming Saints, especially the skinny one in front. He looked more like a flagpole than a leader. As the Mormons drew within earshot, the ruffian who appeared to be the big bug stepped directly into Golden's way, cutting him off.

"We're not lettin' none a ya inna this church." He patted the pistol tucked into the front of his pants threateningly. Golden thought it might go off when he did. Now there would have been a sight: the gun wasn't aimed at the man's head, but it still would have blown out his true seat of reason.

The members flinched, but not Golden. He looked that ruffian square in the eye and, with as much authority as his squeaky voice could muster, said, "Mister, I'm here to preach the gospel of Jesus Christ to my fellow Saints, and we have rented this church for that purpose. Now, if you'll excuse us."

With that, Golden gently pushed him and the other ruffians aside, parting them like Moses at the Red Sea. It was not at all what the mob had expected, and they stood dumbstruck as Golden led the equally stunned members inside. The mobbers remained stupefied until the last member had stepped inside and closed the doors behind him.

The interior was equally as charming as the exterior. Benches of excellent craftsmanship lined a center aisle that led to a pulpit carved from solid oak. Plentiful sunshine from the high windows lining the sides gave it a nice open feel. The chapel was a real testament to the skill of the local craftsmen. The members took their seats quickly. None of them dared speak for fear they might break whatever miracle had just occurred.

Golden was so worked up from confronting the mob that he almost forgot he had to speak until he noticed the members staring at him. He definitely had their attention, that was for sure. But first he owed some thanks. After all, he'd just waded unharmed through an armed mob. He stepped to the pulpit and offered the opening prayer.

The thought formed like an oncoming freight train. You could hear it rumbling along its track for miles before you could actually see it, and when it finally arrived it was with so much noise and force that it was impossible to miss. The flabbergasted look on Chester's face faded, and his brow crinkled together. That skinny fellow hadn't paid him no mind at all. Completely ignored him, in fact. That was downright insulting was what it was. A downright insult. He didn't fight in no war just so a bunch a Yank Mormons could pollute a church, not in his neck a the woods. It was a slight that Chester wasn't like to ignore, no sirree, no how.

Golden finished his prayer. It was interesting to him how trial and danger had a way of increasing the sincerity of your prayers. He smiled at the members. He was still worked up from his brush with the mob and took a deep breath to calm himself.

"My brothers and sisters—" He had no more uttered these opening words when a barrage of gunfire ripped through the front of the building. It sent bits of the door flying and men, women, and children diving for the floor. Random chunks of lead buried themselves in the walls and the backs of pews.

Golden hugged the floor behind the pulpit as rounds whistled by. Wood splintered around him, and he could feel the pulpit tremble as several bullets lodged themselves in its mercifully solid oak.

The firing stopped as suddenly as it had started. The only sounds were the sobs of crying children and the cocking of guns being hastily reloaded outside. Golden checked himself quickly. He was fine. He rose from the floor, running a finger over the holes where several bullets had buried themselves in the pulpit. Smoke drifted through the newly ventilated front door, and whatever décor had been at the back of the chapel hung in shambles.

He looked quickly over the congregation. People were frightened and clustered together on the floor. Mothers covered their children with their bodies, and fathers covered their wives. As far as he could tell, no one was hurt . . . yet. If they were scared before, they were positively terrified now. It was only a matter of time before the mob opened up again. Golden realized that he should be frightened too. But Golden wasn't frightened. He was mad. Plum mad dog mad. The mob may have been "protecting" the chapel from Mormons, but no one was protecting it from the mob's own stupidity.

Golden leaped from the stand, his shoes crunching on splintered wood and broken glass as he stormed down the aisle and right up to the door. It was fractured beyond repair. He raised his size twelve shoe and kicked open the remains. The fractured door split open, nearly falling off its hinges. The startled mob on the other side froze in the middle of reloading their guns, staring flabbergasted at the angry cowboy in a suit.

Chester was closest. Golden grabbed the still-smoking gun from his hand. Winding up like a baseball pitcher, he hurled it as hard as he could. It whirled high over everyone's heads, disappearing into the thick growth of the woods beyond the clearing.

Still driven by pure adrenaline, Golden whirled his full six-foot-plus frame on the man.

"You keep that up, you beef-witted clot-poles, and you're going to kill some of these innocent people here!" Golden was as furious as a hive of hornets shaken by a schoolboy. He shook an angry finger, waving it off in the direction the dragoon had flown. "Now go and find your gun and all of you go home and tell your wives what brave bootlickers you were to come out here and put fear into the hearts of unarmed people!"

The mob leader's fingers wiggled as if they finally realized they were empty. He stared wide-eyed and gape-mouthed at the tall assailant who'd just disarmed him and thrown his pistol into the woods.

Golden's anger faded enough for him to realize that he'd marched solo into enemy lines and was quite literally outgunned. This could get ugly as a mud fence and fast. It was too late to turn back now. He stood staunch, jaw set square, staring down the mob, his eyes just daring them to make a move.

Chester, empty fingers still wiggling, made a faint, disbelieving snort, then turned and hightailed it up the path, quickly disappearing into the forest beyond. He didn't even bother to go after his gun. With their leader gone, the stupefied mob glanced at each other a moment longer, then quickly slinked off higgledy-piggledy with their tails between their legs, fading into the surrounding woods till none were left.

When the last one was gone from sight, Golden realized he'd been holding his breath. He exhaled with a big sigh.

"You and me, Lord," he whispered, glancing heavenward, "You and me." He was racking up quite a debt with the Lord and hoped his credit would hold out a while longer.

He stepped carefully over the remains of the door and back inside the chapel. Miraculously, no one had been hurt. The members rose cautiously, dusting themselves off and peeking over the backs of the pews. They looked at Golden with nothing short of awe, sparing the occasional glance outside as if they couldn't believe the mob was really gone. It was the most amazing thing they had ever seen. Later that night, when he was finally alone and had the chance to really think about what he'd done, Golden's knees would grow washy and almost buckle. But it was okay—he was kneeling to say a very sincere thank you anyway.

For now, Golden returned to the stand and retrieved his scriptures from the floor, dusting them off gently. He set them on the pulpit, looking out over the Saints, who were slowly returning to their seats. "Now where was I?"

It was one meeting no one slept through.

CHAPTER 24

MUSIC AND THE SPOKEN WORD

For my soul delighteth in the song of the heart; yea, the song of the righteous is a prayer unto me, and it shall be answered with a blessing upon their heads.

—Doctrine & Covenants 25:12

Nothing travels faster than the speed of gossip. Since time immemorial, this law has held true and immutable, and the Church in the South was no exception. Word of Golden's feat spread faster than greased lightning. In fact, it traveled just as fast, if not faster among the elders than it ever could have even among the Relief Society sisters. Within days there wasn't a Saint in the entire mission who hadn't heard at least one or two versions of the story. The story got bigger and better with each telling, as stories are prone to do. But the heart of the story remained true, and the message was clear: President J. Golden Kimball meant business.

Of course if you'd asked Golden about it, he'd say it wasn't bravery or inspiration that motivated his actions at all, but stupidity mingled with a general lack of common sense. It takes a real fool to walk up to a group of armed men and pick a fight. He worried that his foolhardiness might inspire similar recklessness among his elders. Fortunately his worries were needless. It turns out that the only person to ever repeat such a rash act would be himself.

As the story spread, other tales about Golden began to circulate as well. It wasn't long before every elder had been impressed and moved by the tale of Golden's involvement during the now infamous Cane Creek Massacre. Or how he'd nearly died himself due to malaria but stayed on to finish his mission regardless.

Two things were soon generally agreed upon by the missionaries: one, after what he went through the first time, the new president was chock-full of sand coming back to these parts again, and two, if the new president was willing to do that, the least the rest of the elders could do was to get out and try to teach. And that's just what they did.

In the end, Golden couldn't have done a more effective job of inspiring his elders if he'd planned it. He didn't need to pull the elders up by their bootstraps after all. Once they learned what kind of man they had for their president, they did it themselves. Dusting off their scriptures, they girded up their loins and fresh courage took, and the work in the South began again in earnest.

As with any endeavor you put real effort into, it wasn't long before the elders began to see the fruits of their labors. That's not to say they were taking in converts by the thousands, but converts did come, and the missionaries were able to see something they hadn't seen in some time: baptisms.

A native of Alexander County, Mabel Rasmussen worked as a seamstress. She had known the Paulson family for years but was quite surprised one day to learn they were Mormons. They seemed so normal. Through their acquaintance, she eventually met the missionaries and obtained a copy of the Book of Mormon. When she read it, the strangest feeling had come over her, a burning in her bosom, as the elders called it. The phrase made her laugh and blush at the same time, but it was an apt enough description, and she had chosen to be baptized. She knew that joining the Church would be quite a change for her. Mormons weren't often treated well, but truth was truth, there was no denying it.

Her baptism was scheduled to take place at Glade Creek on a Thursday before noon. A mere trickle of a stream upriver, Glade Creek joined with the Lower Little River just south of Millersville where it became a waterway worth mentioning. Further on it joined with the Catawba and wound its way down to South Carolina and eventually the great Atlantic. At several places along its length, the banks of the river widened out and the current became calm, ideal places for spending the day fishing or conducting a baptism.

Scattered clouds benignly dotted an otherwise perfectly clear summer sky. Golden stood with Elder Welch, Elder Davis, and a handful of people gathered along the bank. Most of them consisted of the local membership, but a few were nonmember folks from 'round these parts come to see a Mormon baptizing.

Golden was beaming. He was so proud of his elders. This baptism was not only a blessing in Mabel's life, it was also a testament to their efforts. He was proud of Mabel too. She stood in the middle of everyone, looking radiant in a white dress she had sewn herself just for the occasion.

Elder Davis opened with a word of prayer, after which Golden had been asked to give a few words. He stood, looking at the small assembly standing against the river. The sight warmed his heart. What could be lovelier than a group of Saints gathered on a day like this to witness someone joining the fold?

"My brothers and sisters, I am so grateful to be here today to witness this baptism. It thrills me to the very core." Golden paused. He noticed that the congregation was no longer looking at him but were focused on something behind him instead. From the worry on their faces, it couldn't be good. He turned, following their gaze.

You had to give them credit on their timing. The mob knew when to make an entrance. There were ten of them that stepped from the woods this time. Every soul may be individual and unique in the eyes of the Lord, but Golden had seen so many of these types of ruffians that they were all starting to look the same to him. They all seemed to wear the same ragged clothes, walk with the same tough-guy swagger, and smell of the same cologne: liquid courage. The only difference today was that these men weren't armed. That was a relief at least.

The mob crossed from the tree line to the riverbank like a troop of schoolyard bullies. They had the usual mob setup—the leader in front surrounded by a few strong-arm types, their flanks consisting of weaker men who, if not for the ability to hide behind others, would no doubt lack the courage to show their faces at all. It was usually easy enough to tell who the leader was—it was whoever enjoyed the sound of his own voice the most.

"This here a Mormon baptizin'?" the ringleader challenged as they approached.

Golden stepped forward, placing himself between the mob and the Saints. "Yes, it is." Why any man would go out of his way to cause trouble for others instead of going fishing or swimming or doing anything else on a day like today, Golden would never know. Why even bother?

The leader looked Golden and the others over, peering with special curiosity at Mabel and Elder Welch in their white clothing. Maybe it was the first time it occurred to him you could wear white without a pointy hood. As usual, Golden was taller than anyone else there, saint and mobber alike, but it didn't seem to matter a lick to this fellow. He fixed Golden with a mean eye and spoke loud enough for the entire assembly to hear.

"Jess wanna let ya know that if y'all dare to baptize these folks, we gonna up an' toss 'em in the river." He tucked his thumbs into his belt loops and gave a cocky snort. "That's what we gonna do." He looked quite pleased with himself. He had told the good-for-nothing Mormons a thing or two. The men around him nodded in agreement.

Golden paused, not quite sure if he'd heard that right. He

was pretty sure it was supposed to be a threat, but throwing a person into the river when that's where they wanted to go wasn't much of a threat at all. *Oh, please, Br'er Fox, don't throw me in the briar patch!* They may as well have threatened them with a wet willy or a severe Dutch rub. Perhaps this group hadn't attended the same mob school as some of the others.

Still, there was no use in risking unnecessary harm to the Saints, and Golden felt it best to treat the men seriously. Instead of pointing out that the water was where the Saints intended to go in the first place, he answered respectfully. "Fair enough. But before you do that, if it's all right, I'd like for us to sing a hymn."

He waited a moment for a reaction from the men. When none of them made any objection, Golden turned to the members.

"Truth Reflects upon Our Senses." He called out the name of the first hymn that came to mind. Golden had never conducted music before, but the choristers he'd seen just flapped their arms about, and no one paid them much attention anyhow, so he supposed he'd be all right given the circumstances. He raised his hands to begin and then cocked his head back to the mob. "Feel free to join in if you like."

Golden launched into song. The members were a bit shaky at first, but their voices grew in confidence as they gave life to the familiar strains.

> Truth reflects upon our senses
> Gospel light reveals to some
> If there still should be offenses
> Woe to them by whom they come
> Judge not that ye be not judged
> Was the counsel Jesus gave
> Measure given, large or grudged
> Just the same you must receive
> Blessed savior, thou wilt guide us
> Till we reach that blissful shore
> Where the angels wait to join us
> In thy praise forevermore.

It was a rough but ultimately beautiful rendition. Like all great hymns, it illustrated the basic truths of the gospel in a clear and simple manner.

When they finished singing, Golden smiled at the members with satisfaction, then looked at the mob. The leader didn't say anything, and none of them moved. Golden nodded quietly to Elder Welch to proceed, and he took Mabel by the hand. She glanced nervously once at the mob, then followed bravely into the river. It gurgled around their ankles as they entered. They continued in until they were waist-deep in the clear water. The mob remained motionless. Elder Welch held Mabel's wrist, then, looking up at the shore, asked, "If you'll kindly remove your hats."

Astonishingly, the mobbers removed their hats without so much as a peep. A few smoothed down their hair but otherwise stood still, holding their hats respectfully in their hands.

Golden and Elder Davis stood witness as Elder Welch performed the baptism. The smile on Mabel's face as she emerged from the water was so joyous Golden found himself smiling as well. The members met them with blankets and towels as they stepped from the water so they could dry off.

Golden glanced with apprehension at the mob again, but the men still showed no sign of moving. The leader's face was unreadable. Golden didn't know what was going through his mind, but there was no use in risking it any longer. He decided to forgo the closing prayer, opting to get the Saints moving along while they still could. Quickly and quietly, he ushered the members on their way, hastily bringing up the rear himself. They walked up the bank, giving the mob wide berth, circling to where their horses and wagons were tied.

To Golden's alarm, the mob fell in step behind them. Maybe they hadn't gotten away so easily. The hymn had thrown the mob off a bit, but its effect hadn't lasted long.

He thought about making a break for it, but not all the Saints were unhitched or ready to go. They would be caught if they tried to run. Golden had already pushed his luck further than he ever hoped, but it looked like he'd have to push it a little more. Still walking, he drew Elder Davis in close to him.

"Get the Saints out of here." Then he turned to meet the mob. If the mob really wanted trouble, there wouldn't be much he could do, but he hoped to cut them off or at the least slow them enough that the rest of the members could get away. Bracing himself, Golden was prepared for a fight, but he wasn't prepared for what happened next.

The mob stopped no more than a heartbeat away. They were close enough that he could see the color of their eyes. Golden's nerves were jumping like a wild bull, but the mob leader looked even more nervous. He didn't look like he was itching for a fight. In fact, he looked humble. Instead of standing aggressively, he was wringing his hat anxiously in his hands. He glanced at Golden, then down at his own feet.

"We were jess wondrin'," he said softly, "would y'all come back an' sing that song again?"

If Golden had to be honest with himself, which he was because he knew no other way, it was the last thing on earth he ever expected to hear. He exchanged a surprised look with the elders who had stopped behind him, then looked back at the mob.

"Yes, we can do that." Golden was humbled himself by the mob's response. The astounded but relieved members and elders began regrouping behind him.

"An' mister?" The leader looked down bashfully again. When he looked up, Golden was again surprised to see traces of tears forming in his eyes. "Will you teach me 'bout your gospel?"

A warm smile spread across Golden's face. "We'd be delighted."

And that's just what they did.

CHAPTER 25

TESTING THE WATER

Do not go where the path may lead, go instead where there is no path and leave a trail.

—*Ralph Waldo Emerson*

Golden sat at his desk shuffling through papers. To Golden, doing paperwork was akin to sweeping up mouse turds. He was sure that it was the entire difference between the celestial kingdom and outer darkness. The unfortunate souls in perdition would spend eternity looking after small crap while those in heaven would be able to get out and do the real work. He would rather have been out with his elders and among the Saints, for it was there he was the happiest. But for the time being, he was living in a less than celestial world and paperwork was still a part of his duties, so he endured it the best he could.

George Albert sat across from him, reading aloud from a list of recent mission statistics.

"One hundred eight missionaries, nine hundred and fifty-four meetings held," he said, adjusting his trademark glasses. "Sixteen thousand five hundred seventy-six families visited, twenty-two thousand tracts distributed, and seventy-one baptisms held."

"And no deaths and only a few beatings to speak of." Golden added his own stats to the pile. "Not a bad quarter."

Mark Twain once said that there were three kinds of lies: lies, damned lies, and statistics. Golden didn't place too much faith in numbers but acknowledged they could be a reasonable thermometer of the work and right now the temperature was pretty good. Certainly the best it had been since he'd arrived.

"No, not too bad at all," George Albert agreed with a smile. He had quickly gotten used to the president's sense of humor. Though the idea of considering "only a few beatings" a good thing was still odd to both of them.

Golden stood, stretching his legs and reaching to the ceiling. He could nearly touch it when he stretched like that. He turned and looked out the front window.

It was a beautiful day in the South, and the rich soil of the road soaked up the high summer sun. Lookout Mountain stood high above them like an old friend. With the busy effort required by the work and the ever-present threat of mob trouble a constant worry on his mind, it was all too easy to overlook how beautiful it really was down here. Despite whatever difficulties they may have had, things were moving forward again, and Golden was feeling pretty good about it. He turned back to George Albert.

"George, I've been thinking. I have a mind to try preaching a meeting here in the city."

George Albert looked shocked. He knew what consequences preaching in the city could bring. His own experiences here so far and Golden's explicit warnings to the elders had made it more than clear.

For the most part, people tolerated the elders being around as long as their activities remained out of the way. Proselytizing in the city itself might be pushing their goodwill too far. Past attempts to preach in larger cities had never ended well. George Albert imagined a time would come when people's hearts would be softened enough that things would change, but he wasn't sure if that day was today.

"I thought that was considered too risky."

"Hell, down here it's risky just going to the outhouse," Golden answered. "It's just a look-see. I'd like to test the public sentiment, see how they're feeling about us. If it goes well, we'll continue. If it doesn't . . . " He paused. He knew full well what could happen if it didn't go well. "If it doesn't, then we'll wait and try again later."

"What would you like me to do?" George Albert asked. Golden could see that George Albert wasn't as optimistic as he was about it, but Golden was speaking as the president of the mission, and George Albert was nothing if not obedient. Golden really thought a lot of the kid. If he stuck to his guns, he might be somebody one day.

"Send a telegram to Elder Bean and Elder Thomas. They're not far from here. Have them secure us a meeting place for a few weeks from now and get the word out. I'll take care of the rest."

George Albert jotted down his notes, then rose and put on his coat and hat. He paused as he opened the door. "Are you sure you want to do this?"

Golden wasn't entirely sure, but it was worth a shot.

"What's the worst that could happen? Other than getting shipped home in a pine box?"

George Albert nodded weakly and stepped outside.

Elder Bean and Elder Thomas were serving in the area around Ridgeside, on the edge of Chattanooga. They, like all the elders, had a real affinity for the president, so when he asked them to arrange for a meeting place, they had gone whole hog. A few weeks later Golden and George Albert sat with them in the upper room of the Hamilton County courthouse. It didn't get much more "in town" than that. Golden had been hoping to test the waters, not do a cannonball, but here he was.

During the war, the courthouse had been taken over by the Confederates and used as a prison. Afterward it remained in use as Chattanooga's municipal building and jail until the county purchased it and converted it into the courthouse. It had been recently remodeled, but its glory was sadly to be short-lived.

Less than twenty years from the day Golden sat with his elders inside, the courthouse would be struck by lightning in a violent spring storm and burn down. For now it stood tall and proud, its five-story clock tower overlooking the wide grass lawn. Fine brickwork lined the edges where it butted up against the paved sidewalk running along 4th and Market streets.

The room they were in today was not the main courtroom but a multipurpose space, used for public meetings and such. It suited Golden's purpose exactly. A bank of large windows ran along one wall of the room, looking over the street and letting the late morning sun stream inside, creating pools of sharply contrasting light and dark. A simple pulpit stood at the far end of the room from the entrance, and Golden and the others sat on the quilted seats placed behind it on the stand. In front of them stood enough rows of wooden pews to hold two or three hundred adults. They were completely empty.

The elegant stained-oak grandfather clock in the corner began to toll ten o'clock, the hour the meeting had been planned to begin. Its chime echoed inside the barren room. Golden looked over the vacant benches. He hadn't been sure what to expect today. Maybe an empty room was as receptive an audience as he could have hoped for.

"We placed a notice in the paper and handed out tracts on the street," apologized Elder Bean, "People should know about it. I thought at least *someone* would show up."

Golden shrugged. "Well, we tried. I said I wanted to test the temperature of the people, and I'd say we've found it."

As far as Golden was concerned, if the people didn't want to hear the Mormons—and they obviously didn't—it was better to be told by an empty room rather than one full of angry, hateful men. Now he knew, and they could get back to preaching in rural areas as they always had.

"What was your sermon on anyhow?" Elder Thomas asked.

"I thought I'd start out simple, talk about faith and repentance." Golden raised his hands in a what-are-you-gonna-do motion.

"That's a pity. It sounds like it would have been a good sermon," said Bean. "Too bad."

"I can always save it for the next time I have to speak," said Golden. He gathered his scriptures and notes and readied to leave. That's when he heard the sound of boots in the hallway. To Golden's delight, a man walked in. Perhaps people had decided to show up fashionably late. The man had his head down, his face buried beneath the wide brim of his hat. Without so much as a glance at the elders, he took a seat near the back, slouching down in the corner. A moment later a few more men followed him through the door.

George Albert leaned over to Golden with a grin. "It appears you get to give that sermon after all."

Men were filing inside in a steady stream now, and the back few rows were almost completely filled. Golden's initial excitement began to melt into unease as he watched the growing assembly. He shot a glance at Bean and Thomas. From the look on their faces, they sensed it too. George Albert's excitement waned when he noticed his companion's faces.

"What is it?" he asked.

"No women or children," Golden whispered to him.

"What does that mean?"

"Trouble."

George Albert looked out over the crowd again. Only now did he see what the others had noticed right away. Sure enough, there wasn't a single woman or child among the congregation. All in all, about twenty men had come in the room. They were harsh-looking souls, much more so than you would ever expect to encounter on the Chattanooga streets, especially this time of day. Some carried poorly hidden liquor bottles in their coats. It was a sure bet there were clubs or worse concealed there as well. The entire mob was sitting directly between the elders and the only exit. The last man to enter locked the door behind him and took a seat.

They were in trouble, all right. Golden looked quickly around the room. The windows were open and could be used as a last resort, but even if they could make it to one, they were still high on the second story of the building. It was a long way down to the unforgiving ground below.

Golden kicked himself. He had been rash, overconfident in his rush to preach in the city. He was willing to pay the price for his pride, if that was his fate. *But please don't let these good elders come to harm on account of me*, he thought.

He looked at his elders. They were scared too. He looked at the mob. The fellow that had locked the door was staring right at him, sucking his teeth. It was the only noise in the entire room. The men were no longer even bothering to conceal their drinking flasks or weapons. One fellow picked at a calloused hand with a knife so big it was almost a sword.

Golden had seen enough fights in his time, he knew how these things went. Someone was going to make the first move. Guessing that he wouldn't like the mob's move, Golden thought he'd try his first. He'd come here to preach, and that's what he intended to do. He hoped that if he could just give his sermon and invite the Spirit into the room, perhaps it might soften the hearts of the men and he and the elders might be spared whatever evil they had in mind. It was a slim hope at best, but it was either that or the window or worse. As he stood, George Albert grabbed his coat sleeve in protest, but Golden placed a hand on his shoulder.

"I will do the preaching. If they kill me, you need not bother further." He hoped his voice sounded reassuring, because he certainly didn't feel it. He took the pulpit and looked apprehensively over the men, who sat like slavering wolves waiting for something to tear their teeth into.

"The gospel . . . " his voice cracked. There was a mocking chuckle from the back of the room. Golden cleared his throat, which didn't help the tremor in his voice. It was as shaky as his knees, but he was going to keep his nerves if it was the last thing he did, which, he realized, it might be. He opened his mouth and tried again, "The gospel of Jesus Christ is built around the principles of faith and repentance. Faith, in God and in Jesus Christ—"

He stopped. You didn't need a degree to know these brutes didn't have the least amount of interest in what he was saying. He doubted if a single word he'd said had even registered in their ears.

What can you say to men such as this? You can try to reason with them. Maybe try and talk your way out of it, appeal to their better sensibilities, assuming they have any. Whatever you do, you don't want to provoke them further. You definitely don't want to bring up an already controversial hot topic, one so laden with venom, one so divisive in nature that it meant your death just to speak of it. Yet that was just the kind of idea that popped into Golden's mind.

He shook his head and tried speaking about the much safer topic of faith and repentance. But the impression was undeniable, as strong as anything he'd ever felt before.

His brow knit together as he looked at the assembled messengers of hate before him. They were shifty, fidgeting in their seats. The leader took a long swig from his flask. Golden could smell it from across the room. Whiskey or 'shine—something foul. Golden remembered once thinking that the worst thing about alcohol was the smell. He realized he'd been wrong. The worst thing about alcohol was its ability to give false courage to the hearts of cowardly men.

As if he could read Golden's mind, the man set his bottle down on the bench and stood. The others began to follow. Golden was out of time. His grip on the pulpit tightened. To say what he felt was suicide. But so was not saying anything at all. He had only one shot at this.

Golden opened his mouth and took it.

CHAPTER 26

OUT OF THE
FRYING PAN...

Lettin' the cat outta the bag is a whole lot easier than puttin' it back in.

—*Southern Saying*

In September of 1857, nearly forty years before Golden stood surrounded by a murderous mob in the Hamilton County courthouse, a wagon train of emigrants from Arkansas found themselves passing through Utah Territory on their way to California.

The 120-member Fancher-Baker party, as the wagon train was called, had stopped briefly in Salt Lake to restock its supplies, a common practice for wagon trains at the time. The steady traffic helped earn Salt Lake its nickname "the crossroads of the West" and brought a constant influx of people, news, and goods from the east, in part fulfilling Brigham Young's prophecy that one day merchandise would be available in Salt Lake as plentifully and inexpensively as back east. However, the party's timing proved to be tragic.

Earlier in the year, two pieces of bad news reached the Mormons in Utah. The first was that the beloved leader Parley P. Pratt had been murdered while on a mission in Arkansas by a man whose wife had left him to join the Saints as one of Pratt's plural wives.

The second piece of news was that a detachment of roughly one thousand five hundred soldiers of the United States Army had been deployed to come to Utah. No one knew what to expect when they arrived. Drawing from their past experience with persecution and harassment, the Mormons prepared for the worst. Expecting an all-out invasion of biblical proportions, they began stockpiling grain and making ready for a siege.

The Saints at the time had no way of knowing that the army's eventual arrival would be peacefully met with no hostilities on either side. That remained in the future. And so it was in the midst of this paranoid state that the Fancher-Baker party arrived in Salt Lake. They were quickly disappointed to learn that the Saints were unwilling to trade their grain and were forced to depart less well stocked than hoped for. They moved on, heading south, following the Old Spanish Trail that would lead them down past Cedar City and out of Utah.

Rumor quickly began to spread that one of Parley P. Pratt's widows had recognized a member of the wagon train as being present at her husband's murder. The truth of this has never been validated, but gossip has never waited on truth. Hearsay and suspicion continued to follow the wagon party like a plague. By the time they had reached the Mountain Meadows area it was being told that they had poisoned a spring near Corn Creek, killing eighteen head of cattle and causing the deaths of two or three people who had eaten the dead animals. It was also being widely circulated that the party had taunted, vandalized, and harassed Mormons and Native Americans along the route, by some accounts going so far as to claim that they had the gun that "shot the guts out of Old Joe Smith." True or not, these stories spread through the Mormon communities like wildfire through dry brush in late summer.

Their route southward brought the wagon train past the towns of Parowan and Cedar City. Isolated from contact with

Salt Lake, the local leaders held several meetings deciding what should be done with the offensive wagon party. Some were in favor of "chastening" the emigrants, while most opposed the idea, preferring to have the party leave the area of their own accord. The consensus to leave the party alone left a few of the local citizenry disgruntled and, against the will of the local Church and militia leaders, they conspired to act. A plan was formulated to convince the local Indians to attack the company, killing some of them and stealing their livestock. They could then lay the blame for the entire attack on the Indians.

Good readers, at this point, yours truly is going to have to step forward and tell you, in no uncertain terms, that these people are addle-headed idiots. You would think that people would have learned by now that answering an atrocity with another atrocity isn't really an answer at all. Especially people who claimed to believe the gospel of Christ. But if there is one thing we can learn from history, it's that we still haven't learned anything from history.

The Fancher-Baker party arrived in Mountain Meadows expecting several days of rest before making the next push on their journey. A grassy, mountain-ringed valley about thirty-five miles southwest of Cedar City, Mountain Meadows was a well-known stop along the Old Spanish Trail, ideal for watering and grazing livestock.

On September 7, the party was attacked by what appeared to be a group of Paiute Indians. Numbered among the Indians, however, were about fifty to sixty Mormon militiamen dressed as Native Americans. The Indians had initially been reluctant, but the militia leaders had promised them loot and convinced them that the emigrants were part of the approaching army who would kill Indians along with Mormon settlers.

Seven emigrants were slain immediately in the first assault, and sixteen more were wounded. They quickly circled their wagons, lowering them and chaining the wheels together in a protective corral. Shallow trenches were dug and dirt thrown beneath and into the wagons to shore up their defenses.

The attack continued for the next five days, during which time the besieged families had little or no access to fresh water or food. At one point, two emigrant horsemen were discovered a few miles outside the protective corral by some of the Cedar City militiamen. In an effort to contain the situation they killed one of the riders, but the other escaped back to the wagon train with the shocking news that their killers were white men, not Indians. The cat was out of the bag.

The idiots who had thought up the idiotic idea in the first place had now idiotically botched their own plan. The assault was taking days longer than they had counted on, the local military command would soon learn they had disobeyed their orders, and the wagon train now knew that whites were involved in the attack. The only way to ensure that no word of their involvement would ever get out called for one final act of desperate savagery.

On Friday, September 11, 1857, two Mormon militiamen approached the encircled wagons under the auspices of a white flag. They told the Fancher-Baker party that they had negotiated a truce with the Indians and would escort the emigrants to Cedar City, but they would have to leave their weapons behind and turn all their livestock and supplies over to the Indians. The emigrants were suspicious but had no water and didn't have enough ammunition left to fend off another attack. Hesitantly they agreed and were led from the encirclement under the guard of the militia.

The procession had traveled about a mile when a prearranged signal was given and the militia turned and shot down the men and older boys in the party. Some claim that the militia let the Indians execute the women and children, but regardless, the outcome was the same. When all was said and done, over 120 people lay dead, murdered in cold blood. If the wagon party had been guilty of anything, they were denied the very justice that the Mormons themselves had sought for so long.

The massacre is an abomination that will forever stain the history of the Church. While it's true that it occurred at a time of great fear and misunderstanding between both the federal government and the Mormons in Utah Territory, no reason or motive can ever justify the end result.

Official investigations into the incident were interrupted by the Civil War but resumed shortly after the cease-fire. It was as if the whole thing, including the public mistrust and anger, had simply been put on pause. As soon as the investigation resumed the emotional outrage did as well, picking up right where it had left off. Indictments were served, and at least one of the leaders of the massacre was executed but it did little to calm the outrage of the American public. For years after, even the slightest mention of Mountain Meadows was enough to cause an uproar. For a Mormon to mention it, especially deep in the heart of the South, was nothing short of signing his own death warrant.

"Gentlemen!" Golden's voice was as high-pitched as ever, but it was filled with enough authority to make the approaching mob at least pause. Golden continued quickly. "You have not come here to listen to the gospel of Jesus Christ. I know what you have come for. You have come to find out about the Mountain Meadows massacre and polygamy, and God being my helper, I will tell you the truth!"

Why Golden would have the notion to open such a deadly can of worms before an already violent mob, no man knew, including Golden himself. When he opened his mouth, however, that's what came out. It was a jolt to everyone in the room. It wasn't what any of them expected to hear. It surprised Golden as well; it wasn't what he expected to say. But the tiger was out of the cage, and he saw little choice except to continue.

"The massacre at Mountain Meadows, for indeed a massacre is what it was, shall forever be a blot upon both this Church and our great nation. There is no excuse before man nor God for the actions taken by those men in 1857!" Golden was speaking both off the cuff and from the heart, his voice full of spiritual fervor.

Caught off guard, the leader grabbed the closest mobber by the coat, stopping him and the rest of the men. Never taking his eyes from Golden, he motioned for the men to sit down, which they did as silently as they had stood. Mistrust and curiosity mingled in the leader's eyes, but surprisingly he seemed content, for the time being at least, to settle back into his seat and listen.

For the next fifty minutes, Golden preached like his life depended on it, which of course, it did. Every member of the Church, and probably every citizen of the country, was at least moderately versed with the story of the massacre. Golden was no scholar, and while the incident certainly upset him, he had never delved into the matter much. He was sure that he would soon run out of things to say—that either his limited knowledge or his nerves or both would fail him. But his nerves held fast and so did his voice.

"... And any man that claims otherwise is a hypocrite and an enemy to God! In the name of Jesus Christ, amen!" He finished just as fiery as he'd begun. The room was silent as a tomb, silent enough that Golden could hear his own heart throbbing in his chest. He was sweaty from exertion, his throat was dry, and he was huffing for breath like he'd just run a country mile. He had gone on much longer than he believed he could, but he hadn't spoken a minute less than he'd felt prompted to. Or a minute more, for that matter. When he felt he'd said all he was supposed to, he stopped. He knew his words would have an effect. There was no question in his mind. What that effect would be, however, no man knew. At the very least he hoped his elders would get out alive. Most likely he'd just condemned them all to a brutal and undeserved death.

The conviction that had filled him for the last hour was gone now, and he felt completely drained. If the mob decided to attack after all, he wouldn't even have the strength to run for the window. He watched the crowd, hardly daring to breathe lest he disturb the delicate stillness.

For a small eternity, no one moved. Then the mob leader

rose to his feet, the rest of them rising with him. Golden's heart caught in his chest. Without a single word, the leader turned and walked out of the room. The rest of them shuffled out in the same way they'd come in, heads lowered, faces hidden, looking at the floor. The heavy clunk of their boots carried in the hall as they descended the stairs and exited the building.

It took every last ounce of Golden's energy to keep standing at the pulpit. He gripped it like a crutch for fear he might collapse. He was astonished at the things he'd just said. If he hadn't delivered the speech himself, he never would have believed it. But the Spirit had dictated it, and who was he to argue with that?

When the last of the mob left the room, George Albert stood and crossed to the window. He watched in awe as the men filtered out of the building, disappearing among the people on the street. "I don't believe it. They're gone." He looked at Golden, incredulous.

Relief flooded through Golden. He lowered himself slowly to the floor, leaning his head back against the podium, and enjoyed the simple act of breathing. He opened his eyes and realized the elders were staring at him like a miracle worker.

"Are you all right?" asked George Albert. Golden nodded weakly.

"Elders," he told them as serious as a heart attack, "I don't want you to ever repeat that sermon. It'll get you killed." They didn't need to be told twice.

They ate their lunch in the room, enjoying the light that poured in through the large windows. The fresh-baked bread, cold salami, and cheese purchased from a deli across the street tasted like a little slice of heaven. Golden's strength had returned, and the mood in the room was considerably lighter. Watching them all smile as they chatted among themselves, you'd never guess that these men had been in mortal danger less than an hour before.

"I told you it'd pan out just fine," Golden teased them. His mouth was full of food and his soul was full of playful bravado.

"You didn't seem so sure at first," George Albert countered.

"I wasn't!" Golden grinned, taking a bite of bread and slicing off a piece of salami. "I'll tell you, I don't think we'll be preaching in town again anytime soon!"

They laughed. Thank heavens they could laugh about it. *You and me, Lord, you and me*, Golden thought. He took another bite of his sandwich, savoring the taste. As he chewed, he heard a buzzing. It sounded like a bug—maybe some flies attracted to the smell of the salami. But he didn't see any flies, and the sound was growing steadily louder. It occurred to him that it was coming from outside.

"What in tarnation is that racket?" A moment later he realized it was music. Or at least a vague resemblance of it.

They crossed to the windows to see what was going on. To his eternal surprise and delight, an honest-to-goodness brass band had formed in the street below and now stood facing the courthouse honking away and kicking up a row. It was a real ragtag assortment of people and instruments. A tuba oompahed away next to a rusty trombone and a fiddle. Some of the musicians looked as ragged as their instruments. While you couldn't say much for their musicality, their enthusiasm was undeniable. Golden thought they might be playing the new one by Sousa, but it was hard to tell.

Looking the ensemble over, Golden did a double take. "Aren't those fellows some of the men who were just in here?" George Albert and the elders looked closer.

"By Jove, you're right," declared Elder Bean. "I definitely recognize the man on the cornet."

Golden wasn't sure if he was more astounded by the fact that some of the mob had come back or that they could play instruments. Elder Bean leaned out the window as they wrapped up a number, waving an arm.

"Hello, there!" he called down. The band paused and looked up. "Excuse me, but what are you gentlemen doing?"

"We're serenading that tall, skinny fellow who gave us the sermon," one of them shouted back up as if it were the most obvious thing in the world.

"Yeah," pitched in the flutist. "Why, that man's so tough he'd fight a buzz saw and give it three rounds' head start!"

Tall, skinny fellow? Me? Golden peeked his head out the window to get a better look. Seeing him, the band gave a cheer, and several of them threw their hats into the air. Golden waved, and the band launched into another rowdy number. It wasn't any better than the first, but it was certainly louder. Golden couldn't help but smile in spite of himself.

"I've never had a brass band dispense music after one of my talks before," Golden told George Albert, shouting to be heard over the cacophony. He leaned against the windowsill, contentedly tapping a finger to the beat. The impromptu concert attracted the attention of a large number of passersby, and soon quite a throng of people was gathered around watching the band. It occurred to Golden that for once, he had the best seat in the house.

He was enjoying the event when something beyond the band and the throng caught his eye. He almost missed it at first. On the far side of the street, from inside a store window and framed by dead poultry and slices of meat, a face was glaring straight at him. The man was a few years older, the silver in his hair sharper than ever. Golden squinted against the afternoon sun, peering closer. There was no question about it. Golden was looking right into the disapproving scowl of the Reverend Charles A. Weatherbee.

"Well, I'll be . . . " Golden muttered to himself.

"What?" George Albert asked.

Golden didn't realize he'd spoken out loud. He turned to George Albert. "Oh, nothing. I just saw an old friend. I didn't know he was still around."

Golden looked back to the store window, but Weatherbee was gone.

CHAPTER 27

INTO THE FIRE

Never approach a bull from the front, a horse from the rear, or a fool from any direction.

—*Cowboy Proverb*

Brothers!"

The night was unseasonably hot, and the air inside the dimly lit chapel was stifling. The cramped cluster of men packed inside didn't help. It was overheated and suffocating. There were no women or children here tonight.

Reverend Weatherbee stood at the front, his face lit in an eerie glow from the flickering lamps. The light of the flames twitched in his eyes and cast multiple shadows that danced like a convocation of witches across the walls and ceiling. He looked severe enough during the day. By this light, he looked downright frightening.

"A few years ago, half a dozen of these Mormons arrived in southern Tennessee. Now they number several hundred. They are superstitious and oppose the Southern way of life!" His rich voice filled the space easily, his bony fingers holding the podium in a death grip. "They are a threat to Southern womanhood. To virtue. They are a threat to God!" He slammed a fist into the pulpit.

Kenneth hadn't seen the reverend ablaze like this in some

time. He had preached a fiery discourse, railing against the spreading Mormon evil, and the gathered men were fired up. The Mormon threat hadn't gone away at all. If anything, it was growing worse.

One of the men stood, shaking an angry fist, shouting out to the whole assembly, "How about that Joe Smith speaking to God and his angels?" It was Larry Crutchfield, another local coal miner Kenneth knew well. Larry wasn't the brightest star in the sky but was a good Southern man.

"It's blasphemy!" another shouted in return, and the congregated men voiced their agreement.

Weatherbee looked them over smugly. He had spent years building up *his* kingdom. He had sweated and bled among the people of the South. He had seen its once proud foundations destroyed in the turmoil wreaked by the heathens in the North and their war. And now, as a final insult, these Mormons dared spread their sedition in *his* city, to *his* people. They did not belong here. This was not their place. He had made a decision, deep in his mind, firm and irrevocable. He had built *his* kingdom; he would defend it at any cost. Let the Mormons come with their gold bible and their lies. Let them come and see.

The reverend let the men voice their say, then took over again with the raise of his hand.

"Time was, they hid in the woods, preaching in small towns and where ignorant men were foolish enough to listen." Weatherbee held up a copy of the *Chattanooga Times*. The headline boldly declared

Brass Band Serenades Mormon Preacher

"Now they are preaching in the city. Our city! And they are greeted with brass bands and music!" Contempt permeated his voice, and murmurs of agreement rolled through the chapel like the rumble of approaching thunder.

Kenneth knew the reverend was right. If ever there was a time to rid themselves of the Mormons, this was it. The other men knew it too. The reverend slammed the newspaper down on the pulpit.

"We can't have it! We will not stand for it!" His voice was fever pitch. "We must let them and any who support them know that those who blaspheme and those who teach their lies to our people will face the justice of a wrathful God!"

The chorus of "Amen!" echoed ominously in the dead of the night.

Despite the heat, Golden had little trouble falling asleep. One thing about hard work is that it never fails to deliver a solid night's rest at the end of the day. He had barely been able to keep his eyes open before he all but collapsed into bed when they returned home that evening. He was so soundly asleep that he didn't even stir at the muffled noises of men and horses outside the mission home, nor did he notice the sudden blazing of firelight as it blasted through the bedroom window to paint the entire room in its simmering glow.

It wasn't until a large rock shattered the window, showering his bed with broken glass and wood, that he bolted awake. George Albert, asleep in the bed furthest from the window, sat up as well.

"What was that?"

There were shouts outside. Golden didn't even have time to look out the window before all you-know-what broke loose. *BLAM! BLAM! BLAM!* Bullets filled the air, punching holes in the walls and ceiling, shattering the remains of the window. Golden dove to the floor. He grabbed his trousers and shoes, frantically crawling away from the window. Rounds poured into the building in a furious fusillade of flying ferrous fragments, destroying everything in their path. The lantern on the wall shattered, kerosene spilling down the wall and over the floor, its smell mixing with what had to be burning pitch. Bullets tore through the bed where Golden had been sleeping just moments before.

Lying low enough to make the rug jealous, Golden managed to wiggle into his trousers. The large picture frame jumped and fell broken to the floor. Golden looked toward the back of the room. George Albert lay motionless in his bed.

"No!" Panic seized Golden's heart. He scrambled over to the bed.

"George! George!" He grabbed George Albert by the arm. George Albert looked over at him.

"Are you all right?" Golden all but shrieked.

"I'm fine." George Albert was as calm as a toad in the sun.

Bullets were still puncturing the building. Firelight poured in through the new holes, making shafts of light that pierced the smoke and dust like a pincushion. Scattered and drifting feathers alternately caught and blocked the light in a ghostly strobe, falling on the two men like snow.

George Albert's almost freakish calm despite the continuing barrage gave Golden pause. He was glad George Albert was all right, but he was caught off guard by the absolute lack of panic in the young man's face.

"Aren't you going to dress?" he finally asked.

George Albert shook his head. "You promised we'd be fine in God's service, so I'm going to stay right here." Crazy or not, he really meant it.

"Well, don't get killed on my account." Golden sat himself down on the floor beside the bed and crossed his arms. The impact of bullets was a staccato thudding against the wood. After what felt like an hour but was actually less than a minute, the guns stopped.

A deep Southern voice yelled from outside, "We're warning you, you Mormon heretics! We, the vanguard of righteous Southern society and virtue do hereby warn you to cease from any and all proselytizing activity, and you are hereby warned to leave immediately or face the wrath and the justice of God! You have been warned!"

"I think we've been warned," said George Albert.

Golden nodded agreement. "It would have been a hell of a lot easier if they'd just sent a telegram."

BLAM! BLAM! Both elders hunkered down again as the gunfire resumed. If the room weren't Swiss cheese before, it definitely was now. After another minute, the firing stopped and everything grew quiet.

"You all right?" Golden asked again.

"I'm fine. You?"

"Yes. This may be the first time in my life I am truly grateful for being so thin." He was joking, but his voice was clearly upset. Outside the murmur of voices and the sounds of horses grew faint.

"Sounds like they're leaving," said George Albert. Golden nodded. After another few minutes of silence from outside, Golden crawled across the room, carefully avoiding shards of glass and splintered wood. His bed was beyond repair, its stuffing hanging out like a gutted stuffed animal. The bed stand and ceramic bowl were gone. The cup he had given to Elder Shepherd the first night he'd arrived in the South lay broken on the floor. The remains of the curtains hung in tatters on the sides of the window frame. Golden tentatively raised his head, peeking over the sill to look outside.

"Are they still out there?" George Albert whispered, still in his bed.

"No, but I think it was the Klan."

"You sure?"

"Pretty sure."

Outside a large, wooden cross burned where it had been planted in the middle of the street, its flames rising almost as tall as the building and sending ashes high into the night sky. There were footprints and wagon tracks aplenty, but there was no one to be seen. From the amount of tracks, there had been quite a few men. They were lucky the Klansmen didn't decide to storm the building.

"You think they're serious?" George Albert asked.

"We've heard these threats before and endured a lot worse. We'll just have to lie low for a while, until this thing blows over." Most likely the mob had gotten some burr or other under their saddle and had to vent some steam. If they kept quiet for a while, it would go away like it always did. Golden stood and walked toward the door.

"Where are you going?" asked George Albert.

"I'm going to sleep in the other room. My bed's shot to hell."

Outside the cross continued to burn long into the night.

CHAPTER 28

PERSECUTION

Man was created a little lower than the angels and has been getting a little lower ever since.

—*Josh Billings*

Torches and noise. Elder Martin woke in an instant. Someone had kicked in the door. Murmurs, shouts, curses, and white hoods everywhere. They were on him already. He tried to break free. Were they armed? He thought he saw a gun. Their hands were on him, grabbing arms, hair. Where was Elder Fuller? He couldn't see him.

He kicked blindly. His foot connected with someone who fell back, cursing. Martin wrenched an arm free. Several more hands grabbed him. Blows rained on his head. And then he was on the floor. The hits and the kicks came fast and hard. Several ribs went. He could feel his face beginning to swell. He was being dragged across the floor. Out the door. His head bounced against the step. He could feel his legs scraping across the dirt but couldn't get them to move. What was that smell? Hard to smell anything over the taste of your own blood. Torches? One of them had a knife. He was fading in and out—not good—riding the line between consciousness and oblivion. Fire glinted off the knife's blade. He hardly noticed they were tearing off his clothes.

Where was Fuller? Still couldn't see him. Only white sheets.

They were taking something off a wagon. Buckets. Water? Some of the water splashed on one of them, it was steaming and sticky. He cursed. That smell. Not water. Tar.

"That's it! Cover him good!"

In order to be pourable, the tar had to be heated to well over one hundred and twenty degrees. At that temperature, it doesn't just scald. Skin burns within seconds. Blisters form within minutes that feel like years. The burns were untreatable until the tar was removed, a process which took a lot of skin with it, leaving the victim scarred. Victims sometimes died, not from burns but from infections that came later. It wasn't a one-time torture, it affected them for life.

Martin strained to move, but his body betrayed him. Everything below the waist was gelatin. He clawed weakly at the earth, and he was kicked several more times for the effort. He couldn't even tell what was broken anymore. It was all one big ball of pain. A heavy boot pinned him to the ground. He could barely move as it was. The foot was overkill. He was curled in a fetal ball when the searing tar hit him. He couldn't even scream, his mouth stretching wide in a silent rictus of agony. Klansmen jumped back to avoid the splashing tar, its black splatter a sharp contrast against their white robes.

The pain was less now, his mind mercifully beginning its retreat. He was dimly aware of feathers coming down like snowflakes and someone crouching down beside him. The last thing he heard was a voice near his ear, gravelly and thick with accent.

"You tell 'em, boy. You tell the others we're coming for 'em!"

Then all was darkness.

"Five more beaten, three with whips, and four were tarred and feathered," George Albert waved the papers weakly in front of him. "There's at least ten other incidents here."

The downstairs of the mission home had really gotten the little end of the horn. Entire chunks of the walls and framing were simply gone, all chawed up into the layers of sawdust that coated everything. Doors, walls, furnishings, even parts of the stairs had fallen before the assault. The front door was little more than a frame, the remains of the door itself hanging catawampus by a single hinge. That the Klan hadn't rushed in was still amazing.

The major gaps had been boarded over, but light still leaked through the bullet holes, which were everywhere. If Golden and George Albert had been down here during the attack, they would certainly have been killed. He counted it as yet another blessing from God that they hadn't been.

Golden's face was grave, his brow furled with concern. "At least no one's been killed, thank the Lord for that." He stood and started to pace. He wasn't worried about his personal safety and not even worried about the mobs, really. He was concerned with the welfare of his elders. "This is my fault. I should have taken their warnings more seriously."

The assault on the mission home was only the start of a violent storm that continued to rage out of control. It seemed to have inspired other anti-Mormon forces across the region. Elders from Arkansas to Carolina were being harassed, threatened, and worse. Sometimes the mobs were just random hooligans, but as often as not, they were robed Klansmen. Either way, the results were the same. Elders were being attacked, the contents of their valises scattered, their tracts and scriptures torn up and scattered to the wind. Several were tied to trees and whipped. Wounded and beaten elders began to arrive with alarming frequency at the mission home, each one worse off than the last.

It was as if Satan had seen the increase in the Lord's work and had redoubled his own in response. Golden felt George Albert looking at him, his eyes asking the question, "What are you going to do?" What *was* he going to do? If the violence continued at this pace, it was the end of missionary work in the South. But first things first, he had to see to the safety of his elders. He looked somberly at George Albert.

"Call the elders together."

CHAPTER 29

MEETING IN
THE WOODS

*Wolves have howled at the moon for centuries, but it is
still there.*

—Proverb

Golden wanted to gather the entire mission together
in one spot, but that was logistically impossible. The physi-
cal geography of the mission itself was simply too large to make
gathering all the elders practical. Besides, the mission home
wasn't safe, and it wasn't large enough to hold all the missionaries anyhow. The compromise was to call the elders together in
their individual districts. He wanted to ensure that there would
be enough elders in each place that their numbers alone would
discourage any further acts of violence against them. Hearken-
ing back to B.H.'s edict about avoiding large cities, they decided
it best to find rural, out of the way places to meet within each
district. It wasn't as convenient for Golden and George Albert,
as they would have to travel to several places now instead of just
one, but it seemed to be the best immediate solution available.

Over time, Golden had been able to get to know each and
every one of his missionaries. To the last, they were decent,
upright men in the eyes of God. There wasn't one of them he

wasn't proud to know. Normally being righteous men would be a good thing, but if history was any indicator, persecutions had always followed those who taught the gospel, affecting everyone from Joseph Smith all the way to the Savior Jesus Christ himself. In fact, Jesus had suffered more than all of them combined. Why, if Jesus wasn't exempt from persecution, Golden reasoned, there was no excuse for any of them to be exempt either. It wasn't a pleasant thought, but it was a testimony of the truthfulness of the gospel. Why else would the devil fight against it so fiercely?

Golden planned to travel in a counterclockwise direction around the mission. He didn't have much of a plan beyond gathering and visiting his elders but hoped to have something more concrete figured out before he got back around to Tennessee. Heavy decisions lay ahead of all of them, and it was the outcome that worried Golden the most. His first stop was near Rome, Georgia, roughly seventy-five miles southeast of Chattanooga.

Nestled snuggly in the foothills of the Appalachian Mountains, Rome had served as the seat of Floyd County since 1835. It took its name from the fact that, like its Italian namesake, it was built on seven hills with a river running between them. During the Civil War, Rome had been defended against the North by General Nathan Bedford Forrest, who is reputed to have served as a major figure in the postwar establishment of the Ku Klux Klan, a strange irony in light of the current situation. Forrest may have been gone, but his dubious legacy remained.

Golden's train didn't arrive until late in the day, and it was dark by the time he reached the place where the meeting had been planned. The night sky was clear, and the moon was as full as could be, shedding its pale light on the fourteen elders gathered around a modest campfire. Golden and George Albert made their total number sixteen. They were standing in the middle of a small clearing located next to a large stream. Golden listened to the gurgling and bubbling of the water. It occurred to him that it might be a nice place to come fishing, if it were daytime and the circumstances were entirely different. He turned his attention from the stream to the elders seated on logs and rocks on the ground before him. Elders Thomas and Bean were among them. The elders looked at Golden, not sure what they were about to hear. With Golden, you truly never knew.

"Good evening, brethren. Thanks for coming out on short notice. As you know, we have ourselves quite a situation here." He looked over the assembled missionaries. It struck him again how young they were; most of them were in their early twenties. It made Golden wonder if he'd ever really been that youthful. Granted he'd been a bit older when he was called, but still, sometimes he felt as old as Methuselah.

The elders were doing their best to wear brave faces, but they were plenty scared. One look at them and you could tell that much. Stories of trouble had traveled far and fast, but the elders didn't need story or rumor to be nervous—many of them had witnessed firsthand the actions of brutish men or been victims themselves. The call for emergency gatherings could have only increased their fears. Golden had tried to be as reassuring as possible in his letter, but everyone knew the situation was dire. A letter only meant that things were probably worse than they knew.

If they were scared, Golden didn't blame them, not in the least. He was plenty frightened himself. All their lives were at risk. What scared him the most was that the lives of the missionaries were his responsibility. They were looking to him for leadership. If he couldn't find the proper inspiration or chose the wrong course of action, he could very well get someone killed. *Please, Lord, anything but that.*

Golden had been thinking a lot about what he could say. He had a lot on his mind but in the end decided to cut straight to the chase.

"Brethren, I've given this a lot of prayer and thought, and before I say anything else, I want you to know if there is any man in this mission who doesn't wish to be here, you have my permission to go home. You will be honorably released."

The elders sat up and took notice. If he didn't have their full attention before, he certainly had it now. George Albert was as surprised as the rest of them. Golden had spoken with him quite a bit, discussing what things needed to be talked about, but he hadn't mentioned this.

Those familiar with Golden know that when he gave a talk, he often began with an attention-getting line, something strong or funny, just to make sure he had the attention of the audience. He once opened a talk with "Can you hear me?" When there was no response, he turned sideways, illustrating his thinness. "Can you see me?" Another talk began, "The Lord himself must like a joke or he wouldn't have made some of you people." An opener like that would be accompanied by his characteristic impish grin, and the audience would know it was a joke. There was no such grin on his face as he spoke tonight.

Golden knew from the way the missionaries were swapping disbelieving glances that his words had hit home. He knew very well what a temptation such an offer could be to homesick and frightened elders. But he meant it. At long last, Golden finally understood what B.H. had truly meant when he said that he'd rather send Golden home early and alive than in a pine box. It had nothing to do with money.

"Anyone?"

After a moment one elder raised his hand. It was Elder Allred from Layton. Golden had made the offer fair and square, but he was still afraid of this moment.

Elder Allred stood. All eyes were on him. "Excuse me, President, but are you serious?"

"Yes." As a heart attack. "God didn't force you to come here, and I won't force you to stay. If any of you want to go, you may. The rest of us will stay till we get through."

Elder Allred sat back down. He and the other elders remained perfectly still. Golden waited, giving them time to really think it over. He stood watching them look back at him. He wanted them to work it out in their own minds, but they sure were taking their sweet time.

Slowly it came to Golden that the elders weren't quiet because they were thinking it over. They were quiet because none of them were leaving. They were all looking at him, waiting to hear what he had to say next.

"No one?" Golden asked.

"We're staying," answered Elder Thomas.

"I'm not going anywhere," agreed Elder Allred. The firmness of their resolution was evident in their faces. There were nods of agreement from the rest of the elders. Golden couldn't help but smile. It was a tough choice in tough circumstances, and none of them were backing down. His heart filled with emotion as he looked at the men who sat before him.

"I can't even say how proud I am of all of you. I don't think you'll ever know how humbling your courage is to me, brethren. I needn't tell you we face difficult times. The adversary—"

Hearing something, he stopped. From the woods on the other side of the stream came a noise, distant at first but drawing closer. The elders had noticed it too and were all looking in the direction of the sound. It was a common sound, familiar to them all, but horrifying in the dark of night. It was the sound of horses and men. Speak of the devil . . .

The spectral sheets of the Klan moved through the trees beyond the stream. There was a slew of them; Golden counted at least thirty by their torches. They were mostly on foot, with some on horseback and a few in wagons. It was hard to tell from this distance, but he was sure most of them were packing iron. The great vanguard of the old South had come to defend her against unarmed godless heathens yet again. The Grand Wizard rode at the head of them like the marshal of an underworld parade, the green satin of his robe a shadow in the night. From their direction of travel, it was clear they weren't out marching at night just for exercise. They were heading toward the missionaries with specific intent.

So much for meeting outside the city and in large numbers. Golden's care and caution in trying to ensure the safety of the missionaries had been for naught. The mob had come anyhow. Golden wondered how many of the elders regretted their decision now. He did, but it was too late. His heart sank. Never in his life did he regret being wrong as much as he did right now.

The mob stopped on the far side of the stream. They couldn't have been more than a hundred feet away from where Golden stood. They hitched their horses and gathered a large pile of logs and lumber. At the grazing of a torch, the pile erupted into a great blaze, its flames climbing high into the night.

Golden could see bottles of rotgut being liberally passed around, the men lifting their hoods just enough to drink. They made a great show of loading their guns, firing the occasional shot into the night and creating quite a ruckus. The boisterous murmur of their voices carried on the evening breeze as they hooted and hollered like gremlins enrapt in frenzied devilment. Klansmen kept looking across the stream, loudly hurling threats and curses in the direction of the elders, but none had dared cross the stream yet. Several Klansmen took a large cauldron from the back of the wagon. It was a great black iron thing and took several men to place it onto the fire. Before long, a thick aroma permeated the air. Golden sniffed. It wasn't beef stew.

"Tar," said George Albert. Golden nodded. The smell was strong and unmistakable. He could see black ooze sticking to the branch that a Klansman was using to stir the steaming pot. Things were about to take a real turn for the worse. The missionaries were outnumbered and unarmed. The only thing that stood between them and the mob was the stream. It was only about ten feet across and shallow all the way. Crossing it would be no obstacle at all.

Golden turned back to the elders. "Brethren, I want you to go back to your quarters as quickly and as quietly as you can." He kept his voice as calm as he could. "Stick together. I want you to slip off that way." He pointed in the direction away from the Klan and their steaming black pot of pain.

"We're giving up?" questioned Bean.

"No, we're not giving up. But you are going back to some-place hopefully safe."

"What about you?"

"Don't you worry about a thing," Golden said. *That's my job*, he thought. Still he tried to be as encouraging as he could. "I was raised around scum like that. I know how to talk their language. If anything happens, just ship my body home."

The elders started to bellyache about leaving Golden there alone. It was flattering and humbling to know that they were concerned about him as well, but he would hear none of it.

"Do as your president asks," Golden said. "I mean it. Or I'll sock it to you myself." He raised a fist into empty air. Of course, Golden wasn't going to punch anyone and everyone knew it, but the elders saw that he was serious and reluctantly began leaving.

"What about you? I can't let—" George Albert started to object, but Golden cut him off.

"Smith, are you looking for a fight? Get outta here." Golden dismissed George Albert with a sharp nod in the direction the other elders were heading. George Albert paused long enough that Golden wasn't sure if he was going to listen or not. George Albert suddenly leaned in and gave Golden a bear hug, then obe-diently turned and followed after the last few departing elders.

Golden watched them disappear into the night. Their fire had burned down to nearly embers. That was good; it gave them more darkness to cover their retreat. Alone now, the full impact of his fear pressed down on him. He wanted nothing more than to see Jennie and the children, to tell them he loved them. But they were thousands of miles away. He hoped they would understand.

The mob finally noticed that something was going on in the Mormon camp. He could see them pointing and gathering toward the edge of their bonfire. It wouldn't be long before they made the move to cross the stream. Golden would have to keep them distracted long enough to give his elders time to get to a safe distance. He allowed himself one nervous sigh, then stepped out of the trees onto the bank of the stream. The smell of tar was so thick he could taste it.

From where he now stood, he could see the Klansmen's fantastic costumes more clearly than ever. It had never occurred to him before how much they looked like Klowns. The masks weren't frightening. They were something to hide behind. Who was truly scared here? Only a coward has to hide behind a mask, and liquor to boot, as if either could hide you from your own conscience.

Satisfied that his elders were well underway, Golden mustered his bravado, raised his hands to his mouth, and yelled as loudly as his voice would allow, "Hello! Can you hear me over there?"

They most certainly could. Still looking in the direction of the Mormons' dying campfire, it took them a minute to finally notice the tall, skinny shadow standing on the far bank. Even those who weren't looking before were looking now. Klansmen nudged each other, pointing and yelling select obscenities across at him. Golden was in for it now. He had tossed his hat in the proverbial ring. So he did the only thing he could do: he kept yelling.

"We're all finished over here. Do you know who we are?" Golden's voice sounded brave, but his eyes told a different story. Luckily, from where they stood, the sheets-for-brains Klansmen couldn't see his eyes.

"Yer them fobbin' Mormons!" they yelled back. "We warned you to get out. We gonna teach y'all a lesson!"

"That's right, we're Mormons!" Golden was yelling so loudly his voice nearly broke. "And let me tell you something—Mormons have horns!" He pantomimed the horns. "You cross that stream, and we'll gore the hell right out of you!"

There was a noise behind him. Startled, he turned to look. Emerging from the shadow of the tree line was George Albert and the rest of the elders. They had come back. Curse the stubborn elders and God bless them at the same time! He'd never been so grateful to have company before. They fanned out their ranks, forming a line along the bank beside him. George Albert gave him a nervous smile. Golden smiled grimly and looked back at the mob. Whatever was going to happen next, they were all in it together.

The babble among the Klansmen began at once.

"You don't s'pose that's true, do you?" asked a short Klansman.

"I heard it was true," a tall one replied loudly.

"I heard it too," seconded another.

They had all heard stories about the Mormons and their vile ways, but few if any had ever actually met an honest-to-goodness, bona fide, real live one before. From where they stood, they could barely see the Mormons on the far bank, let alone tell if they really had horns or not. They just knew there was a lot of them elders over there, and they didn't seem the least bit scairt. They were staring the enemy down, and the enemy was staring them right back in the eye without even flinching. No matter who you are, that's bound to make you think twice.

It was suddenly obvious to everyone in a white sheet that this wasn't going to be as easy as they thought. Some of them, maybe a lot of them, were going to get hurt. They hadn't come out here expecting much of a fight, and they sure hadn't come out looking to get gored.

"I don't know about you fellers but I got a wife and young'uns at home to think about," the short Klansman said. Several others grunted hasty agreement. "I'm outta here."

"Me too," said the tall one.

Unbelievably the Klansmen turned and began to leave, riding away on their horses or stealing off on foot. Apparently they weren't all that curious to find out if Mormons actually did have horns or not. Like all mobs, their bravery (and stupidity) ran in numbers, and their numbers were suddenly beginning to dwindle.

"Where are you going?" the Grand Wizard yelled, grabbing at several of them.

"I don't wanna get gored," answered one.

"Don't be ridiculous!" the Wizard yelled. "You don't really believe that rubbish, do you?" But the trickle of men was now a full-fledged exodus. The Wizard tried desperately to rally his troops, but still they slipped away. Several of them poured out the tar, smothering the fire and burying the trees in darkness again. The cauldron was loaded on the back of the wagon and driven away, disappearing into the woods. Apparently they did believe that rubbish.

"Wait!" He screamed, practically screeching, pointing skyward, "The moon! It's not quite full! They can't have horns! Come back!"

The large Klansman passed him, and the Wizard grabbed him by the arm.

"Not you too?"

Their eyes locked for a moment, then the broad-shouldered man brushed the Wizard loose and walked off.

The Wizard took a step forward, as if to go after him. He shook an angry fist, then his foot slipped and he found himself on the ground, his legs and robes stained with smoldering tar. With a cry, he whipped off his hood and robe, cursing where his hands came into contact with the scalding muck.

"Cowards!" he yelled into the darkness. But his men were gone. It was over. All alone, he threw his robe to the ground, stomping on it in a fit of rage. He turned to fire one last icy glare at the line of Mormons across the stream.

It was too dark, and they were too far apart, but if Golden could have seen the Wizard's face, he would have been looking right into the burning eyes of the good Reverend Weatherbee.

Maybe it was the night air, maybe it was the alcohol, maybe they had a change of heart, or maybe it was none of these things. Golden would never know the reason the Klan had for leaving; he was always just grateful that they did. As the last of the Klansmen disappeared into the woods, Golden heaved a sigh of relief.

"Well, what do you think of that?" asked George Albert, his voice full of dismay.

"Waste of a good bedsheet." Golden snorted. He didn't have time to say anything else before he was surrounded with hugs and hearty pats on the back from overjoyed elders.

CHAPTER 30

GOING UP FOOL'S HILL ON THE SLIPPERY SIDE

The biggest troublemaker you'll ever have to deal with watches you shave his face in the mirror every morning.

—*Cowboy Proverb*

Weatherbee paced the front of the room like a lion in a cage, his face a contortion of fury. He paused to brood between explosive rants that erupted from a depth of anger Kenneth had never seen in a man before. Spit flew from his lips each time he spoke, and a large vein stood out on his forehead like a pulsing snake. Every time the reverend stopped to yell, Kenneth was afraid it might burst.

The pew felt particularly uncomfortable today, and it had nothing to do with the lack of a cushion. Kenneth shifted where he sat among the assembled core of Reverend Weatherbee's most devout followers. They were the bulk of the men who had attended last night's bonfire near Rome. Most of them were much like himself, laborers from the area struggling against the ever-present threat of poverty. Some of them Kenneth had known for years—good, God-fearing Christians—but some of them were truly brutish characters, hardened and hateful, who weren't the type of company he'd normally choose to keep. He wasn't exactly sure when the latter sort of men had started attending Weatherbee's meetings, but here they were and here he was, meeting with them as he'd been doing for some time now. When had the reverend's parishioners come to be such a coarse bunch? Or had they always been this way? He couldn't recall.

Weatherbee's sermons were usually filled with hallelujahs and amens, but today the men were silent as graves. They sat with their heads bowed, staring at the floor or their feet or the bench in front of them. They looked anywhere but forward, like a bunch of children being chastised, afraid to meet the reverend's eyes lest they catch the brunt of his wrath. Kenneth noticed that a few regulars hadn't even bothered to show up at all. He was rapidly starting to wish he'd been as smart as them.

The reverend continued to berate them as craven fools and dim-witted failures for their inaction against the Mormon elders the night before. Kenneth was wise enough to keep his yap shut, but secretly he was glad it hadn't come to blows. To be honest, this whole business of running around in sheets didn't suit him. Despite his large stature, he had never much favored violence. After what the South had been through, the last thing any of them needed was more of it.

On the other hand, he wasn't rightly fond of the notion of having Mormons around. After the stories he'd heard and the things he'd learned from Reverend Weatherbee, he wanted them gone. Seducers and polygamists and perverters of the laws of God had no place among decent folk. He wanted to be rid of them as much as the next fellow, but what he and Weatherbee's folks were doing didn't sit well with him either.

He'd been lukewarm about the Rome trip from the get-go. The first raid against that church or hive (as the reverend called it) in Chattanooga had been enough. Burning that cross was a bit much, though. Jesus died on a cross like that for our sins. Burning it didn't feel right somehow. Firing on the building had been excessive too, but he guessed it had sent the message. After that and the recent aggressions happening toward Mormons in some of the neighboring states, he had hoped that just turning up in white robes again would be enough to send these Mormons packing.

To his distaste, many of the other men had gone to Rome aiming for more than just scaring the elders off. They had gone looking to inflict some serious harm. The real surprise, and not a pleasant one, had been when the wagon with the tar had shown up. He'd heard that some Mormons had been tarred and feathered in Louisiana, and maybe some of his group had thought it was a good idea. Kenneth didn't like it, but he hadn't been able to bring himself to say anything. He was disappointed with himself for that and disappointed that the reverend hadn't said anything either. He didn't think Weatherbee had planned on it being a tarring, but regardless of what the original idea had been, by the time they'd arrived at the Mormon meeting, that had become the plan.

The Mormons' strong defense at the river had caught everyone off guard. No one had expected it. In hindsight, Kenneth supposed it wasn't all that surprising. Whatever else they might be, the Mormons were still men, and men would defend themselves. Whoever that tall, skinny fellow had been, he was either tough as whitleather to pull a shenanigan like that or he was crazy as a jaybird. Either way he wasn't one to be trifled with. If it had come down to it, Kenneth was sure a lot of people would have been injured on both sides. So when Larry had spoken out, Kenneth had been quick to back him up. If it got everyone out of there without bloodshed, it was good enough.

"How could you all just leave?" Weatherbee was shouting again. Never before had anyone disobeyed him like that. It was mutiny. It was heresy. A betrayal of both him and the Lord.

There are two kinds of questions in this world. Some that require answering and some that do not. Weatherbee's question was more of the second type, but Larry spoke up anyhow.

Kenneth wasn't sure what possessed him to answer. Maybe Larry thought it was the type of question that wanted answering or maybe he just cracked from the pressure of mistakenly sitting right beneath Weatherbee's nose in the front row. Either way, he piped up, his voice small and nervous, "You told us that by the full moon Mo-muns grow horns and become vicious."

"Said so yuhself," nodded the stocky fellow sitting next to him. It was a fairly common rumor in the South and had been going around for years now. Kenneth tried to remember when and where he'd first heard it, but he couldn't quite recollect. He'd always thought the notion of horns was silly as a goose, but apparently not everyone did. Some folks believed it as gospel truth.

"I've never said such a thing," Weatherbee sounded insulted. "How can you believe such an obvious lie?"

"I couldn't risk it. I got my family to think about," Larry tried to defend himself. Weatherbee wasn't aware that it was Larry who had actually started last night's retreat, which in his current state was a good thing for Larry.

"Your family is all the more reason to get rid of them!" Weatherbee spit the words at him.

"But them Mormons is vicious," reiterated the stocky fellow. Lester was his name. "They should be left alone."

"They're not vicious!" Weatherbee snapped at him; several veins on his neck bulged in support of the vein on his forehead.

If Weatherbee had been yelling at him like that, Kenneth would have been upset. A fellow of his stature wasn't used to taking much guff from anyone. Lester definitely didn't have the same stature, but he didn't look the least bit upset either. He simply looked confused. He scratched his head as he slowly mulled Weatherbee's words over. Ponderously and with great contemplation, he voiced the question that rose in his mind.

"If they's not vicious, then why's we after 'em?"

"Because!" Weatherbee bellowed. That was his whole answer. His anger was draining his rationale. He balled his hands into fists, attempting to gather his composure. There had to be a way to show them. There had to be. He had tried to reason with these people, he had tried to warn them of the Mormons and their evil. But they still wouldn't listen. They left him with no choice; there was only one thing left to do.

"Look," he spoke through clenched teeth. He was forcing himself to speak calmly, but the pulse of the vein in his forehead told the truth. He wasn't calm at all, not by a long shot. "I am going to show you people once and for all the truth about Mormons. They want to preach in our city so badly? I'm going to give them the chance!" And with that, he marched out, leaving the men sitting, unsure of what was going to happen next. Whatever Weatherbee had in mind, it was about to be set in motion.

CHAPTER 31

IT MEANS A GLOVE

Most of the trouble in the world is caused by people wanting to be important.

—*T.S. Eliot*

How about these?" George Albert held up a stack of bullet-ridden folders. He was kneeling on the floor, sorting through a tattered crate of papers.

Golden barely glanced at the papers in George Albert's hand. They weren't much more than confetti. "Toss 'em."

George Albert dropped them on the quickly growing pile of trash in the middle of the floor.

The rest of the whirlwind mission tour had gone off without a hitch. To Golden's joy and relief, the missionaries had all opted to stay, down to the last man. He couldn't have been more pleased. For the time being, he asked that the elders remain gathered together in their districts. He also temporarily suspended all proselytizing activities, having them focus on working with existing members and converts instead. The tactic seemed to do the trick for the most part. They still received threats here and there, but most were empty ones and the ones that weren't hadn't amounted to much, thankfully. Direct action by mobs was dropping again. The Southerners had been able to blow off most of their steam, and things were calming down.

Golden was still worried about the safety of the elders, since scaring the Klan off once certainly didn't mean they'd scared them off once and for all. But the missionaries said that they were feeling good about things, so he supposed maybe he should too.

With his focus on protecting his missionaries, Golden hadn't wasted much time cleaning up after the Klan had turned the mission home into a modern art version of Swiss cheese. Now, with mission activities on hold for a while, he had nothing but time. Golden kept joking that although the mission home had been dedicated years before, it wasn't until now that it had become holey.

They had been at it for a few weeks, but the place still looked like a leftover war zone. A large pile of splintered wood and broken fixtures lay in a pile in the corner. A copy of B.H.'s history of the Church and several copies of the Book of Mormon had been thrown away with full honors, having protected the shelves that held them with their lives. The front curtains hadn't been so fortunate and neither had the chairs and benches.

About the only salvageable piece of furniture had been Golden's desk. It was bullet ridden and one leg was shattered, but it could be fixed. Golden dug out the shells that he could, but plenty remained buried deep enough in the wood to tell its story for years to come.

Perched on a trunk by the lopsided thing, Golden grabbed another stack of files. The papers were thoroughly punctured. *Better paper than people*, he thought and then tossed them in the trash pile. He was about to investigate the contents of the heavily splintered armoire when the silhouette of a man traced its way across the light coming through the scarred walls. It moved directly to the front door, which slammed open, shaking dust from bullet holes and blowing loose debris across the floor. With a theatrical flourish, Weatherbee stepped into the mission office. He glanced about with a look of disdain, the slightest smirk tweaking his thin lips as he took in the disarray.

He was the last person on earth Golden ever expected to

see walking through his newly replaced door. Seeing Golden, Weatherbee descended on the desk, completely ignoring George Albert, who sat frozen and speechless. Weatherbee had cooled down, and his overstuffed air of self-importance was once again in full effect. His hands held stiffly behind his back, he stood imperiously in front of the desk, looking down at Golden something mighty blue. Golden's surprise quickly turned to caution.

"You are the so-called leader of the Mormon elders, I presume?"

This was obviously not a social call. From Weatherbee's tone, it wasn't going to be pleasant conversation either. Golden kept his own tone as polite as he could. He wanted to tell Weatherbee that technically the leader of the Mormon elders was God himself but decided against lengthy explanations. "Yes, I am."

"I understand that you've been trying to teach your false doctrine and lies to the good people of this city." It was amazing how much contempt he could inject into a few simple words.

"We teach the gospel to whoever is willing to listen."

"Well, these people have the right to know the truth about what you preach."

"I couldn't agree more," said Golden. These people did have the right to know the truth.

Weatherbee paused, sniggering flatly at the jab. He leaned in toward the desk, stabbing a finger at Golden. His breath smelled like curdled milk.

"I am going to show everyone once and for all the truth about you Mormons and expose you for the vile sinners and liars that you are. When I am through with you, no soul will dare listen to a thing you have to say!"

Weatherbee's words were icy cold, but a fire burned in Golden's bosom, a fierce conviction that spread throughout his whole being. He rose from his seat and met Weatherbee face-to-face.

"You had best leave it alone. You cannot destroy this Church." Golden's voice was calm and deliberate as he spoke, but the words hit with the force of a steam train. The reverend's posture faltered, momentarily taken aback by Golden's sudden ferocity, but he quickly recomposed himself.

"I don't think you understand," Weatherbee said. The haughtiness had returned to his voice, "I am challenging you to a public debate."

"Reverend Weatherbee." Golden looked him right in the eye. "I know who you are and what you teach. I have no desire to debate or argue with you over religion."

"Afraid that your teachings will be revealed for what they are?"

"The truth?" Golden cocked an eyebrow.

"Lies!" Weatherbee hissed.

Golden realized he was starting to get upset and calmed himself down a notch. He knew a skunk when he smelled one, and this one stunk worse than most. There was no point in locking horns with Weatherbee. A man like him had no interest in hearing anything that anybody else had to say.

Had it been a month ago, Golden might have been interested in the chance to preach in the city, but as things currently stood, it was the last thing he wanted to do. "I'm sorry, I am not going to do it." He shook his head and sat back down.

A sneer wormed its way across Weatherbee's mouth. His eyes narrowed cunningly as he played his trump card. "You don't have a choice! The gauntlet has been thrown down!" He pulled out the newspaper he was holding behind his back and slammed it down on the desk. In big, bold black and white, the *Times* headline announced

Reverend Weatherbee to Challenge
Mormon Leader in Public Debate!

The meeting had already been scheduled. It was dated for today. Weatherbee pressed the paper firmly to the desk with one hand, sliding it forward toward Golden. There was some sort of black gunk under some of his nails. Golden could have sworn it looked like tar.

Noticing Golden looking at his fingers, Weatherbee quickly withdrew his hand. "It's in every paper," he announced. "Everyone in the city will be there."

A chill ran down Golden's spine. Golden had witnessed first-hand the power that Weatherbee could exert before an audience. He hadn't earned his notoriety in the South simply because he was anti-Mormon. He was a great orator, powerful and eloquent from the pulpit—a real smooth-tongued devil who knew how to feed the audience exactly what they wanted to hear.

Golden was a simple rancher whose vocabulary only grew extensive when using the cowboy language. He couldn't hope to compete with Weatherbee in a public arena. He was in a real fix, all right. You might as well cover him in raw bacon and throw him to the lions.

"I'll see you this afternoon at the courthouse, and then we'll see how the cat jumps. Don't be late now," Weatherbee gloated. He exited the mission office, banging the door behind him, loosing more sawdust and rubble.

Golden slouched down on his makeshift seat. This was a trap, no doubt about it, but he was stuck between a rock and hard place. He had to go. A no-show would only serve to prove Weatherbee right in the eyes of the people. He was going to have to face Weatherbee this afternoon, one on one. There was no way out of it.

"What are you going to do?" George Albert broke the vacuum of silence left in Weatherbee's wake.

"I'm going to find a dictionary and look up 'gauntlet.'" Golden stood and went upstairs.

CHAPTER 32

SHOWDOWN

*Life consists not in holding good cards but in playing
those you hold well.*

—*Josh Billings*

Golden's second to worst fear was confirmed as soon
as they neared the courthouse. His worst fear was that he
would show up to find nothing but a mob waiting with a hanging rope. There didn't seem to be any sign of that, thank heavens.
His second to worst fear was that his impending humiliation at
Weatherbee's hands would take place in front of a large group of
people. This fear was apparently going to come true: hundreds of
people were gathered around the building.

The weather was pleasant and the citizenry had deemed to
make a day of it. Everywhere you looked, there were people mill-
ing about the lawn. Blankets were spread here and there, some
with parasols and picnic baskets. It reminded Golden of that
painting made out of nothing but colored dots by that French
hombre. Every person in the city had to be here.

"At least there are women and children this time," George
Albert said.

Golden smiled, although his heart wasn't much in it. George
Albert was right. Children of all ages ran about; a lively game
of tag was underway on the north side of the lawn. Mob action

was unlikely, which was good, but for Golden that was about as hopeful as the picture got. The sheer number of people there testified to Weatherbee's undeniable popularity. He had done an astounding job of getting the word out. This was going to be quite a show, a regular three-ring circus. Golden had the sinking feeling he was going to be playing lead clown.

When Weatherbee stormed out of the mission home, he'd left Golden less than an hour to get ready. It was probably generous by Weatherbee standards, but it wasn't much to Golden. George Albert had helped, pressing Golden's suit for him while Golden frantically scoured his scriptures for an idea—any idea—for a sermon.

To say that his speech was hastily prepared was an understatement. For lack of anything better, he decided to talk about thinking of God and faith. It was the topic he'd covered when he'd preached with B.H. from the cage beneath the oak tree. It had gone over rather well then, and he'd been regurgitating parts of it in his talks from time to time ever since. It might not be the best fit for today's occasion, but he knew it well, and considering the amount of time he'd had to prepare, it would have to do.

Golden wasn't really worried about his own humiliation. Well, he had to admit he was. Who wouldn't be? But humiliation has never been fatal. What really worried him was the impact that today might have on the mission. They were just emerging from a really rough patch. Failure here could damage or even end the work entirely for years to come. Worse than that, it could rekindle the flames of hatred, causing further harm to his elders. And that was simply out of the question.

Kenneth arrived at the courthouse early, before anyone else had shown up, including Reverend Weatherbee. He hadn't slept well and had woken early, beating even the rooster out of bed. He'd been to plenty of church gatherings in his time, but for some reason, he felt as if today were more than just a meeting.

Something was troubling him, a vague shadow at the back of his mind that he couldn't quite get a finger on. All he knew was that it had something to do with Weatherbee.

Larry Crutchfield showed up with his wife and young'uns a short while later and joined him in the back row. Kenneth wasn't really sure what he expected to happen today, but he'd left his own family at home. Seeing women and children arrive, he wished he had brought them along. In fact, he felt downright silly. Just what kind of Bible meeting were you attending if you were afraid to bring your wife and kids anyhow? The kind he'd been attending lately, that's what kind.

Kenneth sat up as two Mormon elders entered the room. The first was so tall and thin that he had to be the fellow from the creek. Here in the daylight, up close, he didn't look like much of a threat at all. And he sure as shooting didn't have any horns. They crossed to the front of the room and took their seats on the stand across from Weatherbee.

The courtroom benches were packed with folks from all walks of life. Miners and farmers in their coarse jeans and cotton shirts sat next to city folk in suits and fine dresses. There wasn't a spare seat in the entire room, and still people crowded together to stand at the back of the room and in the doorway and outside in the congested hall. Besides Golden, George Albert was the only other Mormon there.

It had been warm outside, but with the full house, it was steaming in here. Even with the large bay windows open as wide as they would go, it was as stuffy as all get out. Golden was already as nervous as a long-tailed cat in a room full a rockin' chairs; he didn't need the help breaking into a sweat. He'd preached to groups as big as forty, even fifty people before, but this audience was four or five times that size and growing.

Shifting in his seat, he risked a glance across the stage at Weatherbee. He had come a-walking onto the stand like he owned the place. From the look and size of the audience, well, he probably did. He now sat on the far side of the stage, looking just as confident as a fellow could. His shirt and collar were sharply pressed and immaculately worn; he was dressed to kill. If it was hot in here, he didn't seem to notice; he looked cool as a cucumber.

Today felt like the time Golden had walked past Weatherbee's chapel on the first day he'd arrived in Chattanooga. Only this time he knew the verbal assault was coming, and he wasn't able to just walk away. They were in the same room of the courthouse that the mob had trapped them in before. He felt trapped all over again. He dug his finger into his collar. It was too tight, constricting around his neck. He should have worn a bigger shirt.

With each new person who squeezed himself into the room, Weatherbee's air of victory grew and the further Golden sank into his seat. He wondered if it was too late to make a break for it. As if in answer, the grandfather clock in the corner began to toll. It was twelve o'clock. High noon.

As the reverb from the last chime faded, the house fell silent and Weatherbee rose from his seat. He shot a knowing look at Golden, then stepped to the pulpit, gripping the edges in his bony hands. He looked over the assembly before him. All eyes were on him, ears bent to hear his every word. All was as it should be. Weatherbee smiled smugly. This was his home turf, and he was playing for the home crowd. He couldn't lose. He inhaled deeply, then fired his opening salvo.

"Mormons," he paused for emphasis, "are going straight to hell." He wasn't loud. He didn't yell. He pronounced it as calm fact and was greeted with a chorus of hearty amens in response. He let them voice their agreement, then held up his hand in a quieting motion and the crowd fell silent.

"Now, my brothers and sisters, it is not lightheartedly that I make this pronouncement." He placed his hand gently against his breast, an expression of concern creasing his brow. "As a man of the cloth, having wholly devoted my life to God Almighty, it saddens me, yea, it breaks my very heart to see any man lose his soul and be thrust to hell."

Golden had to admit: Weatherbee was good. He was very good. His delivery was polished and smooth as silk. In a matter of a few sentences, he had the audience in the palm of his hand. The only thing Golden had anticipated today was for it not to go well for him. So far Weatherbee was meeting his expectations.

"Yet sadly, to hell is where these Mormons are going if they don't change their ways." Weatherbee continued. Again amens from the crowd. "They say they preach the truth, but they speak only false doctrine and prevarications. Now, in all mercy and fairness, it is likely that they honestly, truly, from their very hearts believe these lies as truth. But even if you believe a lie, it is still a lie. And if you follow that lie, as they do, you are going straight to hell."

His charisma was remarkable. Golden supposed that if he'd met Weatherbee in any other capacity or circumstance he might have actually liked the man. He emphasized and accentuated like a pro. His showmanship was unparalleled. He should have been an actor.

"'Just what false doctrines do we teach?' they ask. What false doctrines indeed. They are guilty of preaching polygamy." The audience booed and hissed. Weatherbee had struck a chord, and they were really responding to him. "They are guilty of stealing the precious flower of Southern womanhood and delivering them into the harems of lecherous Mormon patriarchs. Well, I tell you they've got to quit teaching it! They have got to quit teaching that polygamy." His voice rose dramatically, then fell low again as he repeated the central mantra, "Or they are going straight to hell!"

Another rousing chorus of amens and agreement. Weatherbee was hitting his stride, and the audience was right there with him. He spared a glance at Golden, his eyes glowering with victory.

The reverend was really pouring it on. That skinny feller didn't have a chance, thought Kenneth. If the feller weren't a Mormon, he might have almost felt bad for him. He settled back in his seat, listening as Weatherbee continued his preaching. Kenneth was content to be here and listen, but the shadow still lingered in his mind, vague and undefined. He was barely aware of it, but Kenneth was sitting on a very narrow fence; it wouldn't take much to tip him to one side or other. Whether he knew it or not, today was all or nothing.

If Golden could sink any lower into his seat, he would have been on the floor. Watching the reaction of the congregation, he realized that his rehashed speech would not do—not today, not with this group. Certainly not after the way Weatherbee was working them into a lather.

The last time Golden had sat in this very room he had received a prompting. The words he should say came to him clear as day. He felt no such inspiration today. His mind was blank. It was all he could do to keep from hyperventilating. Never before in his life had he wished so badly that he could vanish or that an earthquake would suddenly hit or a flood or a stampede would tear through town, that something or anything would get him out of this predicament. But the only thing that happened was the congregation continued to soak up Weatherbee's every word while the clock ticked painfully forward.

Tick tock, tick tock. The clock was as relentless as Weatherbee's mouth. He had been preaching for an hour and a half straight and hadn't diverted from his "Mormons are going straight to hell" theme the entire time, not once. The temperature in the courtroom had moved steadily from simmering to boil as the afternoon stretched on, but still he showed no sign of stopping.

The people sat quietly in their seats. The lengthening hour and oppressive heat had stifled their initial excitement. The occasional amen still drifted through the muggy air but lacked the enthusiasm they'd had over an hour ago. Women fanned themselves listlessly. Bored men wiped sweaty foreheads with already drenched handkerchiefs. A portly gentleman in a gray-checkered suit checked his pocket watch. He closed it and tucked it back in his breast pocket with a sigh. The fellow in a bow tie next to him was nodding, fighting off sleep. His head would slump and with a jerk he'd sit back up. He'd no sooner blinked once or twice than his head would begin to sink again, like a slow-moving woodpecker. Everyone was ready for this to be over. Everyone but Weatherbee, that is, who continued to whale away, unfazed by temperature or time.

"A Bible?" His voice still carried loud and strong. "We already have ourselves a Bible! Why, it says right here in the Bible that there will be no further revelation from God, for he has given us all we need to know, that we need no more! These Mormons have got to stop preaching about new revelations. They've got to stop preaching about the gold bible, about Joe Smith seeing God, for that is blasphemy, and they are going straight to hell because of it!"

Golden was roasting in his seat, the wool and cotton of his suit sticking to him in places where it shouldn't. When he first arrived he had wished he could die to save him from embarrassment and failure. Now he wished he could die to save him from heat and boredom. He'd endured priesthood meetings that had been far less arduous than this, even ones where a high councilor had spoken.

Weatherbee was unrelenting. "Polygamy, false revelations, false scripture, deceit, and lies! The Mormons are going straight to hell! And it sorrows me! I confess this man is a good man," Weatherbee pointed a finger at Golden without skipping a beat, "but he's going straight to hell!"

The fellow with the bow tie was out like a light. He'd finally succumbed to the full effect of gravity and was slumped over, his head resting on the shoulder of the man in the checkered suit. He wasn't the only one asleep. The entire room was filled with yawns and blank expressions, their minds numb from heat and verbal overload. And still Weatherbee raged on.

Golden once heard a story of a little fellow who was sick and went to the doctor. The doctor was an herbalist and gave him a bunch of plants and told him to boil them in a quart of water and drink it all.

"I can't," the little fellow protested, "I can only hold a pint."

Golden couldn't speak for the audience, but he knew he couldn't hold any more. He'd had it up to here of being told that his father was going straight to hell. That his mother was going straight to hell. That Joseph Smith was going straight to hell. That he was going to hell and all his elders with him.

"All of them, each and every one, if they don't repent and confess their wrongdoings unto God, they're going straight to hell! In the name of Jesus, amen!" Weatherbee smacked the pulpit with a final, fervent thump.

It took the audience, and Golden as well, a moment to realize that Weatherbee was done. They muttered a final, weary "amen," coming back to life a little now that the preaching was finally over. Weatherbee turned from the pulpit with a self-satisfied smirk. He looked at Golden and mouthed "straight to hell" as he returned triumphantly to his seat.

The audience began to stir, some standing. The man in the checkered suit even put on his hat. They were ready to go. Their look of relief vanished when Golden stood. They had forgotten that there were two speakers scheduled today. There was an audible groan as it dawned on them that the debate was only half over.

Golden was as mad as a hornet. Weatherbee's endless

preening had been absolute bullpucky, but Golden had nothing
to say that would convince the audience otherwise. Even if he
did have something to say, the audience was past its limit. They
didn't want to hear any more, particularly from some Mormon.
Stick a fork in 'em; they're done. Weatherbee's challenge was over
before Golden even had a chance to begin. Well, if a horse is
dying, it's best not to prolong the misery. Golden grabbed the
stand so tightly it shook.

"I have only one thing to say." He waggled an angry finger
high in the air, his voice rising in a screeching crescendo. "I'd
rather be a Mormon going to hell than not be a Mormon and not
know where the hell I'm going! Amen!"

And he sat down.

He regretted it immediately. What on earth did he just do?
Panic gripped his stomach like a vice, and a new layer of sweat, as
cold as ice this time, broke out all over his body. *Tell me I didn't
say what I think I just did.* But he knew he had. It had come as
an impulse, as swift and sudden as a bullet; it had felt right at the
moment, but now that it was too late to take it back, he knew
he'd blown it.

George Albert sat, jaw dropped open. The look of absolute
shock on his face told the whole story. Golden was sunk. He'd
given the whole shebang to Weatherbee in one fell swoop. He
slumped into his chair with a grimace, burying his face in his
hands.

Weatherbee had won the day. The sound of the audience
cheering for him rose like a dull roar in Golden's ears. Golden
shook his head slightly, but the noise was impossible to ignore.
He wished he could block it out, make it all go away. It didn't
seem like it would end, and it . . . it didn't sound right either. It
was like no other cheer he'd ever heard. The sound was curious
enough that Golden looked up.

The audience wasn't cheering. The entire courtroom was
laughing. It wasn't mean or mocking but hearty and loud—the
good kind of laughter, the kind you hear after a good joke. Some

people were in tears they were laughing so hard.

Kenneth exchanged a look of disbelief with Larry. Larry looked as surprised as all get out. Despite himself, Kenneth began to laugh. That was the funniest thing he'd ever heard from a pulpit. He slapped Larry on the back, and Larry began to laugh too.

The man with the checkered coat jumped to his feet. "Why, that's the best sermon I've heard in a long time!" he yelled and started clapping. The sleeping man with the bow tie stood and groggily began clapping with him. Suddenly the entire congregation was standing and applauding heartily.

Now there really was cheering mixed in with the laughter. There were even a few amens and hallelujahs thrown in for good measure. And it wasn't for Weatherbee. Everyone was cheering for Golden.

Golden couldn't believe what he was seeing. His jaw dropped open as wide as George Albert's. It had to be a dream. There was no reason the audience should be cheering for him, yet here they were clapping away. A standing ovation, no less! George Albert, every bit as surprised as Golden, stood and began to applaud as well. Somehow Golden had pulled a coup.

It took Weatherbee as long as Golden to realize just who the audience was cheering for. Like Golden, he simply assumed that the applause had been for him. He stood, ready to take the stand in triumph, quickly reviewing his carefully prepared victory speech in his mind. He hadn't taken more than a step when someone yelled out, "Not you, you flannel-mouthed blowhard! The skinny gent!"

That took the wind out of his sails right quick. He stopped and looked at the crowd as if seeing them for the first time. The awful truth of it hit him like a kicking horse. They weren't cheering for him; they were cheering for that Mormon! How could they? He watched the congregation, flabbergasted. Embarrassment and anger would set in later. For now he was in shock and denial. He had set up the perfect trap. His delivery had been matchless. A finer discourse hadn't been preached in Hamilton County in a lifetime. And that skinny wretch with the mousy voice had swept the victory out from under his feet with that . . . that . . . that wasn't even a sermon! And he, Charles A. Weatherbee, man of the cloth, defender of the South, had lost. He had thrown down the gauntlet and lost.

The laughter and applause began to subside. The show was finally over, and people began to leave, escaping into the fresh air outside. A great many of them lined up to shake Golden's hand before working their way out of the room. They complimented him on everything from his brevity to his charm, saying what a wonderful job he did. Golden thanked them. He still couldn't believe it, but he couldn't wipe the surprised smile off his face if he tried. There was no reason he should have come out on top. Yet here was a line of people waiting to congratulate him. He was so busy shaking hands that he didn't even notice Weatherbee slip from the room and out the back of the courthouse.

CHAPTER 33

LOSING IT

Nature gave us all something to fall back on, and sooner or later we all land flat on it.

—*Cowboy Proverb*

Weatherbee slammed the paper down on the table, pounding it violently. The headline declared the word, and the word was

Mormon Gives Weatherbee the What For!

He was still dressed to a T and looked the same as he always had, but this Weatherbee was an entirely different man than the one Kenneth thought he knew. In all his years, he had never seen Weatherbee behave like this, or any other grown-up, for that matter. Pounding the pulpit was one thing; it was a standard practice of most preachers. But this was more like a tantrum; he hammered the table with both hands as if the paper would disappear if he hit it hard enough. But the paper, like the Mormons, didn't look like it was going to go away any time soon. Any air of authority or even respectability that the man had left was dissipating into the air like steam off a boiling kettle. Frankly the old man was acting like a baby, and one in need of a good spanking at that.

Kenneth sat in Weatherbee's chapel with the remaining

followers. The group today was even smaller than before; less than a dozen men sat on the uncomfortable wooden benches this time around. They were the oldest and closest of Weatherbee's congregation, although "close" was a word best used loosely. Now that he thought about it, Kenneth wasn't aware of anyone that the reverend was particularly close to.

"How dare they print this about me?" The vein stood out on his forehead like Clingman's Dome over the Appalachian Trail. Ink from the newsprint smudged the corners of his hands like bruises. He was beyond furious. Spittle built up in white patches of foam at the edge of his mouth as he ranted. "How dare they? You saw the demon at work!"

How could that simpleton, that country hick, have turned this all around on him? It was impossible. After all his preparation and care. This was more than an affront—this was war. If he couldn't preach the Mormons out, he'd have to purge them from the South. Burn them out like God's cleansing fire. And he knew exactly who would have to be cleansed first.

"Gather the rest of the boys, now! For by God there will be one less Mormon on earth tonight!" He snapped at the men, calling them to action. Instead of jumping to as he expected, they sat gaping stupidly. Worthless. He'd whip them into shape; he always had.

Weatherbee's eyes were so wide that the whites would have been visible even from the back of the building. From where Kenneth sat a few rows from the front, they were positively wild as they darted back and forth across the room. It was a crazed expression, something Kenneth had only caught a glimpse of once before.

When Kenneth was still a youngling, perhaps ten or so, he had gone hunting with his rifle and had come across a raccoon in his father's barn. He chased it around till he got the varmint good and tucked in a narrow stall. The raccoon quickly realized its mistake, but it was too late; it was trapped, and it knew it. That was the first time Kenneth had seen a look like Weatherbee wore on his face today: an expression of desperation so severe it bordered on panic.

In a last-ditch effort, the raccoon leaped at him, clawing and biting savagely. Kenneth managed to knock it off but not before a large flap of skin hung loose and bleeding on his right arm. The wound later became infected, spreading through his arm, and the doctor had to clean it out. The pain had been excruciating. The doctor told him he was lucky; he could have lost his whole arm or even died.

Kenneth fired once at the coon but missed, and the animal fled, forcing itself underneath the jagged wood of the barn wall. The gap was far too small for it to fit. In its reckless state, it forced itself through, leaving behind a large chunk of its own bloody skin against the boards. It had been so desperate that it didn't care what it hurt, including itself, to get away.

Kenneth would never forget that look. On the raccoon it had been scary. On Weatherbee it was downright horrifying. It was a stark contrast to his usually confident manner, as if something wrapped too tightly had come unbound. Kenneth was no coward, but that look had frightened him as a boy, and it frightened him even more now.

"Well? What are y'all waiting for? Go get 'im!" Weatherbee was shouting.

When Kenneth first met Weatherbee years ago, he found the man and his teachings agreeable. He admired the reverend's spirit and had gladly joined his growing congregation. But Weatherbee was out of sorts of late, growing more and more antagonistic as time drew on. Each new aggression of Weatherbee's against the Mormons only fed the growing doubt in Kenneth's mind. Fighting against the powers of the devil was one thing, but beatings and killings? Was meeting evil with evil really the answer? It certainly wasn't what Jesus taught. The means simply didn't fit the message. Weatherbee was out of character. Or maybe this was his character and he was finally flying his true colors.

Kenneth had been too timid to speak up before, but he knew

that he couldn't wait any longer. Things were out of hand. This wasn't exactly the time or place he wanted to bring up what was on his mind, but the fact was there just wasn't another time or place to do it. He stood, unconsciously wringing his hat in his large hands.

"Reverend." Kenneth wasn't sure how to breach the subject. He'd been thinking about this for a while, trying to figure out what he should say and how he should say it. He'd even practiced it over in his mind a few times beforehand. But he hadn't counted on the extent of Weatherbee's rage. He had at least fifty pounds on Weatherbee, but the man was mighty intimidating. Kenneth had been bigger than the raccoon as well, but he still carried the scar from that encounter. He knew that by speaking out now, he risked not only his own safety but the safety of his family as well. If the other men didn't back him up, he could be in real danger. Still, he had something to say, and he was going to say it.

Weatherbee stood looking at him, impatiently waiting for him to speak. Here, now, with Weatherbee right in his face, it was harder than Kenneth thought it would be. He suddenly found a new respect for that skinny Mormon feller—it wasn't easy to stand up to the full weight of Weatherbee's glare at all.

Kenneth mustered his fortitude and spoke his mind. "The boys and I was thinking. We got ahselves problems enough 'round here without having to deal with the Mormons."

"That's right." The reverend agreed. "So get off your duffs an' let's go get 'em!"

Weatherbee had misunderstood. Kenneth struggled to remain as even keeled as possible.

"You see," Kenneth continued, determined to get this off his chest once and for all, "we figured as long as they leave us alone, we got other things to worry about these days."

"Don't tell me you fools are accepting them?" Weatherbee laughed. It was dry and derisive. Kenneth couldn't mean what he was saying. Only idiots and fools would ever do such a thing.

"No." Kenneth struggled to explain his thoughts. "But some of us got families to feed, an' we can't spend all a our time chasin' willy-nilly after Mormons." Now that he'd started, it was easier to keep going. It felt good too, airing his thoughts out. "Frankly, I don't care for the way things are being done 'round here anymore. The others feel the same too."

"What are you talking about?" Weatherbee snapped. Why were they hesitating? There was no time for this! What was wrong with these idiots?

Weatherbee refused to grasp what was being said. There was no other way to word it more clearly; Kenneth dug in his heels and spoke his mind. "We're leaving."

He may as well have spit in Weatherbee's face. The reverend's wide eyes narrowed like snakes, pinning their intensity directly at him. Kenneth took a step back as if he'd been pushed.

"You can't leave me." Weatherbee's voice was a threatening hiss. "Think of everything I've done for you! You know what happens to those who turn against the will of the Lord!"

It was the wrong thing to say. No matter how much he may have feared Weatherbee, Kenneth cared even less for being threatened. It was Weatherbee's turn to take a step back as Kenneth raised himself to his full height and leaned into his words.

"How long we been coming to you now, Reverend?" The words came out almost mocking. "Years? We come to you for the good word of God, but all we ever hear about anymore is Mormons and their polygamy and how wrong they are. Ah don't care about the Mormons! I'm soured on hearing about 'em. I want to hear about God and the sweet gospel of Christ."

"That goes for all a us." Following Kenneth's lead, Larry had found his voice and stood next to him. Larry wasn't a big man, and his balding pate barely reached the top of Kenneth's arm. Weatherbee realized he'd hit an absolute dead end with Kenneth and suddenly turned the full extent of his frustration on the smaller man.

"What do you know, you pathetic moron?" he screamed. Larry quailed, shaken.

Kenneth didn't like using his size to lean on people, but he had no problem with it right now. He stepped out of the pews into the aisle, directly between Larry and Weatherbee.

"Shut yer mouth!" Kenneth yelled. For once Weatherbee did. He took a step backward and found his back against the pulpit. Kenneth stabbed a thick finger in his direction. "Now you listen here. Come next Sabbath, you won't be seeing me here, nor my family. We're gonna find ahselves another minister, one who'll teach about God for a change."

"I teach about God!" Weatherbee shrieked, his rage overriding his fright enough to yell but not enough to stop him from clinging to the front of the pulpit like a drowning man. His neck and face were as red as the devil himself, twisted with fury. True colors indeed.

"Good-bye, Reverend." Kenneth was done. He turned and walked down the aisle toward the door, leaving Weatherbee still howling behind him. Kenneth ignored him. He'd spoken his peace and had nothing more to say. He expected to feel angry or even relieved. To his surprise, he felt sad. A good man once stood where Weatherbee stood screaming himself hoarse. Maybe that man would come back again someday, but Kenneth had no mind to stick around and see. This was no place for him, not anymore. A brief feeling of loss passed through him and then was gone. He put on his hat as he stepped out the doorway and into the light.

Larry's momma didn't raise no fool. Kenneth had been all that had stood between him and the brunt of Weatherbee's animosity. With a last glance at the silver-haired man, he took after Kenneth like a scalded dog.

The remaining handful of men must have agreed with Kenneth or they simply knew the party was over. Whatever their reasons, the result was the same. As one, they stood and followed Kenneth and Larry down the center aisle and out the door.

"What? All of you?" Weatherbee shrieked. His voice trembled with a newfound fear. He had seen people leave his flock before. Every so often some faithless heathen would fall by the wayside. It was an unfortunate loss, but it happened. Even Christ lost disciples from time to time. But a wholesale apostasy like this was unprecedented. It was unthinkable.

"Run then! Cowards! Run to your everlasting damnation!" They had proven themselves unworthy, to be cast off as dross in the refiner's fire. He didn't need them. But still he shouted after them. He shouted until his throat was raw and his voice cracked. He shouted until the last shadows of the day had drawn long around the chapel and the sun tucked itself behind the western ridge of the valley. But there was no one left to listen.

CHAPTER 34

THE MESSENGER

Nothing warms the soul like the sight of an old friend.

—*Anonymous*

The station was beginning to fill with people arriving in anticipation of the daily 3:10. Golden stood in the middle of the platform awaiting a new batch of elders. Most folks paid him little mind, but a few tipped their hats, greeting him politely.

"Afternoon, Father."

Golden nodded and smiled, waving a hand in return. He was excited. Today's arrivals would be the first new missionaries sent here since before the latest batch of troubles. Since the showdown with Weatherbee, things had been going better. Mob activity had decreased, and they'd even had several successful engagements to preach inside the city. There hadn't been any more brass bands, but they hadn't been interrupted by armed men or had the mission home shot up either. Interest in the Church itself didn't seem to be growing much, but at least tolerance of it seemed to be. Chattanooga still wasn't the City of Enoch, but Golden was glad to say that things were definitely improving. They'd even seen a few baptisms from the courthouse debate. The fact that Salt Lake was sending out fresh elders was a good sign for the mission in and of itself.

Feeling high on his oats, Golden had gotten a bee in his

bonnet to test out the incoming greenhorns and see what kind of elders had been sent to him. A shrill whistle announced the train's arrival, right on time. He stepped back, standing near the wall, watching the train as it pulled in, brakes squealing. Large clouds of steam and smoke puffed out from its sides, rising to roll off the high ceiling of the station. It pulled to a stop, and passengers began exiting the cars onto the landing.

It didn't take long before a bewildered group of young men stepped onto the platform, looking rather lost. They were his new elders. There was no mistaking them for anything else; they were as obvious as spots on a cow. Golden didn't remember being that buffaloed-looking when he first got here, but he must have been.

The other passengers went about their business, not wasting any time in making their way out of the station and onto parts unknown, leaving the missionaries huddled together, glancing apprehensively about the now-empty platform, wondering what they should do. They looked so nervous that Golden almost felt bad about his idea.

He adjusted his collar. The stiff white clerical collar was heavily starched and fit differently than the cotton shirts he was used to. The priest's cassock fit him well, even if it was a bit short. There weren't too many people built like Golden, and he'd been lucky to find a costume that fit him at all. It had taken several days to track one down, but he'd finally found one at a local tailor shop. The proprietor, who was a man of good humor, specialized in robes of the priesthood and happened to have an extra set lying around that he let Golden borrow. Dressed in black robes from head to toe, the white square of the collar underlining his protruding Adam's apple, Golden made a convincing-looking Southern preacher.

He raised his head authoritatively and approached the elders, clearing his throat in an exaggerated manner to get their attention. The elders turned, their eyes as wide as saucers, like a cartoon from the newspaper. It was all he could do to keep from laughing and breaking character. Golden lathered on a Southern accent as thick as taffy and genuine enough to fool a born-and-bred local, let alone a bunch of new missionaries fresh from Utah.

"'Less I miss mah guess, y'all'd be Mo-mun elduhs." He looked them over critically. The elders stood frozen, trying to figure out what to make of the tall, skinny priest confronting them, their jaws flapping uselessly.

"Ain'tcha? What's the matta? Devil got yuh tongue?" Golden pressed them further. Much to Golden's delight, one elder in a brown suit boldly stepped forward. Good for him. He had guts. The Lord definitely needed men with backbone down here.

"Excuse me," the elder asked, undaunted, "do you know where we can find the Mormon mission headquarters?" From his tone, he wasn't only asking for information but also letting the priest know that he wasn't afraid. He was square shouldered and had the build of a man who worked hard for a living. Probably a rancher or farmhand. Not much different than Golden had been when he first met B.H. on this same platform nearly eleven years before. Mercy, had it really been that long ago?

Continuing his masquerade, Golden raised an eyebrow and nodded in a cocksure manner as if the elder had just confirmed his deepest suspicions.

"Ah'll have yuh know, Ah have it on good authority that all Mo-muns are going straight to hell." When it came to giving Mormons a hard time, Golden had learned from the best. He launched into a lengthy discourse, quoting scriptures and using every colorful term and euphemism he had learned in his long and exhaustive missionary career in the South, not to mention a few he just made up on the spot.

The longer he spoke, the wider the eyes of the missionaries grew and the further their jaws dropped. He was really giving it to them. There wasn't a single piece of anti-Mormon rhetoric that he didn't throw at them. He railed on polygamy, chipped on Joe Smith, hacked on Brigham Young, bashed gold bibles, and thrashed visions. It wasn't long before the poor boys looked so baffled that he began to feel sorry for them.

He was just about to let them off the hook when the courageous elder in the brown suit cocked back his fist and, *POW!*, socked Golden right across the jaw. It was one of the most solid blows Golden would ever have the privilege of receiving in his life. His hat and bible went flying, and he dropped to the floor.

The other elders, almost as surprised as Golden, suddenly sprang into action, rushing to Golden's side. They may not have known how to react to the argumentative priest, but they knew that punching him out like John L. Sullivan wasn't it. Golden was instantly surrounded by elders, who helped him to his feet, all the while bombarding him with apologies as fast as they could utter them. They brushed him off and quickly retrieved his hat and bible. Golden touched his cheek gingerly. The elder had really cleaned his plow. His nose was stinging and stars drifted in and out of his watering eyes. A pair of elders restrained the stocky elder by his arms. He was still agitated, but it didn't look like he was going to swing again.

"That's quite a right hook you've got there, son." The elders were still too flummoxed to notice that Golden's Southern accent was gone. None of them could have predicted what Golden said next. "I'm J. Golden Kimball, your mission president." If the elders had been shocked before, they were positively floored now. "I wanted to find out what kind of missionaries I was getting. And now I know. Strong ones."

"President Kimball?" the stocky elder stammered, "I . . . I'm so sorry. I didn't . . . I don't know what to say."

Golden was upset. He'd just had his clock rung something fierce, and his jaw was going to ache for a while. If the elder had been a pig, Golden would have had pork chops for dinner. But he couldn't entirely blame the elder either. After all, Golden had egged him on pretty good. The elder may have been a bit rough around the edges, but he was still a servant of the Lord. And Golden knew he was the last soul on earth to criticize anyone about being rough around the edges.

"Young man," his voice was that of a loving father who is

disappointed with the actions of a beloved child, "I believe you are a defender of the truth, but you had better learn to keep that temper in check. Let's take that fighting spirit and point it in the right direction."

"Yes, sir. I will, President." His voice sounded humbled. The elder had learned his lesson, and so had Golden. That was the last time he'd give anyone a hard time like that. At least while he was mission president.

After more proper introductions with the elders were made, Golden led the troop out of the station. It must have been quite a sight: a gaggle of Mormon missionaries being led through town by a priest. Golden knew there were plenty of eyes on them, but it didn't bother him. He was used to it.

They followed along the gully and turned up the road. The red brick buildings of downtown had spread over the years, covering much more of the lush valley than they did when Golden had first arrived as a new missionary. As it always had, Lookout Mountain rose above them, covered in its forest shroud. The route to the mission home was as familiar to Golden now as his nose was to his face. It was with some trepidation that he approached Weatherbee's chapel, but it was empty when they passed. Golden never saw the man again.

Eventually the bruise on Golden's cheek and the slight purple tinge around his left eye healed up fine. The rock 'em, sock 'em elder went out into the field, where he turned out to be a fine missionary, hardworking and a bold proclaimer of the gospel. As far as we know, he never hit anyone else again either.

After a few more months, the mission home was in apple pie order again. Wooden plugs and putty filled most of the holes, and new lumber replaced sections that had been damaged beyond repair. With an updated covering of wallpaper, it was hard to tell anything had ever happened. It made it feel a bit more like home as well. Fresh curtains shaded the new windowpanes, and several pieces of recently purchased furniture adorned the room. The debris pile was gone, and the office had been swept up. Golden even splurged a bit and got a rug for the place. Something practical, nothing too fancy; it was the Lord's money, after all.

Golden sat at his desk shuffling papers. He was glad the work had resumed, but so had the mouse turd sweeping. Oh, well. At least his new chair was comfortable. The old desk was working like a charm too. A few of the drawer faces had to be redone, the shattered leg had been replaced, and a fair share of bullet marks had been smoothed and filled, but it was as sturdy as it had ever been.

The shadow of a man crossed the curtains behind him, moving toward the front door. There was a light knock, and Golden looked up as the door swung open. In stepped a man dressed in a new suit with a derby hat perched on his head. He was clean-shaven and carried a valise. Golden could hardly believe his eyes.

"Elias!" He almost didn't recognize his own brother, "Well, look at you all gussied up in your best bib and tucker!"

Golden jumped up and grabbed Elias in a bear hug. It had been too long since they had last seen each other, and he was thrilled to see him. Elias looked well, but Golden couldn't help but grin at the idea of his brother all cleaned up and citified.

"Why, you look almost respectable." He smiled. "What are you doing here?"

"They want you back in Salt Lake right away," Elias said as if that explained everything.

Golden was filled with sudden concern. "Is everything okay? How's mother?"

It was Elias's turn to be caught off guard. "Haven't you heard?"

"What?" Had something happened? Was it Jennie or the kids? Golden's already anxious nature kicked into overdrive.

"You've been called to serve as one of the seven presidents of the Quorum of the Seventy. I thought you knew already."

"I . . . I what?" Exposure to gunfire must have impaired his hearing. He had been here for three years this time around; a release wouldn't have surprised him, but this?

Elias produced an envelope from his pocket, which he handed to Golden. It was already open.

"I hope you don't mind. I was dying of curiosity," Elias shrugged.

Golden scanned over the typewritten letter. It was addressed to him from the office of the First Presidency and signed at the bottom by President Woodruff himself. Elias wasn't joking.

"Why am I always the last to know about these things?" Golden lowered the letter. "What about my elders? Who's to take my place?"

He realized the answer as soon as he had spoken.

"You?" He pointed a dubious finger at Elias. Elias nodded reticently, and Golden started to laugh. He couldn't help it. Elias serving as a mission president? It was a hoot. Course, that's probably what a lot of folks thought about him serving as well.

"What's so funny?"

"Nothing." Golden patted him on the back with his usual good nature. "It's good to see you. Come on upstairs; we'll catch up on things while I pack."

Golden grabbed Elias's bag for him, and they headed upstairs, chatting excitedly.

Hardly a soul batted an eye at the group of elders gathered on the platform to bid Golden farewell. Elias was there, of course, and George Albert and a few other elders who were serving close by, including Bean and Thomas. Countless others had sent thank-yous and thoughts of fond farewell. Letters would continue to pour into the mission home for weeks after Golden returned to Utah, and Elias would dutifully make sure that each and every one of them made it back to his brother.

There were more than a few tears shed in the train depot that day, but Golden himself remained dry-eyed. He felt sad about leaving. After literally pouring blood, sweat, and tears into something for so long, you can't help but grow to love it. And Golden had come to love the work, he truly had. Despite his stoic appearance, he was going to miss it and especially miss serving with his missionaries. He had come to care for each and every one of them very much. At least he knew that they would be in good hands with Elias.

The good-byes were brief. He gave them all a hug and told them to stay strong in the work and close to the Spirit. George Albert's bear hug nearly knocked the wind out of him.

"Thank you for everything."

Golden smiled and nodded.

"Thank you, George Albert. You take care. Make sure my little brother here stays out of trouble, okay?"

"Will do," George Albert laughed.

Golden would have loved to stay and visit with Elias longer, but he was even more excited to get home to Jennie.

"Any final advice?" asked Elias.

Golden thought for a minute, then nodded.

"Only fully converted members are to be sent to Utah."

Elias looked puzzled, but Golden just hugged him and got on the train. The whistle blew, and the engine started up. Puffs of steam flowed out from its sides like small reflections of the clouds God had painted in the sky.

As the train pulled out, Golden heard music and looked out the window. The elders were joined together in singing "God Be with You Till We Meet Again." They weren't the Tabernacle Choir, but it was a chorus of angels to Golden. It wasn't the quality of their voices; it was the feeling behind it. He loved his missionaries, and he knew they loved him right back. That was just a good feeling, a very good feeling indeed. He waved a final farewell, listening until their voices were drowned out by the sound of the train and by distance. Golden continued staring out the window long after the train had left the station, watching Dixie roll past in all her glory and splendor.

What a long, strange trip it had been. In the beginning, facing the long end of a mission had been mighty tough, let alone two of them. He had honestly felt there was no way a simple, ignoramus cowboy like himself would ever be able to make it through. But he had promised the Lord (and his mother!) that he would go. And maybe that had been faith enough.

In hindsight, the times when the Lord had helped him through were obvious. It was just as obvious when he had dragged Golden kicking and screaming. But the times that stood out the most in Golden's mind were the times the Lord had carried him in his arms. There was no other way of explaining how Golden had gotten through it all.

An overwhelming sense of love came over him, filling him till he felt he would overflow—love for his missionaries, love for the people he served, and more than anything else, love for the Savior himself.

He looked out the window again, this time to hide the tears that began to run down his cheeks.

The train rolled west into the sunset.

CHAPTER 35

THE FIRST OF MANY

Don't squat with your spurs on.

—*Cowboy Proverb*

Malaria had almost killed him. He'd been threatened by mobs that wanted to beat him, hang him, whup him, or shoot him. Heaven knows they'd tried. He'd faced death and been scared half out of his mind more times than he cared to count. But none of that could hold a candle to how frightened Golden felt today.

He was sitting on the stand at the front of the marvelous Salt Lake Tabernacle, surrounded by General Authorities on every side and facing a packed house. President Woodruff sat within spitting distance (not that Golden would ever think of doing such a thing), flanked by his counselors George Q. Cannon and Joseph F. Smith (George Albert's second or third cousin. Maybe fourth; Golden couldn't keep track). Next to them sat the entire Quorum of the Twelve, including a reverently slumbering Rudger Clawson and thirty-eight-year-old Heber J. Grant. Golden had met Heber briefly, but neither man had any idea yet how great a role they would come to play in each other's lives.

Golden had never felt so unworthy of anything in his life. Who was he to be sitting with the likes of such men? He almost wished he hadn't made it back from the South. If B.H. wasn't sitting next to him right now and Jennie and the kids hadn't been in the audience watching, he might have made a break for it—just grabbed his hat and vamoosed.

The choir finished a beautiful rendition of "Behold the Harvest Wide Extends," and President Cannon, who was conducting the conference, stepped to the podium.

"I hope you have enjoyed the beautiful strains of the choir as much as I have." Even though there was no microphone or electric speakers (those wouldn't come along for another thirty years or so), his voice carried easily throughout the building. The room had been designed so that a speaker's voice could be heard in any part of the Tabernacle. You could literally hear a pin drop from the back of the building. Golden didn't want to be a doubting Thomas, but he was so nervous, he wasn't sure his already squeaky voice would carry past the first row.

"We have a bit of official business to attend to," President Cannon said. It was time for sustaining newly called General Authorities.

"If you had anything to do with this, I'm going to hog-tie you," Golden whispered to B.H., who just smiled and patted his friend on the arm. It was above Golden's bend to understand just how an unrefined cowpoke like himself should be called as a Seventy. He knew there were better men; he'd worked with lots of them. But if his service in the South had taught him anything, it was that the Lord truly worked in mysterious ways.

"We'd like to sustain Jonathan Golden Kimball as one of the first presidents of the Seventy," President Cannon motioned from the pulpit, "Those in favor manifest it by raising the right hand."

Golden fully expected no one to lift their hands, but when President Cannon asked, the congregation raised their arms as one, sustaining Golden to his new calling and the next chapter in his life. The people's willingness to sustain him was humbling. When President Cannon asked, "Any opposed manifest it by the same sign," Golden wanted to raise his own hand high in the air, but he figured that he had already been outvoted.

The full weight of the responsibility settled on Golden's shoulders. The magnitude of the calling was mind-boggling. In the mission he had been responsible for several hundred elders, and that had felt like a lot. Now he was going to be responsible for thousands of Saints. For the millionth time since Elias had delivered the news in Chattanooga, he felt insufficient for the task. Golden may have had little faith in himself, but he did have plenty of faith in God. And if this was where God wanted him, then God would help him get through it somehow, just like he always had.

"President Kimball will now address us briefly."

It was a double whammy. Not only was he given a calling he felt completely inadequate for, but he also immediately had to speak before a packed Tabernacle. Without question, this was the biggest audience he had ever addressed. Call it baptism by fire. He should have objected when he had the chance.

He took a deep breath and stepped to the podium. Golden could have sworn the crowd doubled in size from the time he stood up to the time he got to the stand. In his mind, he could hear George Albert saying, "At least there are women and children this time." He was pretty sure this crowd wasn't going to attack him.

Running his fingers over the edges of the woodwork, he looked out over the congregation. President Taylor had been right; he had never felt more humbled in his life than now, standing here, facing the assembled Saints of God. Not that Golden had ever doubted the prophet for one moment. There was just no way to grasp the full truth of his words until you stood here for yourself. Golden couldn't help but wonder if President Taylor had known something more that day than what he'd let on. Golden smiled wistfully at the memory, then decided he'd better start talking.

"My brothers and sisters," he began, "President Taylor once told me, many years ago, that standing here was a humbling experience, but I never had a clue just how humbling until now.

On my mission to the South, I never was afraid of a mob when I had the Spirit of God, but I was scared pretty nearly to death after the Spirit left. Standing here today I feel much the same way I felt then—I'd run, but I have no place to go."

The audience laughed, and Golden relaxed a little. At the very least, he knew that his voice was loud enough.

"I have been called as a Seventy. And to be perfectly honest, I can't really say why. There are three ways a man gets called in this Church—inspiration, revelation, and relation. If I hadn't been related to Heber C. Kimball, I wouldn't have been a damn thing in this Church."

There it was. The "D" word. Carried forth clearly and unmistakably by the magnificent acoustics of the Tabernacle. Golden didn't even notice it had popped out. But the audience sure did. A wave of gasps and whispers and not a few muffled chuckles rippled through the room. Jennie covered her mouth, half embarrassed and half giggling. That was her Golden, all right, through and through, bless him. On the stand, Rudger Clawson stirred briefly, then fell back asleep. Blissfully unaware of the ruckus he'd caused, Golden carried on with his talk. Just like they would for years to come, people sat up and took notice, listening as Golden spoke. They were shocked, but they were also curious to hear what he might say next.

"I have never been ashamed to testify to the divinity of this work, when I felt that I had the Spirit of God. When I was in the mission field, I said to the elders: Whenever you are moved upon by the Spirit of God and in the spirit of testimony, you are to testify that Joseph Smith is a prophet of God, and I promise you it will make you all the trouble you can bear."

There were a few more muffled laughs from the audience. He definitely had their attention.

"I want to tell you in a few words that there is nothing in the world that the wicked dislike so much as the truth. No greater blessing has ever come into my life than serving the Lord." It was the honest truth. Not every minute in the South had been a bed of roses; in fact, a good portion of it had been just the thorns, but the experience was priceless. His personal growth from it was without measure. Golden knew he'd never be able to repay the Lord for all he had done for him. But he was determined to give it his cowboy best. "I am grateful for the chance God has given me to serve the Saints. My testimony, brothers and sisters, is that I know this work is true. I have tested it out. I have tested God out, and he has been faithful and true. I only hope that I can be the same. God bless you all. Amen."

Golden returned to his seat. B.H. patted his arm again in a congratulatory manner, then leaned over and whispered in his ear. Golden's eyes widened. He covered his mouth with his hand, blushing a shade of red that even a western sunset in July would have envied.

And that's how a rough and sometimes crude cowboy came to be a rough and sometimes crude General Authority. Eventually J. Golden would grow to become one of the most beloved Church leaders of all time, a legend in his own right. But that, my friends, is a story for another day.

EPILOGUE

Home. **How** wonderful it was to be here. Jane and Jack ran across the front yard with little Beth in tow, carrying on as children will, shouting and playing games. Golden sat on the porch with Jennie and the baby, admiring the majestic Rockies and the bright Western sky. Jennie leaned over and put her arm around him, holding him close. It was perfect. Only one thing bothered him still.

"I can't believe I slipped like that from the pulpit. In conference, of all places."

Jennie squeezed his hand. "Quit worrying about it so much. You did wonderfully."

"No, really, how is a man like myself supposed to lead anyone?"

"Just be yourself," she said.

"I'm afraid that's all I know how to be."

Jennie smiled that amazing smile of hers, then snuggled in closer and kissed him.

And Golden was happy.

ABOUT THE AUTHOR

Scott graduated from Brigham Young University and is currently enrolled in the School of Hard Knocks. He is a nomad who claims his home in Utah, California, Hawaii, and wherever else in the world he happens to be. The closest thing he's ever done to being a cowboy is dude ranching for a day. He couldn't sit down for two weeks afterward. Like Golden, he's tall and skinny. He also shares some of Golden's colorful vocabulary and his immense love for the gospel.